60.00

NATIVE

TRIBES

OF CANADA

NATIVE TRIBES

Douglas Leechman, B.Sc., M.A., Ph.D., F.R.S.C.

DIRECTOR, GLENBOW FOUNDATION

Illustrated by A. E. Ingram

W. J. Gage and Company Limited · Toronto

O F   C A N A D A

Printed and bound in Canada

CONTENTS

ILLUSTRATIONS

MAPS

Reproduced by kind permission of The National Museum of Canada.

CHAPTER 1

OUR CANADIAN INDIANS

PRAIRIE INDIAN
ON HORSEBACK

INDIANS GATHERING WILD RICE

OUR CANADIAN INDIANS

IT WAS EIGHT O'CLOCK in the morning on Friday, August 3rd, 1492, when Christopher Columbus first set sail from Spain for the west. Though most people in his day believed the world to be flat, for years he had felt sure that it was round and was convinced that he would reach the east coast of Asia if he kept on sailing west across the Atlantic.

He was quite right, of course, but he had not allowed for three facts. First of all, he did not know how big the world really was and that the east coast of Asia was farther from Europe than he supposed. Secondly, he imagined that Asia stretched much farther to the east than it actually does. And thirdly, it had apparently never crossed his mind that there might be another continent between Asia and western Europe.

So certain was he that he would reach China that he not only carried with him letters from Ferdinand and Isabella of Spain addressed to the Grand Khan of Cathay, as China was called in those days, but also an interpreter who could speak Hebrew, Chaldean, and a little Arabic.

On the morning of Friday, October 12th, just ten weeks later, he and some of his officers landed on a small island. The natives spoke neither Hebrew nor Chaldean, and it was soon clear that this was not China, a land of which Columbus already knew a good deal through his study of the writings of Marco Polo, an Italian who had spent a long time in China two hundred years before. There were, Columbus knew, many islands off the southeast tip of Asia, a region then vaguely known as the Indies, and he decided that this must be where he had landed, for such a conclusion fitted perfectly with everything he already knew, as well as with his discoveries since he had left Spain.

WHAT IS AN "INDIAN"?

If, then, these were the Indies, as he now assumed, what was more natural than to refer to the natives as Indians? This he did from the very first day of his landing and, though his mistake is clearly recognized and understood today, their name has never been changed and the native inhabitants of the Americas are still called Indians.

The expression "Red Indian" is often used, especially in England, to mean the Indians of eastern Canada and the northeastern United States. Actually this name was first applied to the now extinct Beothuks, who lived in Newfoundland, and were in the habit of decorating their own bodies and many of their possessions with red ochre. Later on, "Red Indian" was used for almost any Indian, though their complexion is really coppery rather than red.

People sometimes ask if the Eskimos are Indians too. That, of course, depends on what we mean by "Indians". If we mean all the native people of North and South America, then the Eskimos are certainly included. It is a little like saying that we have five fingers on each hand, though we really have four fingers and a thumb. It is true that the Eskimos differ from other natives of North America in many ways, but there are also many ways in which they are very much the same.

In 1506, when Columbus died in Spain, never even dreaming that the mainland of North America existed, he still had no idea of the enormous size of the continents he had discovered, nor had he solved a problem that began to perplex people immediately after his return from the first of his four voyages, bringing back with him natives from the New World.

WHERE DID THE INDIANS COME FROM?

That was the unsolved problem. There are really three separate questions hidden in that one. First of all, had the Indians always been here, just as the trees and wild animals had? Secondly, if they came from somewhere else, where was that place and what path did they follow in their journey from their original home to their present one in America? And, in the third place, when did they arrive?

All sorts of strange and fantastic answers to these questions have been suggested. People have imagined great lost continents, "Atlantis" in the Atlantic Ocean, and "Lemuria" or "Mu" in the Pacific, which were supposed to have acted as bridges of land across which people could have travelled. There is no scientific foundation for either of these ideas.

Others have suggested that the Indians are the descendants of the ancient Phoenicians, the Egyptians, or the imaginary "Ten Lost Tribes" of Israel, or the followers of Prince Madoc, who sailed westwards from Wales in 1170 to found a new colony. There is, we know now, no truth in any of these ideas either.

THE REMAINS OF EARLY MAN

It is much easier to suggest sensible answers to these problems today than it was in the time of Columbus, for we now have far more of the facts needed to form an intelligent opinion. We are able to say "No" quite definitely to the suggestion that the Indians were "always here", because all the early Indian remains that have been discovered are comparatively recent, that is to say, less than twenty thousand years old. That may sound very old indeed until we compare it with the dates of remains found in Europe and other parts of the Old World, where traces of man, quite certainly one hundred and fifty thousand years old, have been discovered and some probably even earlier.

In the Old World, such ancient remains have been found in a great many places and there is no reason why they should not be just as common here if man had lived on this continent in those very early days. As it is, though a few finds have been made for which great age has been claimed, not one of these claims has been satisfactorily proved, and nearly all of them have been quite disproved.

In the Old World, too, we find fossil skeletons of the great apes which are believed by most scientists to be part of the common stock from which the apes and human beings are both descended. No such fossil remains, or living apes, are known in the Americas, though hundreds of thousands of fossils of other animals have been collected from one end of the continents to the other.

Because all signs of the presence of man that have been found in the New World, and there are many thousands of them, are comparatively recent, we have every reason to believe that there were no human beings in North or South America until after the end of the great Ice Age, during which almost all of the northern part of North America was covered with a thick blanket of ice that made it uninhabitable.

HOW DID THE INDIANS GET HERE?

This brings us to our next question: How did the Indians get here? After the childish fancies of Atlantis and Mu had been disposed of, scientists were able to turn to more reasonable suggestions. One was that people had travelled by way of Iceland and Greenland to the east coast of North America, just as the Vikings did about a thousand years ago, at least five hundred years before Columbus reached the West Indies. The objection to that suggestion is that our Indians show no European influence in their appearance, their speech, or their way of living.

Other people suggested that they came across the Atlantic from the west coast of Africa to Brazil. The distance is roughly a thousand miles, about as far as from Ottawa to Winnipeg, but here we meet the same difficulty for the natives show no trace of either Arab or Negro influence in their bodies, their language, or their customs.

Another possibility that has been considered is a route of travel across the Pacific Ocean eastwards to South America. There are certain resemblances in tools and weapons on both sides of the Pacific that make it seem possible that there was some contact between the two continents, but again there is little similarity in physical type or in speech, and some of the resemblances in culture may be explained as independent inventions of the same thing by separate people.

Still others have thought that people could have moved down to the tip of the peninsula of Kamchatka in eastern Asia and then crossed to the Aleutian Islands off the coast of Alaska. This would mean hopping from island to island, with a water gap of about three hundred miles at the widest place. It is not impossible, but the difficulty is that we find no traces of people having lived on the Aleutians, except the present Aleuts and their ancestors who, we know, came from America and not from Asia. It is certain that if thousands of travellers had passed through the islands they would have left some signs of their passage.

THE BERING STRAITS ROUTE

The last suggestion of all is, almost certainly, the right one. That is, that man crossed Bering Straits from the eastern tip of

Siberia to the western tip of Alaska at Cape Prince of Wales. This is a distance of only forty-two miles and one can see the far side from either shore on a clear day. There are two islands, Big and Little Diomede Islands, just about halfway across, which make convenient places to camp for the night or to take shelter in rough weather. That it was possible to cross here in small open boats is quite certain, for there are Eskimos living on both sides and they cross frequently, and have been doing so for centuries past.

Furthermore, as we shall see, the American Indian is, in physical type, the same as the people of eastern Asia. Their ways of life are practically the same, and they even tell their children the same nursery tales, though in a different language.

Perhaps the most conclusive proof, apart from the fact that this route of migration is so easy and is actually still in use, is the resemblance in physique between the people on both sides of the North Pacific. In the Old World, we find many different types, tall men with pale skins and blond hair, short dark men with black hair, black men with crinkly hair, and yellow-skinned men with straight hair, and other variations, but there is none of this diversity in the New World. Here, all the people belong to the same type with minor differences.

PHYSICAL APPEARANCE OF THE INDIANS

The American Indians as a whole have a skin with a coppery tinge, ranging from a light yellow to a deep brown. Their hair is black and straight, abundant on the head but sparse on other parts of the body. Their eyes are brown, sometimes light and sometimes dark, but not blue. Many of the people have eyes with the "Mongolian fold", often called the "slant eye" of the Chinese, and it is especially noticeable in young women and in children. The face is generally wider than in Europeans, and their hands and feet are usually smaller than ours.

Now such a description would fit almost exactly many of the people of eastern Siberia and those of China, Japan, and Korea, but it would not fit any other important group of people anywhere else in the world. In some places, on the west coast of British Columbia for instance, the Indians look so much like Chinese that it is difficult to tell one from another.

WHEN DID THE MIGRATION BEGIN?

Granting then, as all students of the question do today, that this was the main route of travel and quite possibly the only one, when did this movement begin? We have seen that there are no remains of very early man in the Americas, nothing before the Ice Age in fact, so it must have begun after the end of that period. Recent work in Alaska and the Yukon as well as in many other parts of North America leads us to believe that the melting of the great ice sheet began about thirty-five thousand years ago, and that the ice had shrunk enough to allow travel from Siberia into North America about twenty thousand years ago.

Now, we do not suppose that a band of men sat quietly on the beach on the west side of Bering Straits, just waiting to cross. As far as we can tell now, man has not lived in the extreme east of Siberia much longer than he has in North America, and it may well be that the route of migration had actually been open for hundreds, if not thousands, of years before anybody used it. That may be difficult to prove one way or another. However, we do know of traces of man in the southwest of the United States that we believe to be over ten thousand years old, so we may be safe in suggesting that the migration began between fifteen and twenty thousand years ago.

Really, there was not just one migration. It is probable that wave after wave of people crossed over, with intervals of perhaps hundreds of years between them. This would help to account for the variety of languages we find in the Americas and for the little differences in physical type. For some centuries, the flow may have been fairly steady, and at other times it may have stopped completely.

And who were the latest group to come over? We are not sure, but there seems to be some evidence that the people now living in the interior of Alaska, the Yukon, and the Northwest Territories, whom we call the Athapascans, were the latest. Others have suggested that the Eskimos came after the Athapascans and point to the fact that they still have villages on both sides of Bering Straits. However, we know that the present Siberian Eskimos once lived in Alaska and moved westwards, against the stream of migration, back to Siberia. The idea that the people of the west coast, in British

Columbia, were the latest arrivals and that they came by sea is contradicted by their own traditions and memories.

Eventually the descendants of the people who had crossed to America by way of Bering Straits spread over the whole country. There are very few parts of it that they did not occupy, only the most desolate and sterile areas of all, such as the Barren Lands west of Hudson Bay (and even these are scantily populated by the Caribou Eskimos), and the higher parts of the great mountain ranges. All the way down, even as far as Tierra del Fuego at the very tip of South America, the people spread and multiplied.

It has been suggested that they could hardly have gone so far in the time since their arrival, but it is only about twelve thousand miles from Alaska to Tierra del Fuego, so an average movement of two miles a year would allow them to spread as far as that in six thousand years, and two miles is not much more than half an hour's walk. Not that any such steady migration actually took place, but it is clear that the time needed to reach the south is well within the fifteen thousand years mentioned.

THE DISCOVERY OF OLD INDIAN VILLAGES

Naturally, people could not live in all parts of the continent, often for many years in the same place, without leaving some signs of their having been there. Hundreds of such places are known in Canada and many thousands more in the United States. Often the soil round about is stained with powdered charcoal from their long-abandoned camp fires, and there are fragments of bone from their food and chips from their stone working.

To the eye of one not accustomed to looking for such old Indian village sites, there is nothing much to see, and it takes a good deal of care and experience to find them. Once found, however, there is seldom any doubt as to a site's once having been an Indian village, and broken arrowheads, skin-scrapers, stone knives, and, in some parts of Canada, hundreds of bits of broken pottery will be found buried beneath the surface of the ground, sometimes only a few inches down, often more.

Nor are these old villages the only traces of man. True, we have no great ruins of temples and palaces such as are found in Egypt or Greece, but there are houses of stone and bone built by the Eskimo in the Arctic, and on both the Atlantic and Pacific coasts are great heaps of shells, clams and oysters chiefly, which have been thrown away by the people who lived on the beach and fed on these shell-fish.

In some parts of the country, especially British Columbia, old Indian graves are found, and the survivors often buried beautifully made weapons and ornaments with the dead. The bones are still to be seen in some graves, but in most cases they have disappeared and only the things buried with the dead remain to show that they once were graves. The Eskimos sometimes built stone cairns over the dead and placed tools and weapons nearby or inside, presumably for use in the land of the spirits.

The Hurons and some other Iroquoian tribes used to bury the dead all together in large pits called ossuaries at a great Feast of the Dead held every ten or twelve years. Then the bodies of all those who had died and been buried since the previous feast were dug up again, the flesh scraped away, the bones painted red and reburied with ceremonies, feasting, and the giving away of presents.

As well as graves, we find quarries where the Indians dug stone for tools and weapons; workshop sites, where the stone from the quarries was shaped; old Indian trails, many of them still clear and distinct and others still in use even today; pits in which food was hidden or preserved; house sites; and, on the prairies, tipi rings, circles of stones that once were used to hold down the edges of the skin tents.

On the British Columbia coast we find crude drawings pecked in the face of smooth rocks, and in the interior of the province and on the western prairies are drawings in red paint, also on smooth rock faces. Altogether, the evidences of the presence of Indians in the country are numerous and, once your eyes have been trained to look for and recognize them, easily found.

HOW OLD ARE THESE REMAINS?

By studying these relics of Indian life carefully and comparing those found in one part of the country with those from another, we are able to find out a great many things about how the Indians lived before the white man came. One thing offers great difficulty and that is to find out how old these remains are, something that many people want to know. As a rule, the only evidence we have is that some objects must be older than others because they were found at a greater depth in the ground. If we find glass beads or iron along with the Indian things, we know that the site must have been occupied after the whites came, for it was they who introduced the use of iron and glass to this continent. Then, too, we have to remember that beams and planks with large iron spikes in them are sometimes washed up on the beach after a storm, so the coastal Indians may have had a small supply from this source for many hundreds of years.

On the great shell heaps of the east and west coasts, we find trees that must have started to grow after the shell heap was no longer occupied and, by counting the annual growth rings in a stump, we can tell its age. If the tree stumps show four hundred annual rings, the shell heap must have been there at least as long ago as that, but we still have no idea when it first began.

DATING SPECIMENS BY RADIO-ACTIVITY

In the last few years a totally new way of dating things has been discovered. It has been shown that all organic matter (that is, stuff that once was part of a living thing, like charcoal, or wood from a tree, or bone from an animal, or shell from a clam), contains a certain amount of radio-active carbon. Once the plant or animal dies the quantity of this radio-active carbon it contains begins to diminish. Now, radio-activity dies down slowly, so slowly that even after about 5550 years there is still half of it left in any piece of organic matter. If we collect charcoal from an old Indian village site and test it for radio-activity, we may find that it is still strong, which would mean that the charcoal is fairly recent. When the radio-activity is weak, we know that the charcoal must be quite old. Careful measurements tell us just how old the charcoal or other organic matter is, and we are now able to get the date right within ten per cent. The method has been tested, of course, by trying it on very old things from ruins the exact date of which is known, like the town of Pompeii in Italy which was destroyed by an eruption of the great volcano, Vesuvius, in 63 A.D., and the answers have been accurate enough to convince us that this new method really works.

Remains in the village sites tell us a good deal about the people who once lived there, but leave a lot to our imagination. In most cases, the only things left are those of stone, pottery, and perhaps ivory. All the rest, such as things made of wood, or of skin such as clothing, or of horn, or antler, or bone, have rotted away, so that we have left only a very one-sided picture of the possessions of these ancient people. However, there are exceptions to this rule. In some parts of the Dry Belt in the interior of British Columbia, the sandy soil is so dry that it has preserved many things that would have perished in wet soil, and in the Arctic the frost has kept some things as fresh as though they had been put into a huge ice-box.

WHAT WERE THE FIRST PEOPLE LIKE?

From a study of the specimens collected in these places, we are able to get a pretty clear idea of what the first people to cross Bering Straits were like. We believe that they knew how to chip stone to make tools and weapons, how to polish stone, they understood many ways of hunting and fishing, how to make clothing from skins, to light a fire and cook their food, how to make rope and twine by twisting animal or vegetable fibres, probably they knew how to make baskets, and they had the dog as their only domestic animal. They knew little of pottery making, or of agriculture, or weaving. Of the use of the wheel, they apparently knew nothing.

People who came later on brought the knowledge of more advanced methods of making pottery and weaving, but agriculture seems to have been developed independently in this continent, and the knowledge of how to use the wheel never did reach the Americas until it was brought across the Atlantic by the whites. One reason for this was that wheels are not much use till you have roads to run them on, and there were few roads anywhere in the Americas, and none in Canada before the coming of the white man. The use of a spinning disc as a sort of flywheel was known, rollers may have been used to move heavy things such as dug-out canoes, and there have even been found numbers of pottery toys with wheels on them in Mexico. That wheels should have been used on children's toys but never put to work is strange indeed.

The different waves of people who crossed Bering Straits all brought with them their own ways of doing things. As they moved on, into the heart of the continent, they carried these familiar skills and customs with them to their new homes and developed new ones. As a result, we find that there are various customs in different parts of Canada. Indeed, it is by means of these different cultures that we are able to split the fifty tribes of Canadian Indians into convenient groups.

The way in which each group of Indians lived was decided largely by the kind of country they lived in and the nature and abundance of the food available. So much was this so, that the division of the people into culture groups follows almost exactly the division of Canada into geographical areas: the west coast, the interior of British Columbia, the Northwest Territories, the prairies, the Ontario peninsula, the eastern woodlands, and the Arctic.

Each of these seven areas has its own animals, plants, and minerals, its own kind of landscape, and its own weather. They differed greatly in some respects, and very little in others. For instance, the eastern woodlands and the Northwest Territories are alike in many ways, but the British Columbia coast resembles no other part of Canada, and there is no other section of the country like the Arctic.

INDIAN LANGUAGES

In each of these seven separate areas, the people followed similar customs, but that does not necessarily mean that they spoke the same language. On the west coast of British Columbia, for example, there are five distinct languages, not just a little bit different like Spanish and Portuguese, but entirely different just as much as English and Chinese are. On the prairies, four languages were spoken, but in the Arctic the Eskimo tongue was very much the same from Greenland to Alaska, changing only in the south of that territory and on the Aleutian Islands.

There are at least eleven principal languages spoken by the Indians of Canada, split into about fifty dialects. To a white man, these languages are very difficult, for not only are the pronunciations strange to us, but the grammar is most complicated. It would be a great mistake to suppose that, because a tribe has a simple culture, they must therefore speak a simple language. In fact, exactly the opposite is the truth.

Indian languages differ from European languages in many ways. Their grammar is based on ideas that are often strange to us, and their treatment of number, gender, and tense is not in the least like ours. They make great use of prefixes and suffixes, that is to say, of syllables that are tacked on to the front of a word (prefixes), to change its meaning, or at the tail end (suffixes), for the same purpose. In English, if we put the prefix "dis-" before the word "like", and so make it "dislike", we change its meaning, and this is what many of the Indians did, using the system even more than we do. When several extra syllables are added to the main word, a lot of meaning can be crowded into a little space. As an example, take the Thlinkit name for the Northern Lights — *kanyiqkuwate*. The main word is *kan*, which means "fire", and to it have been added three suffixes, — *yiq* (like), — *ku* (out-of-doors), and — *wate* (color). So the Northern Lights are the "colored fire-like things out-of-doors", all in one word.

Not many white men have learned to speak any Indian language correctly, and even those who have made a special study of it, never speak as a native does. Today the two races have mixed their languages to a certain extent. Indians are using more and more English and French words, especially for things that were unknown to them such as cars, radios, aeroplanes, and so on. On the other hand, a good many words that we use fairly often have been borrowed from Indian languages. Moccasin, canoe, papoose, toboggan, tomahawk, wampum, wigwam, tipi, are all familiar and the list could easily be made longer.

One might think that the language differences would have acted as a barrier, preventing the people from understanding each other, and to some extent this was true, but we must remember that there were few tribes that did not have at least some of their men married to women of other tribes, and there were also prisoners of war who had learned the language of their captors. On the prairies, the difficulty was solved by the use of the Indian sign language. An expert in it could talk for hours with his hands, not saying a word aloud, but quite able to express any idea he wished to, and sure of being understood.

HOW MANY INDIANS HAVE WE?

A mistaken idea that we often meet is that the Indians are a vanishing race. At one time there was some truth in this. In 1900, there were about 100,000 Indians in Canada, perhaps a few more. This was just a little less than half of what we believe the native population of Canada to have been before the white man came, that is, 220,000. Since 1900, they have been increasing at the rate of about one per cent a year and in 1953 there were about 146,000.

The decrease in their numbers between the time of the discovery of Canada and 1900 was caused largely by disease. The white men introduced many sicknesses that had not been known to the Indians before and they therefore had not developed any resistance to them. The natives were killed in thousands by smallpox, measles, and influenza, and even now they frequently die from tuberculosis and other diseases brought by the whites.

War, also, took the lives of many. True, there had always been a good deal of conflict among the tribes (though not as much as some history books would lead you to believe), but the introduction

WHERE THE INDIANS OF CANADA LIVED

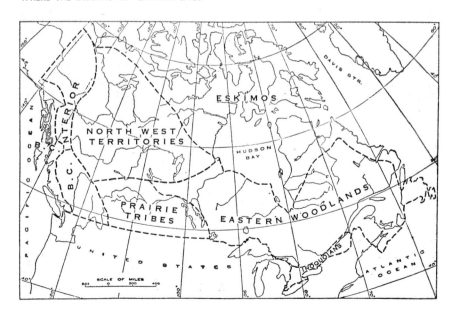

of firearms sometimes gave one tribe a temporary advantage over another and enabled them to wipe out many of their enemies before these, too, got guns.

Alcohol killed many. The effects of a drink of rum or whisky seemed to be much greater when an Indian took it than when a white man did, and if the fur traders gave the Indians free drinks to persuade them to sell their furs, even though the rum was watered down to only one part in eight, as it was at times, the Indians went almost wild. Some of the early traders have described the brawls they witnessed and their accounts are almost beyond belief.

INDIAN CONTRIBUTIONS TO MODERN LIFE

The first white men to land in Canada and the trappers and fur buyers who came after them owe the Indians a great debt of gratitude. It was they who showed the white men the trails and canoe routes through the forests and across the prairies, taught them how to make and use the birch-bark canoe, the sled, the toboggan, and the snowshoe, without which travel was almost impossible. They taught them, too, the habits of the wild animals on which they depended for food and for furs. The Indian women showed them the use of herbs for medicine, which plants were safe to eat and which were poisonous.

Many of the white men found life in the woods with the Indians very much to their taste, and there were plenty of them who refused firmly to live again the dull and unromantic life of city or farm. They married Indian women, who proved in thousands of cases to be hard-working, faithful, and affectionate, and much better able to help in the outdoor occupations of their husbands than white girls who were unaccustomed to life in the woods.

The effect of the coming of the white settlers was profound and often disastrous to the Indians. The old ways of doing things were quickly abandoned. New tools were introduced, new weapons, new ways of trapping. Animals which the Indians had seldom bothered with, because their furs were small and tender and their meat not very tasty, such as fox, mink, and fisher, were now much sought after. The Indians bought food and clothing from the trading posts, so they no longer had to hunt for food or for skins to make clothes from. They trapped only to sell the furs, and the old crafts began to disappear. In a generation or two, the Indians found them-selves quite dependent on the traders and, if the white men had suddenly packed up and gone back to Europe leaving the Indians to shift for themselves, many thousands of natives would have died before they were able to learn once again how to depend entirely on the woods and their own skill for a living.

There are many things we owe the Indians other than the canoe, the snowshoe, and the toboggan. In Canada alone we now produce their tobacco, corn, maple syrup and sugar, squash, beans, buckwheat, pumpkins, artichokes, sunflowers, and turkeys. Farther south, in the United States, Mexico, and South America, the Indians contributed cotton, peanuts, tapioca, vanilla, tomatoes, potatoes, rubber, quinine, cacao, and the chicle used in making chewing gum. Any one of these is much more valuable and important than all the gold the old Spanish Conquistadores ever looted from "the Indies".

COMMON MISTAKES ABOUT THE INDIAN

Today nearly everybody is interested in the Indians and most of us feel that we know a good deal about them. We get our ideas of them from moving pictures, from books and magazines and, some-times, from seeing an Indian on a reservation, in a summer camp, or at an exhibition. Many of the ideas we pick up in this way are far from the actual truth, because the people who produce the movies and who write the books have tried to make the Indians as colorful and romantic as they can and, in doing so, they have twisted the truth a good deal. There are all sorts of things com-monly said about the Indians that are not true at all, and many other details, some of them most interesting, are seldom mentioned.

Some of the mistaken ideas about the Indians go back as far as the first account of them written by Columbus; others are much more recent. In the pages that follow, we shall get a chance to see what some of these mistaken ideas are, and what the actual truth is.

One thing that is quite certain is that the Indians' own ideas about themselves are by no means the same as ours, but even the Indians have largely forgotten what things were like in the old days and they have adopted some of our notions of the Indians of the past, as well as of today. When an Indian takes part in a parade he feels that he must wear a huge feather war-bonnet, because, he believes, that is what the "Indians" used to wear. Actually, these were used by only a few men in one prairie tribe and by nobody else. It is as though an actor felt that he would not look like a "European" unless he wore the traditional costume of a Swiss mountaineer.

One of the commonest mistakes is to assume that Indians "are all the same", that anything true of the people of northern Quebec must be equally true of the Indians of British Columbia. Nothing could be farther from the fact. There are seven principal groups of Indians in Canada alone, and many more in the south, all very different from each other, different in language, clothing, customs, in everyday life, and in their degree of civilization. They are no more alike than are the various nations of Europe.

These differences seem to be based, at least in part, in the origin of the people themselves, that is, in the culture of the group they originated in. Secondly, the people were influenced by the kind of country they lived in. The Iroquois, who settled in a rich and fertile area where farming was easy and profitable, were highly organized in comparison with the natives of the Northwest Territories, where game was often scarce and the climate severe, and who had made much less progress. Again, the natives of the British Columbia coast, who lived in a warm climate where there was plenty of food, had developed art and social organization to a high degree. In the following chapters we shall examine each of these seven separate groups in turn, for each of them has its own special characteristics.

CHAPTER 2

THE EASTERN WOODLANDS

CONE-SHAPED
WIGWAM

Beothuk
Micmac
Malecite
Montagnais
Naskapi
Algonquin
Ojibwa
Cree

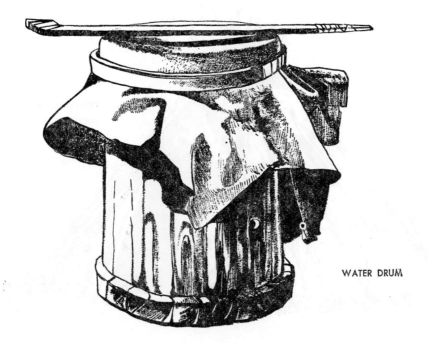

WATER DRUM

THE EASTERN WOODLANDS

IN THE EASTERN HALF of Canada, from about the western boundary of Ontario to the Atlantic Ocean, lived a number of native tribes who spoke dialects of the same language, Algonkian, which gets its name from one of these tribes, the Algonquins. These eastern woodland people occupied a larger area than did any of the other native groups in North or South America, and they were one of the strongest in numbers.

In addition to the Algonkian-speaking people in Canada, there were others in the United States, some groups of them still large today, others few in numbers, some now extinct and remembered only by their names. They were a wandering people, always on the move in search of food, but each group stuck to the country it was familiar with and each separate family and band had a clear idea of where its boundaries were. Living in such a large area as they did, their habits naturally varied from place to place but, taking them as a whole, they make up a logical sub-division of the native tribes of Canada, speaking related languages, and making their living in much the same way. One of the things that is notable about them is their dependence on birch bark for a host of uses.

Starting in the east and working westwards, these are the eight principal Algonkian tribes of Canada:

The BEOTHUK, who once lived in Newfoundland, are extinct now, the last of them, a girl called Nancy, having died in captivity in 1829. Her Indian name was Shanawdithit. The Beothuks were relentlessly persecuted by the whites and by the Micmac Indians who lived on the mainland opposite the Beothuks, and at one time there was even a bounty paid on Beothuk scalps. These were the original "Red Indians", and they were given that name because of their habit of coloring themselves and many of their possessions with red ochre. Later the name was extended to all the Indians of the eastern part of the continent. Another remarkable thing about the Beothuks was that they had no dogs, the only people of North America, as far as we know, of whom this is true.

The MICMAC occupied Nova Scotia, the eastern part of New Brunswick, the nearby part of Quebec, and Prince Edward Island.

Today most of them do a little farming and some make baskets. They have intermarried a good deal with white people.

The MALECITE (pronounced Mally-seet) lived in western New Brunswick, the nearby part of Quebec, and the northeastern part of the State of Maine. They used to grow Indian corn, which most Algonkians did not do, and were much like the Micmacs though their language was somewhat different.

The MONTAGNAIS and the NASKAPI are two tribes who lived in what is now Quebec. The Montagnais were west of the Naskapi, along the north shore of the St. Lawrence to as far east as Seven Islands, and the Naskapi lived to their east, extending far into northeastern Quebec. The Montagnais area is heavily wooded but the Naskapi lands are more open, a tundra-like country. Although these people were among the first to meet the early European explorers, such as Champlain, those of them who live in the interior are still among the least advanced of all the Indians of Canada.

The ALGONQUINS, from whom both the language and the whole group of tribes take their name, Algonkian, lived to the west of the Montagnais in the large area drained by the Ottawa River. They are the most typical of all these people in their way of living.

The OJIBWA were still farther west. They are sometimes called the Chippewa, which is really the same word spelled a little differently. It is pronounced to rhyme with "way". In fact, Ottawa used to be called Ottaway, which is closer to the original word, meaning "traders".

The Ojibwa lived along the north shore of Lake Huron and Lake Superior and on west as far as the Lake of the Woods near the Manitoba boundary. Their country runs far back up the rivers to the north, as far as the height of land between the north and south drainages. These Indians were once the strongest of all the Algonkian people and perhaps the largest tribe in all of Canada. Their only possible rivals in numbers were the Cree. There were several sub-divisions of the Ojibwa, such as the Mississaugas, the Ottawas, and the Potawatomis.

The CREE occupied the northern part of the district, all round James Bay and up as far as Churchill. In fact, they penetrated even farther, going right across the upper corners of Manitoba and Saskatchewan towards Great Slave Lake, though few of them lived there permanently. Their name is a shortened form of a French word for them, Kristineaux. There are two large groups of Crees: the Swampy Cree of whom we are speaking now, and the Plains Cree who live out on the prairies, though they once lived in the forests too. They will be described later on in the chapter on the prairie Indians.

POPULATION

We can not tell now how many Algonkians there were when white men first came to Canada, but about fifty thousand of them are living in Canada today, and only a few thousand less in the United States. Many of them are of mixed blood and are classed as Indians chiefly because they live on the reserves. Other groups, such as some Naskapis in the interior of Quebec, are still almost pure-blooded Indians and do not live on reservations.

WHERE THE INDIANS OF THE EASTERN WOODLANDS LIVED

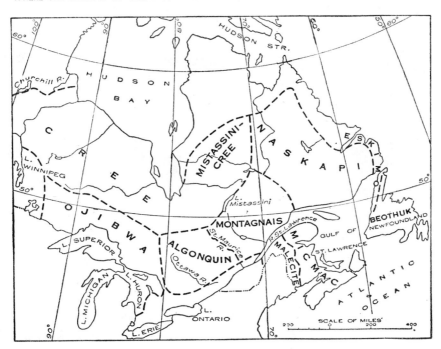

PHYSICAL TYPE

We are no longer quite certain what typical members of some
of the Algonkian tribes looked like, because so many of them are
now of mixed blood. Early paintings make them look very like
Europeans in features and coloring. The skulls and bones we have
found in their graves show them to have been fairly tall, (about
five feet eight inches on the average) and to have had rather
long narrow heads. Their noses seem to have been heavy and
prominent, but not the hawk-like noses of the Sioux, which we often
think of as being "really Indian". Their cheek bones were high and
strong and their faces somewhat large. Of course, within such a
numerous group, occupying territory nearly two thousand miles
from end to end, there were a good
many variations in personal appearance. Sir Alexander Mackenzie once
said that he thought the Cree women
were the most beautiful natives in all
Canada.

POTTERY
COOKING VESSEL

ALGONKIAN
WOMAN AND
CHILD

BIRCH-BARK
VESSEL WITH LID

THE COUNTRY

The area most of the Algonkians lived in is of the type often known as "northern woods". It is a land of rock and muskeg, covered with a dense forest of spruce and other coniferous trees, or else a bare tundra with dwarf vegetation, scrub willows, lichens, and moss. Jacques Cartier didn't think much of it, for he wrote: "The land should not be called the New Land, being composed of stones and horrible rugged rocks, for along the whole of the north shore [of the Gulf of St. Lawrence] I did not see one cart-load of earth and yet I landed in many places. In fine I am rather inclined to believe that this is the land that God gave to Cain."

Everywhere there is a tangle of lakes and streams, and in summer the only way of getting from one place to another is by canoe. In winter, one can go straight across country by toboggan and snowshoes over the snow. On the whole it is barren and rugged, and agriculture is not possible except in a few favored areas, such as are found in the Maritime Provinces.

THEIR FOOD

The people in the northern parts of Algonkian territory lived almost entirely by hunting and fishing. They ate moose and caribou, deer and porcupine, rabbits (which are really hares), beaver and bear, and those of the tribes in the east who could get down to the sea coast on the Gulf of St. Lawrence also killed seals and white whales. They caught lots of fish too, inland during the winter by fishing through the ice, and in the rivers, lakes, and sea in milder weather. Shell-fish were collected and, in fact, anything at all that could possibly be eaten.

The Micmac and Malecite grew a good deal of Indian corn and were less tied down to hunting and fishing than were some of their northern relatives. The Algonquins, too, practised some agriculture and grew corn, as well as squash and beans. They and the Ojibwas used quite a lot of vegetable food, and these latter also had wild rice and maple syrup. We are not certain whether they made maple sugar too before they got iron or brass kettles from the white man. Their agriculture was rather primitive and they could not rely entirely on what they grew, but eked out their crops with wild food whenever this was possible.

The Cree had much the same food, but many of them would not bother with fishing. This occupation, they insisted, was not worthy of a hunter or a warrior, but they did not hesitate to hunt ducks and geese, grouse and ptarmigan, whenever they were to be had.

In spite of this apparent abundance of food, life was not always easy. In a bad year, hunting might be poor for weeks on end, and there are many cases on record of families being so starved that they have become cannibals, eating their dead relatives and sometimes even killing members of their own families for food so that the others might live through the famine. Naturally this was just as horrible to them as it would be to us, and Indians who went through such an experience could never forget it.

COOKING

In the southern part of their country, the Algonkians made pottery to cook in, but in Newfoundland and the north, pottery was either unknown or very scarce. People who had no earthenware pots cooked their food in vessels made of birch bark, so skilfully sewn that they were watertight. Stones about the size of a man's fist were heated in the camp fire and then lifted by means of a couple of sticks and dropped into the birch-bark vessels containing

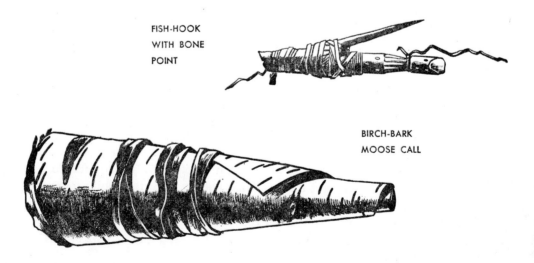

FISH-HOOK
WITH BONE
POINT

BIRCH-BARK
MOOSE CALL

meat and water. This brought the water to a boil, and so the food was cooked. This way of cooking is well known to many primitive tribes all over the world. Some of the Algonkian people who had no birch bark used a bag of skin to hold the water instead. Others used watertight baskets, woven of vegetable materials.

HUNTING

Any group of people who have to depend entirely or even largely on hunting for their daily food naturally become quite expert at it and know many different ways of killing wild animals, some best in one set of circumstances, and others in other situations. The Algonkians had, for instance, many ways of moose hunting, some of which we have adopted and still use. One way was to use a moose call, a little trumpet made from a cone of birch bark. An expert could make noises with one of these that sounded so much like a real moose that any other moose within earshot would come to investigate and was thus drawn close enough to the hunter to be killed. Moose calls are still used in a good many parts of Canada.

Later in winter, when the snow was deep, hunters would follow the tracks of a moose and run it down. The moose would sink in the soft snow and be unable to travel as fast as the hunters on their snowshoes, who soon caught up and killed the animal while it struggled to escape. In summer, if a hunter found a moose swimming across a lake, or feeding, as moose do, on the lily roots in the shallows, he would paddle up in his canoe and spear the moose in the water before it could get to shore. Some moose, too, were simply followed by tracking till the hunter came upon the animal, feeding or sleeping, and shot it.

When a moose was killed it was often easier and less work for the hunters to move their camp to the moose than to carry all the heavy meat out of the bush, so they simply built a new wigwam and lived beside the moose till it was all eaten.

Caribou were hunted in the northern and more open parts of Algonkian territory in much the same ways, except that they were not so often taken in deep snow. Bows and arrows were used a great deal but they were not the only ways the Indians had of killing game. They also had traps and snares. A trap is a mechanism by which an animal is caught when it releases a baited trigger, and a snare is a slip noose which catches the animal by the neck or, more rarely, by a leg.

Snares were used a great deal for rabbits, and the catching of these was generally left to the girls and women. The snare was usually made of sinew or of *babiche*, a tough thong of rawhide. These snares were used for larger game too, even bears, caribou, and moose. Babiche is very strong, and when several of these thongs are twisted together they make a snare that not even the strongest animal can break.

The commonest type of trap was a deadfall, in which the animal, trying to take the bait, disturbed a trigger which let a heavy log fall on its back, killing it. Many of the traps they used were very ingenious, and there were special ones for lynx, for bears, for beavers, even for squirrels and birds.

Sometimes crude fences were built, running for miles over hill and dale through the woods, along which the moose or deer would travel, trying to find a way through. Now and then there would be an opening in the fence, and snares would be hidden in these gaps to catch the game as it tried to get through. Many animals might be caught in this way.

The Naskapi used to catch seals along the Gulf coast in summer, using harpoons with toggle heads. A toggle is something that holds firm, when a strain is put on it, by turning crossways, like the barrel-shaped buttons on heavy winter coats. When a harpoon of this kind is driven into a seal, the head of the harpoon (fastened to a strong babiche line) comes away from the wooden shaft but stays firmly embedded in the seal. Now the hunter has the seal captive on the end of his line so he may pull it close enough to him to kill it.

FISHING

Fishing was almost as important as hunting for all the Algon-kian people, except the Cree who would have little to do with it. Just as with hunting, there were all sorts of different ways of going about it. Sometimes they used to fish at night, using a bright light in the bow of a canoe. The fish were attracted by the light and would swim towards it. The fisherman would spear them when they came close enough. This way of fishing, known as jacklighting, is against the law now.

Some fish were caught in large permanent traps and others in wicker baskets, something like lobster traps, that are still used. Nets, hooks, and harpoons, and also fish spears with bone points were in common use. In winter, people fished through the ice on inland lakes and caught a great many fish in this way. This is still done by both Indians and whites and is a very popular sport.

There were a great many kinds of fish that the Indians could catch and they were all good to eat. There were trout, salmon, suckers, pike, pickerel, eels, muskelunge, sturgeon, whitefish, perch, bass, and many others, as well as cod and other salt-water fish in the sea.

CLOTHING

As you can imagine, proper clothing was most important to these people who lived in a cold climate and often had to be out-of-doors for hours on end. Most of their clothing was of skin, and they had extra robes of fur for the winter. In summer, they wore as little as possible and often smeared their bodies with grease to keep the mosquitoes away.

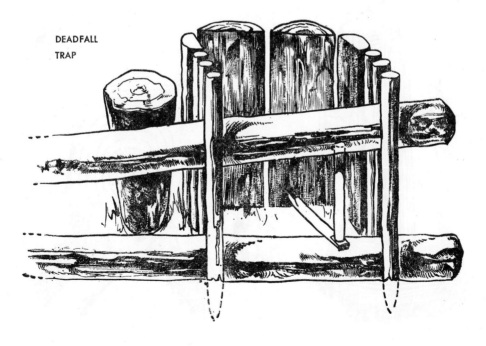

DEADFALL
TRAP

The interesting thing about most of their clothes was that they were tailored, just as ours are. That is to say, the women cut pieces of skin to the shape they needed and then sewed them together with a needle of bone and sinew thread to fit the person who was to wear them. Sinew is a strong thread obtained from the tendons of such animals as the deer and the caribou. The Eskimo made tailored clothes too, but few other natives of the Americas did so, though this method was well known in the Old World. The patterns used were quite intricate, and little differences in local fashions sometimes made it possible to tell where somebody came from by the cut of his clothes.

The usual garments were moccasins, leggings, and sleeves which were added to a tunic in cold weather, a breech-cloth for the

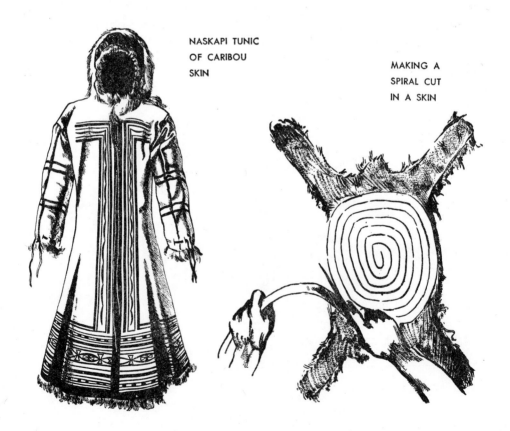

NASKAPI TUNIC
OF CARIBOU
SKIN

MAKING A
SPIRAL CUT
IN A SKIN

men, and sometimes a cap. The men's tunic came down to the thighs, and the women's fell below the knees. Some of the Naskapi, whose clothing was much like that of the eastern Eskimo, had a hood on the tunic, which could be brought up to protect the head and face. Mittens were worn in cold weather, and most people had a big fur robe which they wrapped round themselves when it was very cold, and which they used also for sleeping in.

There were also other materials from which they could make clothes. One of the most important of these, and the closest approach to weaving that they knew of, was made of rabbit skins. The skins, with the hair still on them, were cut into long strips about half an inch wide, by following a spiral cut round and round. This made a strip twenty or more feet long. A number of these were tied end to end, twisted a little, and rolled up into a large ball. As soon as a woman had enough, she made a simple square frame on which she wove the strips of rabbit skin in and out of each other, just as one weaves a little mat from strips of paper. The finished sheet of woven skins was light and warm and could be used as a robe for sleeping in, or it could be made into clothing.

DOME-SHAPED
WIGWAM

Some winter clothes were made from caribou skins with the hair left on them. The Eskimo used these too, and there seems to have been a good deal of borrowing of customs between the two people.

There was not much attempt to make their clothing beautiful, though the Beothuks used to smear a mixture of red ochre and grease on their clothes, and the Naskapis painted their tunics with very fine designs. A good many of the people wore charms on their clothes for good luck in hunting, rather than for decoration.

DWELLINGS

People who have to move camp as often as the Algonkians did need a portable house or one that can be built quickly from the materials at hand. This problem was solved neatly by the wigwam, a word that means "dwelling" in their language. There are two kinds of wigwams, one shaped like a cone, the other like a dome. They were both built in much the same way. Stout saplings were cut and their ends thrust firmly into the ground. They were tied together where they met at the top if the conical form of wigwam was wanted, or bent right over in a hoop if a dome was to be built. A doorway was left at a convenient place. The framework was made more firm and rigid by tying a strong ring, made by bending a sapling into a hoop, to the poles about halfway up inside.

The wigwam frame was covered with sheets of birch bark, which had been strengthened by fastening rods across the ends, to prevent their splitting. Sometimes mats woven from rushes were used for covers and at other times, especially in the north where both rushes and bark were hard to get, caribou skins would be used.

In any case, the essential point was that when the family had to move, they rolled up the covers of the wigwam and took them along with them, but the poles or saplings were just left standing, for the Indians could count on finding others wherever they camped next. That is what makes the chief difference between a wigwam and the tipi of the prairie Indians. Tipi poles are very valuable and the prairie people would never dream of leaving them behind but always took them along with them when they moved.

The sheets of bark or the mats might easily blow away in a high wind, so they had to be fastened down with ropes that passed over the outside of the wigwam, or by poles that leaned against it. A house of this kind could be put up very quickly and, as the men always made the framework in just about the same way, the women knew just where each mat or sheet of bark would fit best. If the weather was bad, or if the people expected to stay longer than usual in one place, the wigwam was built a little more carefully than one to be used for a day or two only.

The cone-shaped wigwams were like the tipis of the prairies, and the dome-shaped ones remind us of the snow houses of the Eskimo.

FURNITURE

There wasn't much in the way of furniture in a wigwam, for the Algonkians had to carry everything they owned with them every time they moved, and so they were careful not to burden themselves with anything they could do without. The floor of the wigwam was the bare earth in summer and snow in winter, but they managed to keep it dry and warm by covering it with a layer of spruce boughs on which they laid mats or skins. The various cooking vessels were close at hand on the ground; they were mostly made of birch bark, though some people in the south used pottery, and in the north some of the Crees used soapstone pots like

WOODEN SPOON

WOODEN BOWL MADE FROM A BURL

those of the Eskimos, because there was but little birch bark to be had in their part of the world. Some vessels, such as bowls, were carved out of wood, and skin bags were used to carry things in. The Algonkians had no tables or chairs and everybody sat on the ground.

TOOLS

Both men and women had their own sets of tools which they needed for making their few possessions. The men had knives and awls and hammers, made from stone or bone in the early days, but of iron as soon as they could get it from the white traders. The women had wooden spoons and ladles, knives made of stone or bone, bone needles for sewing and for lacing snowshoes, bone awls, and skin-scrapers which might be of stone or bone. Sewing was done with sinew thread, and larger things, such as birch-bark vessels or canoes, were sewn with *watap*, the name in the Algonkian language for the prepared roots of spruce and other coniferous trees. Watap looks much like the rattan cane strips that are used to make seats for cane-bottomed chairs.

Both men and women carried their tools in skin bags which kept them all together so that they were easy to keep track of and which would take no harm when they were thrown into a canoe or lashed on a toboggan.

TRANSPORTATION

Travel was one of the really important things in Algonkian everyday life. Each family had to be able to move quickly and easily when it needed to, and those of them who lived in the northern woods, and that was most of them, were seldom in the

BIRCH-BARK CANOE

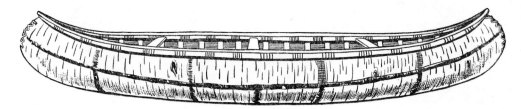

same camp for more than a few days at a time. This meant that almost everything they owned had to be carried with them each time they moved. Naturally they would not carry their toboggans with them in summer or their canoes in winter; these were cached in some safe place till they were needed again, but everything else had to go along.

In summer, the Algonkians travelled by canoe, and in winter on snowshoes, often dragging a toboggan. The birch-bark canoes of these people are now famous, and our modern canoes are built on patterns very like the Indian originals. The word canoe itself is Indian, and it was one of the first that Columbus learned in the West Indies. Canoes vary a little in shape from one Algonkian tribe to another and an expert can tell them apart at a glance, but today few Indians build their own canoes, for suitable birch bark is difficult to find and it is quicker and cheaper for them to buy a canoe than to build one.

The Indians of the northern woods were experts with a paddle and were much in demand with the big fur trading companies, such as the North West Company and the Hudson's Bay Company, to bring the long brigades of canoes loaded with furs out of the woods, returning in the autumn with supplies and trade goods for the far-flung trading posts.

In winter, travel was on snowshoes; when the snow is deep it is almost impossible to go far without them. There were several different patterns, one of the most usual in the east being the bear paw, a rounded shape that looks awkward and forces the wearer to straddle his legs wide apart in walking. However, long experience

TOBOGGAN

has taught the Indians that this is the best shape for walking through thick bush and on the loose powdery snow they so often had to travel over.

A man who was hunting would go out on his snowshoes carrying only a bow and some arrows, a knife, and a little food. When the whole family was on the move, things were different, and they loaded all their possessions on the toboggans. A toboggan differs from a sled in that it has no runners under it, but is merely three or four thin flat boards lashed side by side with their front ends turned up so as to lead easily over the snow.

It was the women and children who pulled the toboggans, for a man must be free to go at once in pursuit of any game they met or to defend himself or his family from possible danger. It was not laziness that got the men out of the hard work of pulling the heavy toboggans, but plain common sense and wise precaution.

People who are not accustomed to snowshoes find them very tiring and painful at first, but once they have become used to them they find they can not do without them.

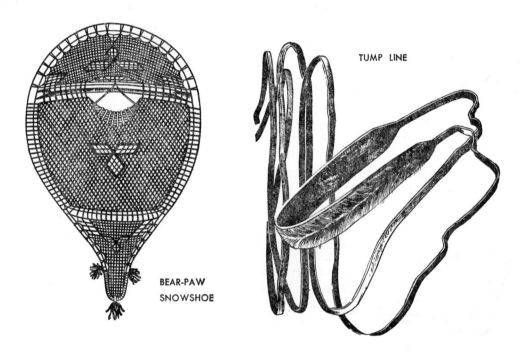

BEAR-PAW
SNOWSHOE

TUMP LINE

The Algonkians had some dogs, but as they were seldom able to get enough game to feed many of them, these people never developed the dog-driving techniques of the Eskimos, and whatever was not carried on the toboggans had to be back-packed. For this, the Algonkians used the tump line, a broad leather strap shaped like a sling. The wide loop of the sling passed over the packer's forehead, and the two ends were used to tie up the pack itself and to hold it so that it rested comfortably on the man's back. A tump line puts a great strain on the neck muscles, and people who are not used to it find it quite unbearable at first. Once accustomed to a tump line, a packer will seldom do without it, and white men who spend a lot of time in the woods often use one.

Another important form of transportation was the way of carrying the babies. They were wrapped in a moss-bag, which was a bag of leather or, later, cloth, open at the top and down the front. This was laced up to keep the baby safely inside. There was a loop at the back so that the bag could be hung up or carried about, and in some tribes the moss-bag was lashed to a small board in such a way that the baby stood upright, resting its feet against a little shelf at the bottom. A hoop of wood over the upper part protected the baby's face if the cradle fell over, and charms were sometimes hung from this hoop to keep the child amused and protect it from evil spirits. The bag was packed with dried moss which kept the baby clean and comfortable. Some cradles were highly decorated, and the mothers took great pride in them, passing them on from child to child and from one generation to the next.

SOCIAL ORGANIZATION

Each family had hunting grounds that they felt were their own and their claim was usually admitted by the other families of their band, but there was nothing much in the way of government to regulate such things, only public opinion. There were chiefs, in a sense, that is to say men who had a little more influence than others, but simply because of their stronger personalities, not from any system of election or inheritance. No chief had any actual authority, and he could not order people to do anything or stop them from doing what they wished to. As a matter of fact, the medicine men often had more real power than the chiefs did.

When anything serious came up that required discussion, as many important men as possible would meet together and talk things over. It was usual for the younger men to sit quietly and say nothing. Only if a growing boy had proved his manhood by killing a bear or a moose would he venture to give an opinion.

Each of the tribes was divided up into small bands made up of closely related families, all of whom spoke the same dialect. In some tribes there may have been more formal council meetings than in others, in part at least because of the influence of the Iroquois tribes who lived so close to them to the south and who had such a strong political organization. Now and then a few neighboring tribes would organize themselves into a confederation, modelled after the Five (later Six) Nations of the Iroquois, but these did not last long or work very well.

There was another form of organization which affected all the Algonkian tribes and many other natives of North America, and this was the division into clans. A clan was a group of people belonging to a single tribe who all claimed descent from the same ancestor, real or imaginary. The clans were not religious or political groups, but purely social. The important point was that a man belonging to one clan was not allowed to marry a woman of the same clan, so a man of the Turtle clan could not marry another Turtle, but must marry a woman of the Deer or some other clan. A child was of the same clan, and had the same totem, as its mother and never of the same clan or totem as its father, but in some tribes these rules were just the other way and then a child did belong to his father's clan. A totem is the badge or emblem of the clan, often an animal, and it is from this animal that the clan claims to be descended.

The number of clans varied from one tribe of Algonkians to another, some tribes having few clans and others, the Ojibwas for instance, having twenty or more. Among the best known clans were the Turtle, Deer, Loon, Bear, Beaver, Duck, Sturgeon, and Water-snake.

The Algonkians had no marriage ceremony such as we have, but a young man who wished to marry would live in the girl's household for some time and hunt and work for his future father-in-law as if he were already one of the family.

WARFARE

We often think of the Indians as being in a constant state of war, but this is far from correct. It is true that all the Algonkian people were at war at some time or other, especially after the arrival of white men who wanted to take their land away from them, but most of their time had to be spent hunting and making a living, so warfare was the exception and not the rule.

The French people usually got along very well with the Algonkians, but English relations with them were less harmonious.

DECORATED BACK OF A CRADLE BOARD

MOSS-BAG

Among themselves, the various tribes were in conflict now and
then: the Naskapi fought with the Eskimos, the Micmacs used to
attack the Beothuks, and the Montagnais fought the Micmacs and
the Iroquois; the Algonquins, too, used to fight with the Iroquois.

We must not think of these as great battles with thousands, or
even hundreds, of men engaged. They were small-scale affairs for
the most part, short-lived, and not many people were killed. The
most dreadful part of Indian warfare was the ghastly torture they
would sometimes inflict on their prisoners. Some tribes were more
ferocious in this way than others, the Montagnais being particularly
cruel. The Ojibwa, though they were good fighters who killed and
scalped their enemies, taking no prisoners, thought the Iroquois
custom of torturing their prisoners quite intolerable.

Scalping seems to have been a fairly common custom, and
in many cases the enemy's head was cut off too. Sometimes the
hands were cut off and there are even records of eating the dead
man's heart so that his courage might be passed on to his
conquerors.

One of the reasons why the wars were usually not large was
the difficulty of feeding the men who were fighting. They had few
reserves of food that they could use to support an army in the field,
and their organization was not perfect enough to enable them to
control or direct an army of men.

The weapons they used in warfare were the bows and arrows
and the knives that they used in everyday hunting. Some of them
also had shields and war clubs, which we call tomahawks, and

DOUBLE-BALL
AND STICK

SNOW SNAKE

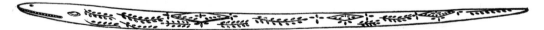

spears were sometimes used too. Some tribes made armor, using slats of wood laced together to make a sort of tunic that protected their chests and backs.

SOCIAL LIFE

Travelling as they did in small bands and meeting other people only now and then, there was not much chance for social life of any kind. Each family was a unit by itself and supplied its own recreations and amusements. Children had few toys, though dolls were made occasionally, and there was not much of the kind of playing we see among our children. The youngsters spent most of their time in helping their parents.

Among the western and southern Algonkian tribes there was more community life, and annual feasts attended by many people were held. Singing and dancing went on all through the night and great quantities of food were consumed. Other smaller feasts were given on special occasions; when a boy killed his first game, for instance, always an important event in his family. The game was cut up so that everybody present had at least a small piece of it in recognition of the fact that the young hunter was now a man and able to support a family, at least in theory.

Among the Ojibwas, the annual sugaring time, when the maple sap was running in the spring, and the wild rice harvest in the autumn, were two occasions for large gatherings of the people. A sort of picnic spirit prevailed at these times. Naskapi families, by contrast, saw other people on rare occasions only, such as the two or three times a year when they all got together to trade goods and supplies.

These different festive occasions were not thoroughly organized. It was largely a matter of much talking, eating, singing, and dancing together, and now and then the men engaged in wrestling matches, the boys ran races, and so on. They also had big gambling games, often playing for high stakes. In some tribes, the men played lacrosse, which is a native Indian game. Catlin, who visited the western Algonkians about 1830 to 1840, saw lacrosse games in which there were eight hundred or a thousand men on each side, the goals were as much as half a mile apart, and there were practically no side boundaries. The referees were the medicine men, and the women urged the men to play harder by switching them.

The women of some Algonkian tribes played a game called double-ball, in which two balls a little larger than our golf balls and covered with buckskin were linked together by a leather strap three or four inches long. The balls were thrown with a curved stick, something like a hockey stick, and the game resembled lacrosse, the aim being to get the balls through the other team's goal.

Another game, seldom seen now, called "snow snake", was played in winter. The snow snake is a rod of wood, quite straight and three or four feet long, the front end lifted a little like the head of a snake. The head is weighted with stone or, in recent years, lead, and the whole snake is highly polished. The game was to slide the snakes over a smooth snow field, and the man who sent his snake the farthest won. If there were five men on each side and all

DECORATED BIRCH-BARK
BOX WITH LID

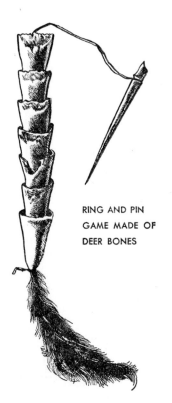

RING AND PIN
GAME MADE OF
DEER BONES

five snakes of one team went a great distance, but one single snake of the opposite team went a little farther, the one in front won the game for his side. The record throw is something over half a mile.

Another game, which could be played by a single person or by two or three, was jackstraws, in which a handful of thin small sticks was thrown down in a heap. Each player had a little scoop or lifter, and the game was to lift the sticks off the pile one by one without moving any of the others, even the slightest bit. It is not at all an easy thing to do.

The ring and pin game is one in which a ring or some other object with a hole in it is tossed in the air and the player tries to catch it as it comes down, on a short stick held in his hand. The ring and pin are fastened together by a short string, and the player scores a point for every successful try. This, too, is much more difficult than it looks. Both of these games had the advantage that the equipment needed to play them with took up very little room and so could easily be carried about with the family possessions. Then, too, they were quickly and easily made.

ART

Art was not highly developed among these people. They were too busy most of the time, and again they could not do much in the way of any art that required extra tools, for they already had as much to carry as they wanted and more. Some of the tribes decorated their birch-bark containers by scraping away the outer layer of bark in such a way as to make a pattern; flowers, as a rule, or leaves, or some simple motif. The Micmacs decorated their baskets with dyed porcupine quills arranged in patterns, and they still sell a good many of these as souvenirs. Other tribes, such as the Ojibwa, also did quill work and some used moose hair for embroidery. There is a tuft of pale, stiffish hair about seven inches long, between the shoulders of the moose. These hairs were dyed in various colors and used for decorating snowshoes, moccasins, and many other things. Not much of this work is being done today. In recent years, for quite a long time in fact, under the influence of French nuns, the Indians have turned to embroidery in silk and beads rather than with moose hair or porcupine quills as they did in the old days, partly because the older materials are now difficult to get and partly because the newer ones, besides being fashionable, are readily available at the nearest store or trading post.

The Naskapi decorated their clothes with most elaborate patterns in red, blue, and yellow. The colors were mixed with fish glue to make them stick and were applied with a curious implement

REPEAT PATTERN MADE BY
FOLDING AND BITING BIRCH
BARK

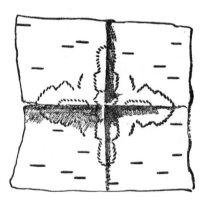

NASKAPI DESIGNS

BIRCH-BARK BOX
DECORATED WITH
PORCUPINE QUILLS

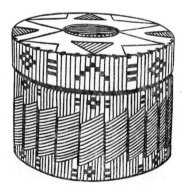

made of bone which looked something like the rockers from an old-fashioned chair, but only about three inches long. Other tribes, too, used to paint their clothes, the Beothuk smearing them liberally with red ochre, and most of the natives using paint in some way. Many of them used face paint in war and also in summer to help keep away the hordes of mosquitoes and black flies.

These people had an ingenious way of making new designs. They would take a very thin sheet of birch bark, not much thicker than tissue paper, and fold it four or more times. Then they would bite a design into the folded bark, using their eye teeth so that they got a good sharp impression. When the bark was unfolded they found the original design repeated four or more times, depending on how the bark had been folded. You may have seen similar patterns made by folding a sheet of paper several times and then tearing it to make a pattern when unfolded.

MUSIC

The art of music was no more highly developed than the other arts, and the Algonkians had few musical instruments. The most important was the drum, which might be of the tambourine type with only one head, or might be double-headed. There was also a water drum made like a small barrel with a skin head at one end. The barrel was partly filled with water which gave the drum a queer echoing note that carried a long way.

The bull roarer might be considered a musical instrument by some. It was a slat of wood about two feet long shaped into a slender oval with notches cut into its sides. A small hole for a string at one end finished it, and it made a weird roaring noise when it was whirled round and round at the end of the string.

Rattles of various kinds were used by the medicine men in their ceremonies and, as different rattles had different tones, they could be made into some sort of rhythmical musical accompaniment for singing.

TALES AND LEGENDS

The Algonkians had an endless store of legends and tales that the mothers told their children, much like our own nursery stories. There were tales that explained how the world was made, and how

the animals we know today got the skins they live in, how the birds
were colored, and so on. There were stories, too, about Nanabozho,
the great spirit that made many of the things about us, the rivers
and lakes, and had all sorts of strange adventures. Many of these
stories are still told round the camp fires in the winter, and some of
the older women can remember dozens of them. To us, many of
them seem rambling and pointless, but the Indians know them well
and still laugh heartily every time Nanabozho gets into trouble yet
again.

MEDICINE

The Algonkians were not good doctors. The medicine men, as
we call them, depended more on magic for a cure than on science,
and their efforts to heal people took the form of loud drumming
and singing and shaking of rattles. The doctor would pretend to
pull a bit of wood or a stone, or even a small living snake perhaps,
from the sick man's body. The women knew something of herbal
remedies, some of which were probably a good deal more effective
than the medicine man's songs. They used plants for food, too,
as we have seen, and also as a source of vegetable dyes which
they used for decoration.

The medicine man claimed that he had spirit helpers and that
they kept him in touch with the supernatural world, a privilege
obtained by much prayer and fasting. The borderline between
science and religion was very thin, as is common among primitive
people.

One thing that did seem to do some good was the sweat lodge,
still used by many of the native tribes of North America. It is a
little hut, just about big enough for a man to get inside comfortably,
covered with bark or blankets or mats to make it almost air-tight.
The man who is to take the sweat bath heats some stones red hot in
a fire outside the sweat lodge and then rolls them inside with a
couple of sticks. Then he closes the entrance and sprinkles a few
drops of water on the hot stones. Dense clouds of steam arise and
the man, who has taken all his clothes off, is soon in a heavy perspir-
ation. After he has stood it as long as he can or cares to, he dashes
out and plunges into the cold river nearby. The old Indians believed
that this purified the body and was good for many sicknesses, and

there is no doubt that it really was useful in some cases, but many Indians died from the effects when they tried the sweat bath as a cure for measles for instance, for the shock, when they plunged into the cold water, was too great.

EDUCATION

There were no true schools or classes of any sort, but a medicine man might teach a pupil some of his magic. Other

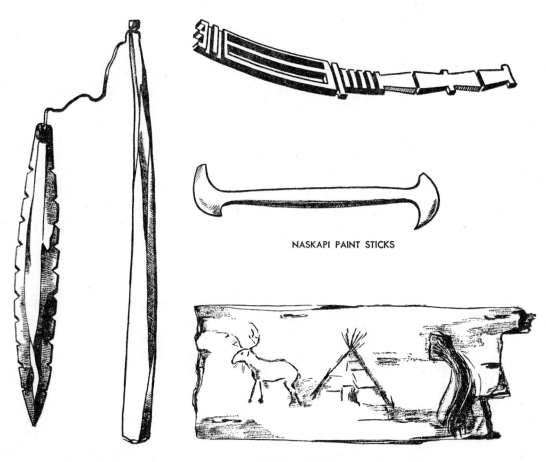

NASKAPI PAINT STICKS

BULL ROARER   PICTURE DRAWING ON BIRCH BARK

children just lived with their families and helped with the many
things that there were to be done. It was hard to know where
the line lay between work and play. None of the Indians could read
or write before the white man came, and they did not even know
that such things were possible. Some of the Algonkians had got as
far towards writing as to draw little pictures on birch bark and
attach a definite meaning to them. If, for instance, in a certain
ceremony a man must sing three songs, one of which mentioned a
deer, the next a wigwam, and the third an enemy's scalp, the singer
might scratch pictures of these three things on a slip of bark to
remind himself, or even to tell somebody else, which songs were
to be sung and in what order.

RELIGION

Religion was not a very important thing in the lives of the early
Algonkians. They believed that there was a spirit, called a
po-wah-gen, in every animal and tree; that many places, such as
waterfalls and great cliffs, might have spirits who lived in them;
and that there were weather spirits too. Some of these beings might
be controlled by a medicine man, and a few of them might be
persuaded to help people or, at any rate, to leave them alone.
Other spirits were feared or felt to be dangerous. The spirit that
lived in the great Chaudière Falls at Ottawa was always offered a
gift of tobacco by passing Indians, who asked the spirit of the falls

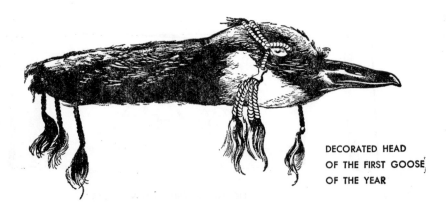

DECORATED HEAD
OF THE FIRST GOOSE
OF THE YEAR

not to harm them or their canoes. Most spirits, they said, were quite indifferent to man and his affairs.

Another name for spirit, *manitou*, is still to be found in such place names as Manitoba and Manitoulin. Another being they all believed in most firmly, the *windigo*, a horrible supernatural cannibal, was usually the ghost of some unfortunate person who had been obliged to eat human flesh in order to stay alive. The windigo was believed to haunt the woods, especially in bitter weather, seeking victims so that it might satisfy its endless hunger for human meat. Of course, no such beings really exist.

Much more real and important to most Algonkians was the need to treat the remains of game animals with respect. Bears especially were treated courteously, the hunter sometimes singing a special song to assure the bear that he is being killed only because the hunter and his family need food. The bones, and especially the skulls, of bears and of beavers were put in a safe place where the dogs could not get at them, and the skulls were carefully cleaned,

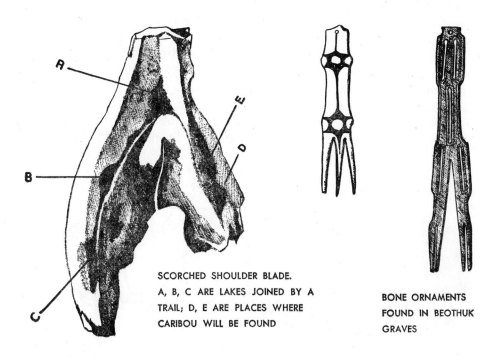

SCORCHED SHOULDER BLADE.
A, B, C ARE LAKES JOINED BY A
TRAIL; D, E ARE PLACES WHERE
CARIBOU WILL BE FOUND

BONE ORNAMENTS
FOUND IN BEOTHUK
GRAVES

with the jaws tied together, and then placed high on a pole or in a tree safe from harm. Sometimes there would be dozens of such skulls on a single pole near a camp.

There were all sorts of taboos and semi-magic rites that a hunter must observe if he hoped to be successful, and every last man of them carried a little bag of charms, such as the skin from a bear's chin, the skull of a weasel, or a bird's beak or claws. The first goose of the season was treated with great respect by the Cree of James Bay. The head was cut off, carefully dried, and decorated with beads. Then it was kept till at least the next year, as a kind of charm. These people would sometimes decorate the hide of an animal with paint as a mark of respect, believing that if the dead animal reported to living friends that he had been well treated, they in their turn would be less reluctant to allow themselves to be killed.

Foretelling the future was a favorite ceremony or recreation, for it was on the borderline between the two. One way was to hold the shoulder blade of a rabbit so close to the camp fire that it scorched. As it did so, the bone would crack and split in the thin parts, and the fortune teller would pore over these cracks and burns and then tell the people what the weather was going to be like or where they might expect to find game.

A more elaborate way of seeing into the future was by means of the Conjuror's Lodge, a hut built of sheets of birch bark or of mats. Into this the medicine man was carried, often bound hand and foot. After an interval of loud singing, the lodge would begin to shake violently, till everybody thought that it must soon fall down. Then the thongs with which the man had been bound would

ROLL OF BIRCH BARK WITH REINFORCED ENDS

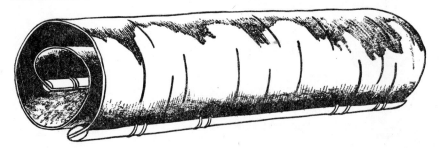

suddenly be thrown out and, in a loud voice, the medicine man would answer the questions of those who wanted to know what the future held for them.

Most people believed firmly in witchcraft and went to a lot of trouble and expense to rid themselves of the spells which they believed had been put upon them. Witches and wizards were thought to be numerous and always ready to work spells against people for the most trivial reasons. Even now there are plenty of Indians who believe that such things are possible. Just as a witch could put a spell on somebody, they believed, so could another witch take it off again and prevent its working.

Nearly all boys, and some girls, when they were thirteen or fourteen, would go off alone into the woods and stay there for several days, eating very little or nothing at all and seeking a vision in which they would meet some spirit or animal which would become their guardian or helper in later years. Many of them believed that they really had seen some such vision and it is quite likely that they actually did feel some unusual experience, for when one is weak from hunger and lack of sleep many strange things may be seen or imagined. In any case, these visions, no matter how real they may or may not have been, were of great importance to the people who believed they had experienced them.

Among the Ojibwa and, to a slighter extent, among their neighbors the Cree, membership in the *midewewin*, or Grand Medicine Society, was eagerly sought. Only men who were well regarded could be members in this secret society, partly healing and partly religious. There were four degrees through which the members progressed in a series of initiations. There are still a few old men living who are members, but the organization is not nearly as strong as it was years ago.

Burial was a difficult matter in a country where the soil was so rocky, and frozen hard for nearly half the year. The Algonkians therefore had to find other ways of disposing of the dead. The Beothuks used to wrap the bodies in sheets of birch bark and place them, as if they were sitting up, in shallow graves. With them they sometimes placed strange ornaments carved from bone or ivory and (being Beothuks) decorated of course with red paint. We are still not sure what these things were used for.

The Micmacs buried their dead in the same way but instead of the carved ornaments they would often put other things in the graves, such as a man's knife and his bow and arrows. With a woman they might place some of the things she used during her lifetime, perhaps her sewing kit or her cooking vessels.

The Naskapi were more likely to wrap the dead person in birch bark and then put him high up in a tree just as they did the skulls of the animals they had killed. In such a case, things were seldom left with the dead person. The Ojibwa, on the other hand, buried many objects with the dead, their tools, their clothes, and even the scalps they had taken. With these, too, they sometimes put food, usually what was thought to be enough to satisfy the dead person for four days in the land of the spirits, for four was a magic number.

CONJUROR'S
LODGE

PRESENT DAY

Many, if not most, of these old customs have now disappeared. Every day the Indians are growing to be more and more like white people and to live as we do. They dress in our clothes and eat our food, except in remote places where they see few white people and have little opportunity of buying white man's food and clothes. Many of the Algonkians have married with whites and now it is often difficult to tell Indians from white men. Some live by farming, or act as guides for white hunters and fishermen. Some few make part of their living by handicrafts, such as beadwork and basket making, but this seldom brings in enough to support them without other work. In the west, round about the Great Lakes, many of the men still trap in the winter and hunt and fish in the summer, but every year the trapping seems to be less profitable. It may not be very long before most of these interesting people become fully absorbed into our white civilization.

How Nanabozho made the land

A Legend of the Eastern Algonkians

In the early, early days, so long ago that nobody can possibly remember them, when Nanabozho, the creator-magician, was still a young man, there was nothing but a vast sea of water. There was air above it, of course, and high above that the stars shone through the scattered clouds at night and a cool wet wind blew softly.

There was only silence. There were no trees in whose leaves the wind could sing, there were no streams to murmur as they ran down the hillsides, for there was no land, only water as far as one could think.

Nanabozho himself was in the water too, for there was nowhere else for him to be. For a long time he was there alone, but at last he grew tired of this and decided to create some animals to keep him company. He created Turtle, and wrapped him up in a safe hard shell. Then he created Muskrat and gave him long fur that trapped bubbles of air in it when he dived so that he could breathe by putting his nose down in his fur.

Then Nanabozho created Otter, who swims so well and strongly, and last of all Beaver with his big flat tail and dense brown coat. Now Nanabozho had companions in the great sea of water, and they all paddled about together happily enough. This went on for a long time, but at last they had done everything they could think of to do, and said everything there was to be said, and Nanabozho began to feel bored.

"This will never do," he said to himself. "I've got to have more amusing companions than these."

He thought about this for a minute and then he began to blame himself for finding them dull.

"After all, it was I who made them, and if they are dull it must be my own fault. I'll see to it that the next ones are a bit brighter."

Nanabozho thought about this for a long time. The real trouble, he decided at last, was the water. When there's nothing but water, one is so limited. There are only certain things that can live in the water, and he'd seen enough of them already.

"It's not solid enough," he said to himself. "I want something I can rest my feet on. I believe that if I could stand on something solid and then put one foot in front of another, I could walk about. Even go pretty fast if I wanted to. Much faster than swimming, at any rate."

Now, he knew, he was beginning to get the first hint of an idea.

Something solid. Where could he find anything except water?

One day, the answer came to him. He had been racing with Otter at the time and Otter dived down and swam deep under water, meaning to put on a spurt when he was so deep down that Nanabozho couldn't see him.

"That's it," Nanabozho shouted. "Under the water! Of course, there must be something solid there or all the water would run away. I'll have to get some of whatever it is at the bottom of the water."

So he took a long breath and dived down as far as he could. Down, down, he went, deeper and deeper till it grew so dark that he could see nothing at all, but the bottom seemed as far away as ever. At last, his lungs nearly bursting, he turned back, shot to the surface, and lay there gasping.

"Where ever have you been?" asked Otter. "You had us all scared stiff. You have been gone a very long time."

"Yes," admitted Nanabozho. "I wanted to see what was at the bottom of the water."

"Well, that's a foolish notion," laughed Beaver. "More water, of course."

"Ah, yes," Nanabozho agreed. "But under *that*. What's under that?"

"Still more water?" suggested Muskrat.

"I don't think so," said Nanabozho. "Look here. If there was nothing but water it would all run away. When you take a drink, the water goes down into your stomach and, if there was nothing to hold it in, it would all run away again. So there must be something at the bottom of the water to keep it from running away."

"Well, it does sound reasonable when you put it like that," Otter admitted. "Why don't you go down and see?"

"That's just what I tried to do," replied Nanabozho, "but it's too far for me. I thought my lungs would burst."

They all looked at each other, wondering what to do next.

"I've got an idea," said Nanabozho.

Otter scratched his back most carefully, and Beaver and Muskrat turned and swam quietly away. Turtle, as usual, was asleep and hadn't heard anything. They all kept quiet and said nothing at all, for they had already found out that when Nanabozho had an idea, somebody was in for trouble.

"I said I have an idea," repeated Nanabozho, "and it's this. You, Beaver, come back here and let me tie my fishing line to your tail."

Beaver didn't want to, of course, but Nanabozho was a great magician and if he said that something had to be done, it just had to be done.

"What do you want to do that for?" asked Beaver.

"I want you to dive as deep down as ever you can and see what there is at the bottom of the water."

"Well, I don't mind trying, but what's the fish line for?" asked Beaver with a worried look.

"Oh, that's to pull you back again in case your lungs burst."

Beaver looked at him sadly and then turned round so that Nanabozho could tie the line to his tail.

"All right. Off you go."

Beaver looked at Nanabozho, and Otter, and Muskrat, and at Turtle, who was just waking up. Then he turned over in a graceful curve, slapped his tail to show that he knew there was danger, and dived deep into the water.

For a long time nothing happened. The fish line paid out from Nanabozho's hand and it seemed endless. Then it stopped and went slack. The four companions watched the line, and then turned their eyes on each other. Nanabozho began to reel it in.

Minute after minute went by and at last the pathetic little body of Beaver floated to the top, the line still tight about his tail.

It was days before Nanabozho could bring himself to try again. This time it must be Muskrat.

"Look what happened to Beaver," said Muskrat when Nanabozho told him what he had in mind.

"Yes, I know, but you've got air caught in your fur and so you can breathe under water."

"Yes, for a few minutes, I can," admitted Muskrat, "but not for ever."

"You won't have to do it for ever. Just till you reach the bottom and come up again. I've got a new fishing line, even longer than the old one and I can tie them both together, and pull you back if anything goes wrong."

"All right," said Muskrat quietly. "I'll try it."

Nanabozho tied the line to his tail and Muskrat looked round sorrowfully at his friends, just as Beaver had done, and then he dived.

At first the line went out very quickly, because Muskrat was trying to swim down so that he might get there sooner. Then it went more and more slowly and at last it hardly seemed to be going at all.

They waited and waited for the longest time, and at last Nanabozho tugged gently on the line. No reply. No little jerk in answer, so Nanabozho reeled the line in slowly. Hours went by as the long, long line came in, and at last they saw the white fur on Muskrat's belly gleaming down there in the water.

Nanabozho pulled the poor little corpse to the top of the water and then he saw, between the front paws clasped tight together, a little lump of brown sticky-looking stuff.

Nanabozho scraped it carefully away and laid it on the edge of Turtle's shell to dry. He smelled it, and tasted it, and thought for a long time.

"I believe it's mud," he announced at last. "And if it is, I can do things with it."

He waited till it was nearly dry and then took it off Turtle's shell and began working it between his fingers. The little pellet of mud grew larger and larger as he worked and kneaded and molded it until at last he had a huge ball of land so big that thousands of people and animals could live on it. There was room for trees to grow and rivers to flow. The ridges in the mud made mountains and the hollows made lakes and, because Nanabozho had been in too much of a hurry to wait till the mud was quite dry, there were big stretches of wet land that we call muskeg, and these never will be dry.

CHAPTER 3

THE IROQUOIANS

POT SUPPORTED
OVER FIRE

Hurons
Tobacco Nation
Neutrals
Seneca
Cayuga
Onondaga
Oneida
Mohawk

CORN MORTAR
AND PESTLE

THE IROQUOIANS

THE IROQUOIANS WERE a group of tribes who spoke dialects of the same language, and lived largely by farming, which no other Indians in Canada did. They can be divided into two main groups, only one of which lived in Canada. This group was composed of the Hurons, the Tobacco Nation, and the Neutrals. The second group lived in what is now the United States, south of Lake Ontario and along the valley of the St. Lawrence River. They were organized into the League of Five Nations, and their names are familiar to most of us: the Seneca, the Cayuga, the Onondaga, the Oneida, and the Mohawk. About 1720, the Tuscaroras entered the Confederation and from then on it was known as the League of Six Nations.

It was once thought that the Iroquoians had come from the Ohio River valley, but we know now that this was not the case and that their ancestors have lived in the part of the world where we first found them for many generations. Though they all spoke the same language, various Iroquoian tribes were frequently at war with each other, especially the Hurons and the Iroquois. When the latter got firearms from the Dutch about 1640, the two tribes fought so bitterly that the Hurons were almost exterminated, and the Iroquois drove them right out of their country, the survivors taking refuge wherever they could find it.

Partly because they lived in permanent villages and had a large settled population in a comparatively small area, the Iroquois were able to organize themselves into a strong confederation and dominate their neighbors.

The first Indians that Jacques Cartier met in 1534 were Iroquoians, probably Hurons, and he met them again the following year at Stadacona, one of their more important villages, which is now called Quebec. When Champlain landed there in 1603 he found that the Huron Indians had moved and their old fields lay empty.

The name Iroquois is from the Algonkian language and means "real adders", which was a way of saying "bitter enemies", for the Algonkians thought the Iroquois were as dangerous as a poisonous snake. They had good reason to think so, too. The Iroquois' own name for themselves means "the People of the Long House".

The more important Iroquoian tribes were the following:

The HURONS, who lived between Lake Simcoe and Georgian Bay. They were divided into four sub-tribes, the Bear People, the Cord People, the Rock People, and the Deer People. These last were also called the White-eared People, because the white ears of the deer are so conspicuous. These four tribes with a few small dependent groups, formed the *Wendat*, a confederation something like the League of the Iroquois, but not so large or powerful.

The TOBACCO NATION or Tionontati or Petuns, who lived to the south and west of the Hurons, between Lakes Huron and Ontario. These people grew large quantities of tobacco, far more than they could use themselves, which they traded with other tribes.

The NEUTRALS, who lived south of the Tobacco Nation between Lakes St. Clair and Ontario and along the north shore of Lake Erie. They were called Neutrals because, for a long time, they remained neutral and would take no part in the war between the Hurons and the Iroquois, even though their own country lay between the two enemies. The Hurons were at last defeated, and the Neutrals were

MAP SHOWING WHERE THE IROQUOIANS LIVED

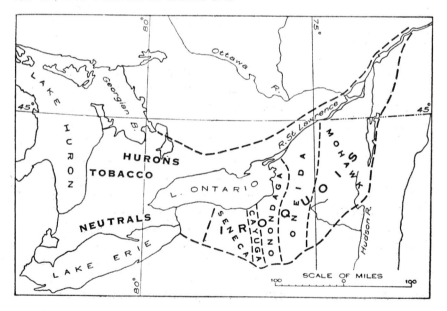

exterminated soon after. Another name for the Neutrals was *Atti-wandaronk*, which means "stammerers". The Hurons called them stammerers because they spoke a little differently from them. The Neutrals returned the compliment and called the Hurons by exactly the same name, for the same reason.

The remaining Iroquoian tribes lived in the United States, but they were so like the first group and the histories of the two are so closely interwoven that we have to consider them as if they were Canadian Indians. They were:

The SENECA, perhaps the largest tribe of the Five Nations, who lived farthest to the west and were the most active in the attacks on the Hurons, because they lived nearest to them.

The CAYUGA, who lived east of the Seneca. Many of them moved to Canada after the American Revolution.

The ONONDAGA, who lived east of the Cayuga, along the east side of Lake Ontario and to the south. Their principal village, Onondaga as it also was called, was the capital city of the League.

The ONEIDA, who lived to the east of the Onondaga and up the St. Lawrence River.

The MOHAWKS, whose name means "man eaters", lived still farther east towards the Champlain Valley. They were the most war-like and aggressive of all the Iroquois.

POPULATION

We are not sure how many Iroquoians there were when the first explorers reached them. Champlain said he thought the Hurons must number about 20,000, and there were said to be about 16,000 Iroquois in 1685, so we may guess that something like 35,000 altogether will not be very far out. Their habit of adopting many of their prisoners into the tribe makes it almost impossible to say how many of them were truly Iroquoian by blood. Today the mixture is even greater, and it is quite possible that there are some people living as Iroquois who have no Iroquois blood in their veins at all.

PHYSICAL APPEARANCE

The Iroquoians, like many of the Algonkians, could often pass for Europeans. There was a slight reddish-brown flush about their skin, and their cheek bones may have been a little higher than in most of us, but the few portraits we have of early Iroquoians, both men and women, certainly do not show us a people who are distinctively Indian. The men seem to have averaged five feet six inches in height, and they varied in build from tall, thin, and long-headed to short, stocky, and tending to fat. Dressed as Europeans they would hardly have been noticed in London or Paris; dressed in a breech-cloth and war-paint, they were Iroquois and no doubt about it.

THEIR COUNTRY

The Iroquoians lived in one of the most fertile and beautiful parts of Canada. It is a rolling hill country, watered with many streams, and originally covered with a forest of timber, mostly hardwoods. The climate, while severe in winter, was milder than in most of the rest of Canada, and the summers were long enough and hot enough to ripen corn, which fact alone made their agricultural way of life possible. It is one of the most healthful climates in the world, neither too hot nor too cold, and the seasonal changes in the weather are thought to have the effect of stimulating the physical

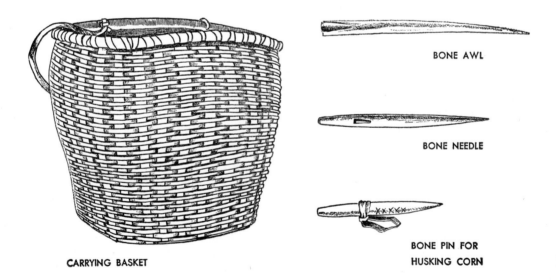

BONE AWL

BONE NEEDLE

BONE PIN FOR
HUSKING CORN

CARRYING BASKET

and mental development of those living there. It is quite certain that the Iroquoians were not lacking in either bodily or mental strength.

Many of the early pioneers spoke and wrote with pleasure and affection of the lakes and forests of the Iroquoian territory, and to-day it is still a most delightful part of the world. The Iroquois on the south side of Lake Ontario occupied a very similar type of country, now one of the richest parts of New York State.

FOOD

The Iroquoians, alone among the Indians of Canada, seldom had fear of famine. They raised large crops of Indian corn and vegetables, and the forests abounded with game and fish. There were some differences in habits from tribe to tribe. The Hurons, for instance, depended more on their crops than did any others of the group, whereas the Neutrals, who lived not far to the south of them, relied more on the great herds of deer which lived in the forest.

The winter, often a time of severe hunger for others, caused the Iroquoians little anxiety, for corn could be stored and so could many of the other crops they raised. They also dried a great deal of meat and fat for winter provisions.

Among the principal game animals they hunted were deer, elk, bear, beaver, and porcupine. There were also turkeys, grouse, geese, ducks, and many other birds. Fish of several species were plentiful and they ate them in large quantities. Among the wild vegetable foods were plums, raspberries, strawberries, blueberries, cran-berries, and cherries; they gathered acorns, walnuts, hickory nuts, butternuts, and beechnuts, and they had also syrup and possibly sugar from the maple and birch.

In their fields they grew great quantities of Indian corn, as well as beans, squash, pumpkins, and artichokes. Tobacco was grown extensively, especially by the Tobacco Nation, and also sun-flowers, which were the source of an oil that they used on their food as we use catsup, and which was also used as a cosmetic. An oil was extracted, too, from walnuts and hickory nuts which formed a thick cream much like butter and which they used in a similar way. Many of our recipes for cooking Indian corn came from the Indians, for they had corn on the cob, hominy, succotash, and even popcorn.

Most of the corn was ground into a fine meal or a coarse flour, and they used it just about as we use wheat flour, for baking bread and thickening soups.

Bear's grease was used as we use butter, and wood ashes served as salt unless they could get real salt from the tribes who lived on the coast. The Iroquoians usually had one principal meal a day, though the Hurons seem to have preferred two, but actually members of the family ate whenever they felt like it. A big bowl of soup was prepared in the morning, and they dipped into it as they desired. Many ate standing up, for the alternative was to lean against the wall or sit on the edge of the sleeping bench or on the ground.

Varied though the Iroquoian diet was, it had one most serious defect. It ruined the teeth of the people who ate it. Iroquoian skulls from old graves show that nearly all the people had very bad teeth and, as all the other natives of Canada had exceptionally fine teeth and used a diet with much more meat and little or no Indian corn in it, we must think that it was the soft boiled food and perhaps the maple sugar that caused the damage to their teeth.

AGRICULTURE

The farming methods of these people were rather primitive and, though they had several varieties of corn, beans, and squash, the yields they got were less than those we now get from the same soil. For one thing, they knew nothing of the use of fertilizers, so the important elements in the soil were soon exhausted and new land had to be cleared, either close to the old fields or on a new site, perhaps miles away.

The land was cleared by the men, who chopped down the trees and cut the brush. Big trees were sometimes burnt down. A scaffolding of saplings was built round the tree trunk, about three feet above the ground, and sods were piled on this close about the tree. Then the sods were thoroughly wetted and a fire was built below them to burn through the tree. It was a slow process, yet quicker and less tiring than chipping away with the blunt stone axes they had before they got steel ones from white men.

When the men had cleared the land, leaving the tree stumps where they were, the women worked the ground, loosening the soil and piling it up in little mounds between the stumps. Corn and beans were planted in the mounds, so that the corn stalks would support the climbing beans, and the squash, which was planted at the same time, grew on the flat ground between the mounds. These three plants were so closely associated and the help they gave each other was so easily seen that they were called the Three Sisters and a woman's society was formed, based on this friendship of the plants. The women used wooden digging sticks for the planting and also a hoe with a deer's shoulder blade for the cutting edge.

Once the land had been cleared and the crops planted the men usually went away trading, hunting, or on the war path, leaving the women to look after the fields, keep them weeded, and gather the harvest. The corn cobs were collected in large baskets, with tump lines to help in carrying them from the fields to the houses, which might be quite a long way off; the corn was stored in large boxes of bark which were kept indoors. Sometimes underground pits were dug and lined with bark, and the corn was stored in these. Some families kept the place where the pits were a secret, for fear that people would steal some of their corn.

In planting, the women used neat little seed baskets divided into three compartments for the corn, beans, and squash so that they could carry all three without getting them mixed.

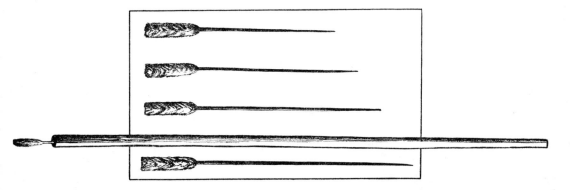

BLOW-GUN AND DARTS

Squash and pumpkins were also stored in pits and they would keep cool and solid till they were needed later in the winter, just as things keep well in our root cellars on the farm. The sunflower and tobacco crops were important, too, and enormous quantities were grown. Many of the farms were quite large, several hundred acres for many villages in fact, and the work of looking after the fields kept the women very busy. It was well worth while, however, for corn removed the danger of famine and made the building of more or less permanent villages possible. About seventy per cent of the food of the Iroquoians came from their crops, and the other thirty per cent from hunting, fishing, and the gathering of wild foods such as acorns, berries, and wild roots.

HUNTING

Deer, which were abundant in the forests, were hunted almost daily and formed the largest part of the meat in their diet. Deer are not very large animals, as compared with cattle for instance, and it took a good many of them to feed a village of a hundred people or more.

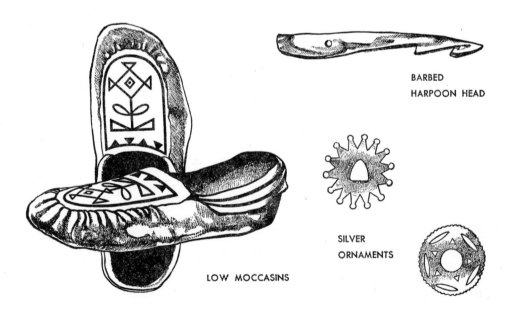

BARBED
HARPOON HEAD

LOW MOCCASINS

SILVER
ORNAMENTS

Bows and arrows were the principal hunting weapons, but traps and snares were used too, and the custom of building fences along which the deer were driven was well known to the Iroquoians. Sometimes the fences ended in a circular corral which the deer could not get out of, and snares were often set in gaps in the fence too.

There were variations in the customs among the tribes which made up the Iroquoian group, but in all of them the skilled hunter was highly thought of, and rightly so, for the food obtained by his skill was of the first importance to the people. Like most hunters, they put a good deal of faith in charms and taboos. Taboos are things one must not do, and they are not unknown even to us, for there are still a good many people who feel it is not wise to whistle while they are fishing, and a well-known charm is the custom of spitting on the bait. One of the charms the Iroquois observed was to avoid the killing of female bears, and the Neutrals had the strange and senseless custom of killing every living animal they could, so that it could not run away and warn other animals of their danger.

The Iroquoians were the only Indians in Canada who used the blow-gun, though it is common as far away as South America. This is a wooden tube, about four feet long, with a bore roughly half an inch in diameter. The darts it shoots are of wood, about the size and shape of a knitting needle. One end of the dart is wrapped with thistledown so as to make an air-tight fit in the gun. The dart is blown out with a sudden puff of breath, short and strong. This is by no means a toy, for it will shoot hard and straight. In experiment, it was quite easy to hit a piece of two-by-four at thirty yards or so, and the dart stuck tight in the wood, so that it had to be twisted hard to get it out. The Iroquoians never poisoned their darts as was the custom in South America.

FISHING

Their ways of fishing were pretty much the same as those of the Algonkians. They used nets and hooks, traps and weirs, as well as spears. That these ways of fishing were successful seems to be proved by the abundant fish remains found in the rubbish of old Iroquois villages. Pickerel, catfish, pike, buffalo fish, carp, gar pike, and chub were all represented by bones and scales, and other kinds have been found too. Fish were boiled or roasted, and large quantities were smoked and dried for winter. Dried fish was crumbled up and added to soups and stews, making them thicker and more nourishing as well as more tasty.

CLOTHING

In the warm weather of summer, the Iroquoians wore as little as possible, but in winter they had to put on a good deal more. The men practically always wore moccasins, with soft soles and extra long flaps which could be turned down or laced up round the ankles, as they wished. Leggings, a breech-cloth, and a shirt with sleeves, which were often detachable, were also worn when the weather was cool. Women wore a skirt and sometimes a jacket, and a one-piece long dress for women was also used. These were all made of buckskin or some other soft leather, smoked and tanned, soft and fine or heavy as circumstances required. In winter, large fur robes were used as an outer wrapping, sometimes of woven rabbit skins like those used by the Algonkians. Some of the people wore moccasins of braided corn husks, but we are not sure just what advantage these had over the leather ones. Moccasins are still worn by some of the Iroquoians. They seem always to be the last bits of native costume to be given up, probably because they are so comfortable and inexpensive. Today they are often decorated with bead-work or silk embroidery.

Few Iroquoian garments were tailored, except the moccasins. Other clothes were made from pieces of skin of about the right

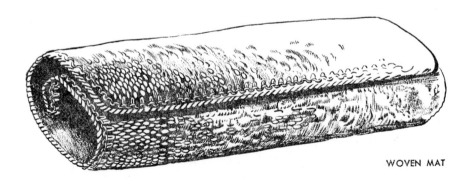

WOVEN MAT

size and shape, but they were laced loosely together instead of being first cut to pattern and then sewn. Few specimens of old Iroquoian clothing still exist, even the oldest museums in Europe having almost none.

Decoration, in the old days, consisted of paint and porcupine quill embroidery, and also beads, made laboriously from stone or shell. Large quantities of these beads have been found in some of the old graves, and it is evident that they were used a great deal. More recently, the Iroquois have used glass beads and silver ornaments, made for them by silversmiths in Montreal and Philadelphia.

Few hats or caps were worn, though the fur robe could be pulled up over the head in cold weather. Men often shaved their heads, or left the hair standing up in a ridge down the middle, and they frequently tied a feather or some other ornament in their hair. One early writer told of an Indian who had a hole pierced through the lobe of his ear in which he had threaded a small green snake. Today the people dress like whites and they are not thought of as looking unusual in any way.

DWELLINGS

Because they lived in more or less permanent villages, the Iroquoians could take the time and trouble to build more solid houses than did the Algonkians, who often moved off the day after they had put up a wigwam. The Iroquoian houses were larger too, and more convenient, but it is doubtful if they were much more comfortable. Early travellers often spoke of the cold drafts, the smoke which swirled through the house and stung their eyes, the lack of privacy, the snarling dogs, and the fleas. The Indians seem to have been much less concerned about their personal comfort than we are and would seldom complain about such little things as a cold draft or smoke in their eyes.

The houses were often quite large, measuring as much as a hundred and fifty feet long and forty or fifty feet wide. There was a passage down the middle, ten or fifteen feet wide, and along this middle line were built the fires at which the women did their cooking. Each fire served the two families living opposite it, for the sides of the houses were divided into cubicles, each occupied by a separate family. So, families Aye and Bee, living in cubicles opposite each other, would use the two sides of the fire built in the central passageway between them. At the back of each cubicle was a platform, raised about three feet above the ground, on which they sat in the daytime and slept at night. The roof of the cubicle formed a wide shelf, below the roof of the house itself, and on this the people kept such things as baskets and hunting gear. Ears of corn hung from the roof, and pieces of meat or fish swung above the fires where they would be smoked and dried.

The framework of the house was of strong poles and these were covered with sheets of bark, cedar, or elm. The bark was held in position with ties of basswood or other fibre, so that it could be taken off if necessary and used again. There was a doorway at each end of the building and a hide hung over this in stormy weather to keep some of the wind out. There were no windows, for they had nothing to use as glass, but holes cut in the roof carried off at least some of the smoke.

In a good many villages, perhaps all of them, there was a special building, known as the Long House, reserved for community affairs, meetings of the various societies, and for council meetings. The Long House is still a prominent building on many Iroquoian reservations, and it is felt to be an important link with the old ways.

The separate houses were grouped fairly closely together and the whole village was often surrounded by a palisade of poles or logs. These varied a good deal in size, sometimes being as little as three inches thick, at others eight inches or more. Nor were they always set close together; though some might be almost touching each other, others would be a foot apart. It is thought that there may have been brush woven between the uprights, or sheets of heavy bark may have been lashed to them. Some villages had two or three rows of palisades to make the defences stronger.

The villages were usually built in the forest, near fertile soil, and away from the larger rivers. They preferred places where palisades could be built easily, and took advantage of swamps and other natural obstacles. There had to be a supply of fresh water, and this was generally inside the palisade so that it could not be cut off if the village were besieged by an enemy.

Because they used no fertilizer, the soil in their fields became exhausted after a number of years, and they had to move the whole village to a new site. This might be only two or three miles away, or it might be ten or more. Another reason for moving was that the supply of firewood in the neighborhood became used up, for they depended almost entirely on dead and dry wood, found either lying on the ground or still standing. The women would complain that they had to walk miles to find wood and then carry the heavy loads all the way back to the village; when their complaints became really serious, it was time to move. This might happen as frequently as at ten-year intervals, or they might be able to stay in a good place for as long as thirty or forty years. Today, of course, the villages are not moved.

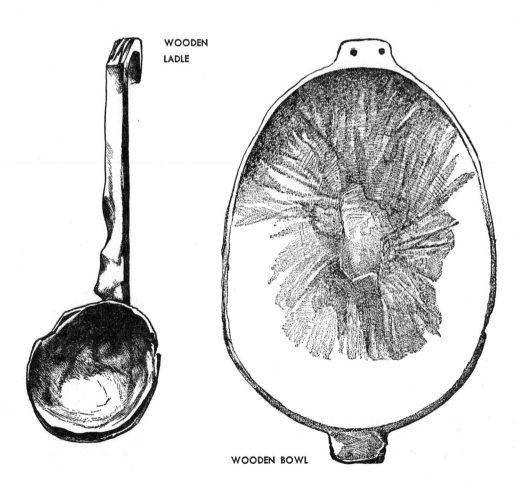

WOODEN LADLE

WOODEN BOWL

FURNITURE

Large and permanent though the houses were, there was surprisingly little in them in the way of furniture. Tables and chairs, which we find so necessary, were unknown, and everything that was not put up on the shelf above the cubicles or laid on the sleeping platform was simply left lying on the ground. Mats of woven rushes or of corn husks were used for sitting on and were sometimes put on the ground near the fire, so that the women could lay their spoons and ladles down on them. They also had paddles of wood for stirring their stews, and for lifting corn bread out of the hot ashes. Bowls were made of birch bark or carved from wood. There were also large storage boxes made of bark, and baskets for carrying and keeping things in.

Pottery was a most important feature of the Iroquoian way of life, for it made the rather slow and unsatisfactory way of cooking with hot stones unnecessary. A pottery vessel was watertight and could be put right on the fire, supported by three or four large stones between which sticks of firewood could be slid, and the food could simmer away there as long as the cook liked. There were pots of different sizes and shapes, some of the best of them most graceful in form and decorated with intricate designs.

Another conspicuous piece of household equipment was the big mortar for crushing corn. Most of the people who ate a lot of corn ground it with stones, but here it was pounded in a wooden mortar made from a hollowed section of tree trunk. The pestle was a heavy, double-ended affair and often two women would work at one mortar at the same time, one pestle coming up as the other came down. The corn was ground to a meal, coarse or fine as required. A pair of stones for cracking nuts generally lay somewhere handy.

TOOLS

Both men and women used tools for various jobs, many of them made of stone. The men had axes, adzes, hammers, and knives of stone, as well as whetstones. Skin-scrapers, for scraping and dressing hides, were also of stone. One might think that stone tools would not be much good, and it is true that they were not as efficient as tools of steel. They were by no means useless, however. Some years ago the experiment was made of building a rough cabin using only Indian stone tools. It took just a little longer than it would have done if steel axes and saws had been used.

The women used some stone tools, too, chiefly knives and skin-scrapers, but the Iroquoians are noted for the great use they made of bone and antler. They had bone awls and needles, bone husking pins, bone spatulas probably used in pottery making, bone netting needles, antler wedges, and also bone handles for their stone knives.

One interesting tool is the pump drill, and it is so surprising to find it in use among these Indians and unknown to all their neighbors that there is some argument as to whether they may not have learned its use from the whites. The pump drill was used for making fire by friction, much as the Boy Scouts do it, and also for drilling holes in such things as beads. They also made fire with the ordinary hand drill, the bow drill, and by striking flint and pyrites together, catching the spark in dry tinder.

TRANSPORTATION

In winter, most things that had to be carried were put on somebody's back, generally with a tump line to take part of the weight. In some cases things were rolled up in a pack and tied with the ends of the tump line, but other people preferred to carry

STONE
NUT CRACKERS

goods in a specially shaped basket which fitted the back quite comfortably and to which a tump line was attached. Others used a pack-board and tump line, and many white men who travel in the bush a great deal say that this is the best of all ways of back-packing.

Toboggans were used, but not very extensively. The Iroquois country seems to be as far south as the toboggan, so well known in the north, ever spread. Travel was largely on foot, and snowshoes were used when needed. These were not the rounded bear-paws of the Algonkians but a longer narrower shoe.

In summer, things were very different, for now travel was usually by canoe if not on foot. There are few birch trees in the Iroquois part of the country tall and straight enough to yield a sheet of bark suitable for a canoe, and so the Iroquoians bought most of their canoes from their Algonkian neighbors. They occasionally made one themselves from elm bark, but these were crude affairs and none too safe. Dug-outs were made too, heavy, slow, and clumsy craft compared with the birch-bark canoes.

DECORATED COOKING POT

WOODEN
STIRRING
PADDLE

The Iroquoians travelled a good deal during the summer, once the crops were sown, and they went on long trading expeditions down the rivers. The Hurons used to sell corn to the Ojibwas, getting furs, drugs, and canoes in return, and the Tobacco Nation sold great quantities of tobacco for furs, hides, and porcupine quills which they used for decorating baskets and clothing.

Little children were carried in cradles much like those of the Algonkians, and these are still used in some remote villages.

DOMESTIC ANIMALS

Like all the other native peoples of Canada, the Iroquoians knew only the dog as a domestic animal. Now and then a crippled bird or animal might be kept about the village as a pet till it died of neglect or ill treatment, but the dog was the only animal usually to be found. Early missionaries wrote often of the many ill-tempered, half-starved curs that slunk about between the houses, and compared so unfavorably with the friendly intelligent pets that they had known in France.

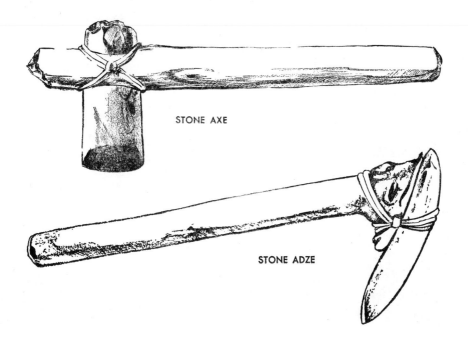

STONE AXE

STONE ADZE

Dogs were seldom put to work. They sometimes went out with the hunters, and in some places they occasionally were forced to help pull a toboggan. As a rule they did nothing but lie about the village. In times of scarcity, it was not unusual to use dogs for food, and this may have been one of the reasons for keeping them at all.

In the great mid-winter festival, it was the practice to sacrifice a white dog on the fifth day. This was done by strangling the dog, and it was believed that the dead animal carried away with it all the wrongs that the people had been guilty of during the year.

SOCIAL ORGANIZATION

None of the other Indians of Canada had such a genius for social organization as the Iroquoians. When they were first discovered by white people, there were at least three confederations of Iroquoian tribes: the Neutral Confederacy, of which we know little; the Huron Confederacy of four tribes, called the Wendat; and the League of the Iroquois (or Five Nations), the best known of them all.

The League of the Iroquois seems to have been founded about the year 1570, largely through the efforts of Hiawatha and Dekana-wida. Hiawatha was a Mohawk who became a famous statesman and reformer. His name, which means "he makes rivers", is an inherited one used by the chiefs of the Tortoise clan of the Mohawks,

BONE BEAMING TOOL

BONE SKIN SCRAPER

and the Hiawatha we are speaking of was the best known of all the men bearing this name.

The Hiawatha in Longfellow's poem is the same man in name only, for Longfellow got his Indians badly mixed and the hero he writes about was not Hiawatha at all but Nanabozho, the mythical Ojibwa creator-magician.

The League of the Iroquois started with three tribes, the Mohawk, Oneida, and Cayuga; then the Onondaga said they would come in if the Seneca would. That made up the Five Nations, and years later (about 1720) the Tuscarora joined the League, making it the Six Nations. Most of the details of those early days are lost now, and the whole story is so mixed up with legends and fables that we can hardly tell what is truth and what is fiction. At any rate, the League was well organized when we first came in contact with the Iroquois and it continued to work well for a long time.

The affairs of the League were debated several times a year in the Council, which consisted of fifty chiefs: nine Mohawks, eight Senecas, fourteen Onondagas, ten Cayugas, and nine Oneidas. This was in the early days before the Tuscarora came in. Some of these chiefs, or *sachems* as they were called, held special positions, such as the speaker, the fire-keeper, the door-keeper, and the wampum-keeper whose duties were like those of a recording secretary. Affairs were talked over carefully and at length, and the various tribes all had well recognized rights to give an opinion or to refuse to act in certain matters.

The organization of the League was repeated in the organization of each tribe and clan, every one of them having its own council, and each giving up some of its own rights of action for the good of the larger group. Thus a clan could not take any action that might harm the tribe as a whole, and no tribe could so act as to endanger the League. We are trying to organize the same kind of thing in the United Nations today. It was the clans of the tribe who had the right to elect a sachem to attend the Council, and the election was really in the hands of the old women who were the heads of the clans. One might think that this would give them a great deal of political influence, for they could depose a chief just as easily as they could elect one, but actually they do not seem to have had much effect on the Council.

The Council discussed everything that concerned all the tribes in the League or any one of the tribes, except for minor matters which were purely the affair of a single tribe. They had well established laws and they recognized various legal rights of individual citizens, such as the right to own and inherit property and the right to inherit certain dignities of position. They preserved the safety of the individual, his right to the exclusive use of his own name, to marry as he wished within the permitted bounds, to wear what he wished, to hunt and fish in the territory recognized as his, to his proper place in moving camp, and many other such rights.

CHILD IN CRADLE

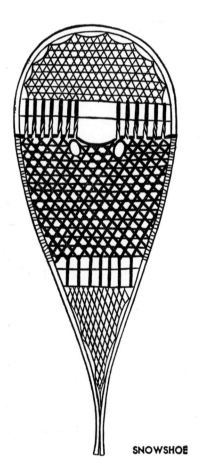

SNOWSHOE

The Council could punish offenders too. If a man was convicted of theft, or of injuring another, of sorcery, murder, or treason, or some other serious crime, he was punished by the loss of his rights of citizenship. This meant that he was no longer protected by law, much like the outlaws of England during the time of Robin Hood, and anybody who felt like it could attack him in any way he wished to. This was always at the risk, however, of finding the guilty man ready to defend himself, so people were a little careful of what they did, even to a convicted offender.

All these legal rights were granted immediately to those prisoners, taken in war, who were adopted into the tribes. This was an important privilege and it had a great deal to do with keeping the League strong, for they lost so many warriors in battle that they would soon have dwindled to almost nothing if they had not adopted

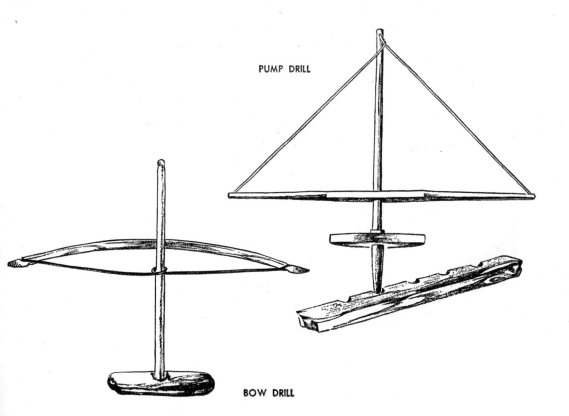

PUMP DRILL

BOW DRILL

this way of keeping up their strength. Only a comparatively few prisoners were tortured as part of the victory celebrations; most of them became new members of the tribe of their captors.

The Iroquois sachems who made up the Council were skilled diplomats and fine statesmen, as our own leaders soon discovered. They often out-witted our side and were very quick to see the advantages and disadvantages of any proposal offered them. They entered into treaties with the white men only after full and careful investigation, and the terms of the treaty were thoroughly gone over, memorized, and then recorded in wampum belts.

Wampum is a shortened form of the Algonkian word *wampumpeak* which means a "white string", or a string of white shell beads. The beads are made from the thick shell of a kind of clam, most of it white, but one part purple. The shells were cut up into little blocks about a quarter of an inch long and an eighth of an inch square. Then they were drilled from each end till the holes met, strung on a string, and rolled on a rough sandstone block till they became rounded. The white beads, which were the more numerous, were worth only half as much as the purple ones. Wampum had several uses: it served as a medium of exchange, as beads for decoration, for making records of such things as decisions of the Council and treaties.

Wampum, when it was to be used as money, was done up in strings of a certain length. When the whites first settled in the New

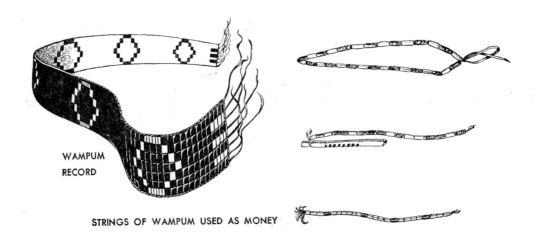

WAMPUM
RECORD

STRINGS OF WAMPUM USED AS MONEY

England states they brought few coins with them and not many more came out of the old country, so they decided to use wampum just as the Indians did. In 1637 wampum was given a legal value of six for a penny, and in 1640 it was ordered that white wampum pass at "4 a penny" and blue or purple at "2 a penny", and not more than twelve pence in shells need be taken at a time. For some time this worked out well and it was quite usual to pay small bills with wampum. After a while some of the settlers began to make their own wampum, and they could do it so cheaply and quickly that the market was soon flooded and the use of it as money had to be stopped.

In making records of treaties and other such agreements, a wampum belt was made, with designs woven in, using the white and purple beads. The designs reminded the record-keeper of what the belt represented, but the idea that each bead stood for a single word or phrase is quite wrong. A belt might show a white man and a dark man connected by a band, and this would remind the record-keeper that it was a treaty linking the whites and the Indians. Sometimes more complicated ideas were woven into the belts, but they were never more than a way of calling to mind what had been decided in council or in making a treaty.

WARFARE

The chief purpose of the League of the Iroquois was to stop the fighting among the tribes and bring about universal peace, and they fought like demons to attain this goal. It sounds like a most contradictory way of going at it, but at times the best way to make somebody stop fighting is to fight him till he does stop. The Iroquois were exceptionally good warriors and they had such an efficient organization that their enemies could seldom resist them successfully. There was a separate series of chiefs and leaders for warfare, and they planned their expeditions with great skill, taking advantage of every imaginable scheme and ruse. Their tactics included ambush and surprise attacks and other methods which were not often used by the European troops who fought against them, so we often hear charges of treachery and unfair fighting brought against the Indians. Actually, they were not treacherous at all, but desperate men fighting to protect their country and willing to do anything that would help them to win. When European officers planned a surprise attack against the Indians or an ambush, they did not feel that they were doing anything that could be called treacherous.

The Iroquoian warrior travelled light. Bows and arrows and a wooden club were their principal weapons, and these they nearly always carried with them in peace as well as in war. Some of them wore armor made of slats of hardwood lashed together and a few had shields of wickerwork covered with tough rawhide. Many of them carried a light braided cord with which to tie their prisoners. The cord was hardly strong enough to hold a man, but it was the custom for a prisoner tied in such a way to admit that he was captured, even though he knew he might be tortured when he reached the village of his captors.

The Iroquoians practised ferocious cruelty towards some of their prisoners, making them suffer as long as they could, reviving them when they fainted, and even stopping the tortures to feed them so that they might live longer. It was considered the proper thing for the prisoner to suffer in silence or else to sing loudly, insulting and scorning his tormentors. Even women and little

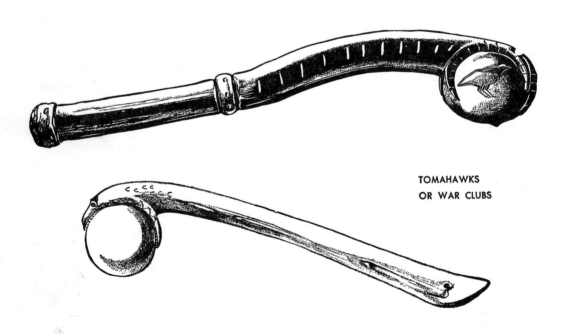

TOMAHAWKS
OR WAR CLUBS

children were sometimes tortured, but most of these, most prisoners in fact, were adopted into the tribe of their captors.

War parties were made up of volunteers, and there was no such thing as compulsory military service. A man could join a war party if he wished and leave it when he wanted to, and nobody would think anything of it unless he was obviously afraid. Then he would have to face the contempt and ridicule of everybody.

One of the great advantages the Iroquoians had over many of their enemies was Indian corn. This was ground into flour or meal, and a small bag of it would keep a man going for days. It was not even necessary to stop to cook it. A man who was in a hurry, or who feared the smoke from a fire might show where he was, could mix some of the dry corn with a little water and make a good meal out of it.

Many of the Iroquoian villages, especially those which might be attacked, were well fortified. A strong palisade, sometimes as much as thirty-five feet high, would be built round the houses, with platforms about four feet below the top on the inside. From here, the defenders could hurl rocks on the attackers down below and pour water over the palisade if it were set on fire. The enemy would try to set the roofs of the houses alight with burning arrows, but these were generally seen in time to put them out.

The Mohawks, in the east, waged war against the Montagnais to their north. The Senecas, who lived in the west, were the people who most frequently attacked the Hurons to the north, even though

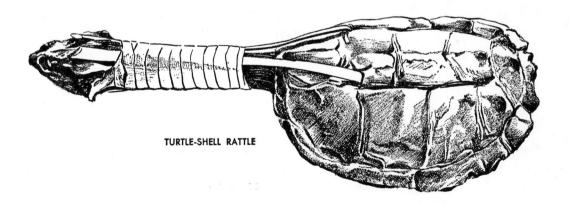

TURTLE-SHELL RATTLE

the two tribes spoke almost the same language and were closely related. The Hurons, in reprisal, sent large war parties against the Iroquois and managed to hold their own till the Iroquois got firearms from the Dutch in what is now New York State, and then the Hurons had but little chance of winning, and the Neutrals went down shortly after.

Equally bitter were the wars the Iroquois fought against the whites. They were the determined enemies of the French and firm allies of the British. One of the methods of warfare practised by the whites was to destroy the crops of the Indians, and the old records show that this destruction was sometimes wholesale. In 1687, Denonville destroyed

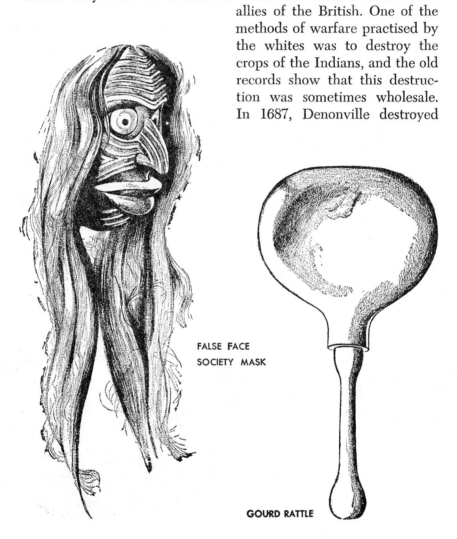

FALSE FACE
SOCIETY MASK

GOURD RATTLE

the standing crops of four villages and it took his soldiers seven days to do it. General Sullivan, in 1779, ruined the crops on not less than two hundred acres, and destroyed many granaries. Forty Indian villages were burnt, together with 160,000 bushels of corn and many other vegetable stores. Such methods as this made it most difficult for the Indians to live through the long cold winter, and hunger, together with the superior training and strength of the whites, defeated them at last.

SOCIAL LIFE

Living in almost permanent villages and having reserve supplies of food on hand made it possible for the Iroquoians to devote more time to social activities than could the Algonkians, for instance. We read so much about their continuous wars that we get the impression that they did little else but fight, but this would be far from the truth. War was the exception, not the rule, and most of their time was spent peacefully enough. The men hunted and fished, cleared land, went on trading expeditions, built their houses and kept them in repair, made canoes, tools, and weapons. The women made pottery, looked after the crops, did the cooking and the housekeeping, gathered fuel, wove baskets and mats, picked berries and other wild fruit, made rope and cords, and looked after the children.

There were dances and festivals, more by a good many than among most of the native tribes of Canada. One of the most important was the mid-winter festival, celebrated when they could see that the sun had begun to rise earlier and the darkest days of winter were past. It lasted seven or eight days, and it was on the morning of the fifth day that the white dog was sacrificed and ceremonially eaten, to wipe out the misdeeds of the people.

Another series of festivals was connected with Indian corn; there was one seven-day celebration when the corn was planted in the spring; another almost as long when the plants first turned green; and a four-day festival when it was harvested. There was another feast, held in the winter, called Dream Fulfilment, at which a fire was built in the middle of the largest house in the village, and people came from many miles around to take part in the masquerades and to pray for blessings in the new year to come.

There were several more or less secret societies among the Iroquoians, and these too held annual festivals. Some of them are not very clearly remembered now, but we do know that there was a Dark Dance, a Medicine Society, and a Little Water Society.

They had also secret medicine societies, such as the False Faces, who wore hideous masks in the performance of their ceremonies. These masks were wooden representations of the "Faces", mythical beings which, the Iroquois believed, lived far away at the rocky rim of the world and in dense forests. Many an Iroquois hunter told of seeing these strange bodiless faces floating about among the trees, their long hair blowing in the wind. They never harmed the hunters, but only wanted a little tobacco or some of the white meal mush.

The False Face members professed to be able to cure diseases, just as the "Faces" themselves did. Anybody who dreamed of them, or was cured by them, might join. They visited the sick, shaking

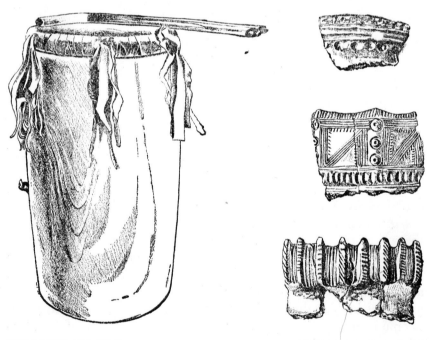

WATER DRUM AND STICK   DECORATIONS ON POTTERY

turtle-shell rattles over them and sprinkling them with hot ashes, which they were apparently able to handle without burning themselves.

Dancing and singing to the accompaniment of water drums and rattles were the most obvious features of the festivals. There was always plenty to eat, and in some cases it was customary for the singer to give away presents as he sang.

Marriage was a good deal more formal than among many of the other tribes of Canada. The bride was usually chosen by the young man's mother, who arranged matters with the girl's mother, frequently without consulting either of the two fathers or the bridegroom himself. If everything seemed satisfactory, the two families exchanged presents and the marriage was accomplished. The young man went to live with his bride's parents, but there was no set period of service expected of him. There was a feast, of course, and one interesting custom was that of giving the bride bundles of firewood as wedding presents. The older women knew that going out into the forest to get firewood was one of the most tedious tasks facing the newly-married girl.

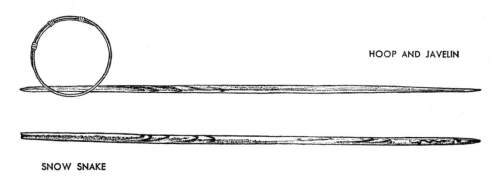

HOOP AND JAVELIN

SNOW SNAKE

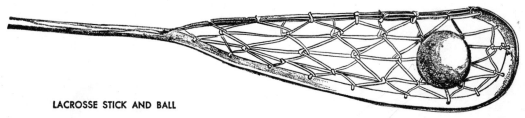

LACROSSE STICK AND BALL

This way of arranging a wedding without consulting the two people most concerned sometimes led to trouble, especially if a young girl found herself married to a much older man who was not acceptable to her, as sometimes did happen. Divorce was simple, either of the two simply picking up all personal belongings and walking off, but though it was easy, divorce was considered shameful, and neither the husband nor the wife would decide on it except for a good reason.

Children were well treated. When they were bad, they were sometimes punished by having cold water thrown suddenly in the face. The name given to a child at birth was confirmed before all the people at the next mid-winter festival or the next green corn festival, whichever came first. At the age of fifteen or so, this name was given up and another was selected and announced at one of the same festivals. This second name was generally kept for the rest of the person's life.

The Iroquoians, in spite of their reputation for cruelty and fighting, were a peaceful and kindly people among themselves. They were most affectionate and showed keen sympathy for any friends or relatives who were sick or in want. Women were well treated too, and held an important position in the family and the clan. There are many cases on record in which white people, who had been taken prisoner by the Indians and forced to live with them for a number of years, firmly refused to go back to their own

INDIANS PLAYING SNOW SNAKES

families when given an opportunity. Life as an Indian must have had a good deal in its favor.

GAMES

Games were popular with both men and women. Lacrosse was played by whole villages and so was the women's double-ball game. Snow snakes were eight or ten feet long, instead of three or four like those used by the Algonkians. Another popular sport was the hoop and javelin game. A wooden hoop, about eight inches across, was rolled slowly along a flat strip of ground. A moment later a slender stick, the javelin, was slid along the ground after the hoop. The player's aim was to make the hoop fall across the javelin when they both stopped. These things are easy to make, and it is a fine game for the summer.

Gambling was very prevalent. Dice were not used but a good substitute was made by scorching six or eight plum stones on one side, so that they had a dark side and a light side. These were shaken up in a shallow wooden bowl and then tossed into the air so that they all fell on a little mat on the ground. If all the dark sides were up, the score was so much, less if only some showed dark and so on down to no darks at all. Similar "dice" were made from bits of broken pottery trimmed into discs about an inch across, with a pattern on one side but none on the other.

Smoking was not only a religious ceremony, but a pleasurable thing too, and the many pipes, made of stone or of pottery, that have been found in the old village sites show that it must have been very popular. We know that very large crops of tobacco were grown every year.

Many of the Iroquoians were first-class athletes. One of the best known was Tom Longboat, a long distance runner and Olympic champion, from Grand River, Ontario, and a medal named in his honor is still awarded for athletics in the Indian schools of Canada.

MUSIC

Singing was the principal form of music and it accompanied their dancing, their prayers, and their healing ceremonies. Drums of two kinds, the tambourine and the water drum, were used as well as rattles made of several different kinds of things such as rawhide, bark, gourds, turtle-shells, and small plaited baskets.

A six-holed flute was played by young men to please the girls they were courting, but it sometimes found another use. If somebody discovered that the enemy were near or were trying to surround the village, a young man would stroll along between the houses as though unaware of any danger, but playing a certain tune which was recognized as a warning by his friends but not by the enemy.

ART

None of the arts as we know them achieved much success. Perhaps the most advanced was pottery decoration, and some of the designs they used are most attractive. The figures modelled in clay or carved in stone for tobacco pipes were amusing, and some excellent work was done in wood carving, especially of masks and miniatures used in witchcraft. The embroidery in porcupine quills of the old days has been replaced recently almost entirely by work in beads and silk.

LITERATURE

There was no true literature among the Iroquoians in our sense of the word, for these people could not write, but they had many legends which have a distinct literary interest and their skill as orators was famous. The early European officers and statesmen who had to deal with them in making treaties and other such official business were surprised at the cleverness of their arguments, the vividness of their expressions, and the force and dignity with which they spoke.

They had many songs, too, which were used on social occasions, for religious rituals, and for healing ceremonies. War songs, songs of peace and of love, and lullabies have all been recorded from the Iroquoians.

SCIENCE

What little science they had was the province of the medicine man, who was at the same time doctor, priest, and magician. They understood the difference between healing by medicinal herbs and by magic, and it was generally the women who used the herbal remedies, leaving the curing by means of blowing, sucking, and singing with rattles to the men. Some cures were attempted in which the patient was cut with small knives to let the blood out and then massaged with warm ashes.

Medicine men had other duties too, for they were expected to be able to find lost articles by magical means, to be able to control the weather, foretell the future, as well as cure the sick. Some medicine men said they were able to turn themselves into animals when they wanted to, and many people believed them for there was a general feeling that animals were really men wearing animal clothing and that they could show their true human side whenever they wished to. As they believed that animals were actually human, it was not difficult to suppose that men could become animals.

RELIGION

For the Iroquoians, religion was very much a part of everyday life. The festivals which were so popular and so numerous were not only social occasions but had also definite religious meaning. Prayers were said during the more solemn parts of the proceedings and sacred tobacco was crumbled up and sifted into the fire burning in the middle of the lodge. The supernatural world was felt to be all around, and everybody wore charms to keep off witches and evil spirits and called on the medicine man in every emergency.

Boys, and a few girls too, when they were thirteen or fourteen, would go away alone into the woods to fast and pray, seeking for a spirit helper that would be their personal guardian in later

SIX-HOLED FLUTE

life. Their belief in these guardians was very strong, and an unusual success in any undertaking was always said to be because of the strength of the guardian spirit.

Everybody believed in witchcraft, and efforts to bewitch people for wrong purposes were severely punished. When somebody fell sick, or met with an accident, the first thought was to get the medicine man and find out who had bewitched the victim and then remove the spell. Dreams were considered most important and many men were strongly influenced by what they had dreamed, believing in them with almost religious conviction. A bad dream was quite enough to make a man turn back from the war path and nobody would think of blaming him.

They believed that there were large numbers of spiritual beings living in the woods, in trees and rocks, in rapids and waterfalls, and that these beings were human in a way, but yet not quite human. Their own society was so well organized, with clans and tribes, and leagues and confederacies, that it was easy for the Iroquoians to suppose that these spiritual beings were organized in the same way. They felt there must be a chief of all the Good Spirits and a chief of all the Bad Spirits and that all the others must be under the authority of one or the other, though but few of the Indians actually gave much thought to the matter.

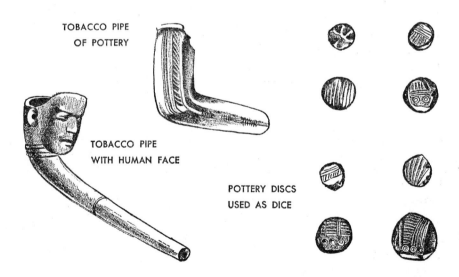

TOBACCO PIPE
OF POTTERY

TOBACCO PIPE
WITH HUMAN FACE

POTTERY DISCS
USED AS DICE

Both men and women fasted for ten days after a death in the immediate family and did not remarry for a year. Among the Neutrals it was the custom to blacken the face in mourning, and also to blacken the face of the dead person. They also tattooed the body before burying it and decorated it with feathers and other ornaments.

That the Iroquoians believed in a future life of some sort seems evident, for they buried things with the dead, presumably for their use in the next world. Just what this future life was like, they did not know. The bodies of the dead were wrapped in furs and placed in a grave, sometimes lined with bark. Others were placed on high platforms. Among many of these tribes, the feast of the dead was celebrated every ten years or so. All the bodies that had been buried since the previous feast were dug up or taken down from the platforms and the bones were scraped clean and decorated with red paint. Then they wrapped them up again and reburied them in a common grave which we call an ossuary. Some of these burial pits have been discovered and excavated, revealing thousands of human bones, with many ornaments and tools that had been buried with them. Sometimes the bottom of the ossuary was covered with a layer of red ochre.

PRESENT CONDITIONS

Today the Iroquoians are among the most progressive of the Indians of Canada. Many of them own fine farms and others are in business for themselves. Some of the Mohawks of Caughnawaga, a few miles outside Montreal, make their living by putting up big steel bridges and buildings, rivetting the beams and girders together, far above the ground and quite unafraid of the dizzy heights. Nearly all the people living on the reservations dress like white men, except for a few who still prefer to wear moccasins instead of shoes.

There are about eight thousand Iroquoians living in Canada, and an equal number in the United States. More and more of them leave the reservations every year as they find opportunities of working outside. A high proportion of Iroquois enlisted in both the Great Wars and, like most other soldiers of Indian origin, were both efficient and unusually brave men.

Wild boy and the cave of animals

A Legend of the Iroquois

Thousands and thousands of years ago, soon after the world was made, there lived on the banks of a great river an Iroquois hunter and his wife and their little boy. The man's name was Kanati, which means Lucky Hunter, and the woman's name was Selu, meaning Indian corn. What the little boy's name was, nobody can remember any more.

Kanati wasn't called Lucky Hunter just by chance. Indeed, he did seem to be either very fortunate or very skilful. Never did he go out hunting without carrying back a deer or a turkey or something else good to eat. His wife never seemed surprised at his success. She would take the game down to the river side, clean it carefully, throw away the parts that were not good to eat, and wash away the blood.

The little boy had nobody to play with while his mother was busy in the house, so he used to go down to the river bank and amuse himself there happily enough. One day, when his mother came to the shore to get some water, she thought she heard him talking to somebody. She stopped and listened, and it certainly did sound as if he were talking and as if another child answered him, but when she got to the spot there was nobody else to be seen.

When Kanati came home, Selu told him what she had heard, and they decided to ask the boy about it.

"Why, yes," he answered at once. "He comes up out of the water nearly every day to play with me. He says he is my elder brother, because we both grew from the same food."

His parents looked at each other without speaking but later on, when the little boy was asleep, they talked about the other boy, wondering who he could be.

"I think I understand it," said Selu. "He told our little boy they were brothers because they both grew from the same food. I think he must have grown out of the bits of meat and the blood that I throw into the river."

"That does sound likely," agreed her husband. "And in that case, he is probably a strong magician, and he might do the boy some harm. We'll have to see."

Selu certainly didn't want any harm to come to her son and so they decided to try to catch the strange boy, but every time they went down to the river bank he dived into the water and vanished before they even saw him.

Then they determined to try a trick. They told the little boy to challenge his playmate to a wrestling match and then hold him till they could come and help. This the little boy agreed to do, because he didn't like the way the strange boy disappeared every time his parents tried to talk to him.

The next day, when they were playing on the river bank as usual, the little boy suggested that they try a wrestling match. This idea pleased the other well enough and soon they were locked in each other's arms and rolling about on the sandy beach. When the little boy felt that he had got a good firm hold, he began to shout loudly.

"Daddy, come on! I've got him. Come on, quickly!"

Kanati and Selu ran down the path to the shore as fast as they could, urged on by the little boy's cries.

"Hurry up, I can't hold him long. He's much too strong for me. Do hurry up!"

Just in time they got there, and the three of them managed to hold the strange boy and prevent him from slipping back into the water.

"Let me go!" he shouted angrily. "Let me go! It was you who threw me into the river in the first place. Now let me go back again!"

In spite of all his cries and struggles, they carried him back to the house and tied him up.

For the first day or two he refused to eat anything, but when he found that they were not going to do him any harm, he gradually grew tamer. Just the same, he was always wild in his ways and well deserved his name of "Wild Boy".

After a little while he began to eat the food that they gave him, and when they felt quite sure that he wouldn't try to run away, they set him free and he and the little boy played together happily day after day for months.

One day Wild Boy watched Kanati as he came back carrying a fat buck and a turkey.

"I wonder how he does it," he said to the little boy. "I believe he must be a magician."

"Oh, no, I don't think so," the little boy said. "It's just that he really is a lucky hunter."

"No, there's more to it than that. A hunter might be lucky day after day, even for weeks perhaps, but not for ever. Kanati has never failed to come back with game even in the worst weather. I think we ought to follow him one day and see just where he goes and what he does."

So, a few days later when Kanati started off with his bow and arrows, the boys waited till he was out of sight and then followed behind him, careful not to be seen, but staying close enough to make sure they didn't lose sight of him.

Kanati travelled very fast. His feet seemed to have magical moccasins on, and the two boys were badly out of breath when at last Kanati started up the side of a steep grassy slope. There were no trees here and the boys knew they would be seen if they left the shelter of the forest. All they could do was watch and hope that Kanati wouldn't go out of their sight.

They were fortunate, for the Lucky Hunter stopped when he was only a little way up the slope, where a large round boulder stood right in the mouth of a cave. He rolled the boulder aside and then stood waiting with an arrow on his bowstring. He had hardly had time to get ready when a fine large deer jumped out of the cave and ran off along the hillside. Kanati drew his bow, the arrow sang through the air, and the deer fell dead.

He rolled the big rock back into place, picked up the deer, and started off home.

The two boys stayed hidden behind some thick bush till he had passed and then they too started for home, taking a roundabout way so that they would not be seen, but running fast so as to be there before Kanati got back.

"So that's how he does it," said Wild Boy when they were alone. "He has all the deer shut up in that cave and lets them out one by one, just as he needs them."

This was a wonderful secret and of course the boys just had to see if they could shoot deer as easily themselves. One day, when they knew that Kanati wouldn't be going out for meat, as there was plenty in camp, they took their bows and arrows and followed the trail that led to the big cave.

It was all the two of them could do to roll it aside. Before they could stop the trembling of their arms and get their bows ready, a deer had jumped out of the cave and was off along the hillside. Then came another, and another, and still another, one by one, and then in pairs, and at last in dozens and hundreds, so many of them and running so fast that the boys couldn't collect their wits and shoot even one of them.

Then came moose, and elk, and caribou, and all the kinds of four-footed animals there are, more and more till the whole landscape was black with the herds of running beasts, all pouring out of the cave. Then came the birds, eagles, and owls, and turkeys, ducks and geese, and grouse, all the birds known to man, till the sky was thick with them, and the sound of their wings and the running feet of the animals made such a noise that the boys were terrified.

Miles away, Kanati heard a sound like distant thunder in the mountains. He looked about him, but the sky was clear, not a cloud to be seen. He listened again more carefully, and knew that this was not thunder, for the roaring sound went steadily on, growing louder and louder.

"Those bad boys of mine are in some sort of trouble," he told Selu. "I'm going to see what it's all about."

Kanati grabbed his bow and a quiver full of arrows, his knife and his club, and ran off up the trail towards the magic cave, for that was where the sound seemed to be coming from.

He hadn't gone far before he met the first of the escaping animals. As he saw more and more of them, he guessed what had happened, and ran faster than ever, hoping to put the big boulder back in place before all the animals got out.

He was too late, of course. When he got there nothing was to be seen but the huge empty cave and two very frightened small boys.

Kanati looked sternly at them and scolded them for a long time. What he had to say to them was never forgotten.

"Up till now," he said, "we have lived in ease and comfort. If we were hungry, all I had to do was to come here to the cave and shoot a deer or a turkey and carry it home to your mother. Now, I shall never be able to do that any more. From now on, I'll have to hunt for our food and so will you, forever, till you die, and so will all other men. There will be many days when you'll not be able to find any game at all, for the animals will always run away as soon as they see you, just as they did today when you opened the cave. From now on, for ever, all men will have to hunt for their food and work hard, and even then not always get all they need."

And so today there are no more Lucky Hunters and even the best sometimes come back empty-handed.

CHAPTER 4

THE PRAIRIE TRIBES

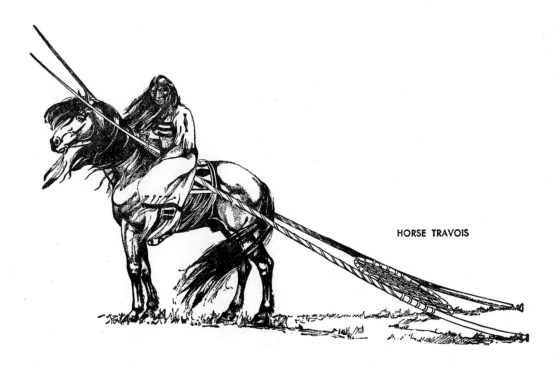

HORSE TRAVOIS

Blackfoot
Blood
Piegan
Gros Ventre
Plains Cree
Assiniboine
Sioux
Sarcee

EAGLE FEATHER
WAR-BONNET

THE PRAIRIE TRIBES

O<small>N THE WIDE OPEN PLAINS</small> of the middle west lived tribes of Indians who depended very largely on the bison or buffalo for their everyday needs. Their food, their clothing, their dwellings, and their tools were supplied in large part by this one animal. The people all seem to have been new-comers to the areas they lived in when first discovered by white explorers. They all lived in much the same fashion and had the same ways of doing things but, unlike the Algonkian people and the Iroquoians, the prairie tribes did not all speak the same language; there were, in fact, four separate tongues spoken on the plains. The Blackfoot, Gros Ventres, and Plains Cree spoke dialects of the Algonkian language; the Assiniboine and the Sioux spoke Siouan; the Sarcee spoke an Athapascan dialect; and the Kootenays, who now live in British Columbia, spoke their own language, Kootenaian.

The B<small>LACKFOOT</small> were a loose alliance of three smaller groups, the real Blackfoot, the Bloods, and the Piegans. These three together made up one of the strongest and most aggressive of all the prairie tribes, frequently at odds with their neighbors and spending much of their time on the warpath.

Their native name is *siksika* which means "black feet". Some people say that they used to color their moccasins black, and others think that they got this name because their moccasins were often dark with the ashes of prairie fires. Their home was east of the Rocky Mountains in the high plains where Edmonton and Calgary now are, but actually they paid very little attention to tribal boundaries and would have promptly attacked anybody who questioned their right to live and hunt wherever they wished to.

The B<small>LOOD</small> Indians or Kainah (from *ah-kai-nah,* which means "many chiefs") lived to the southwest of the real Blackfoot, closer to the foothills of the Rockies.

The P<small>IEGAN</small>, whose name means "poorly dressed skins", lived to the south of the Bloods round about where Lethbridge and Medicine Hat are today.

As a rule, these three tribes acted together in war or in making peace. Their only allies were the Sarcees and the Gros Ventres;

with all the other tribes these three were anything but friends.

Centuries ago, the Blackfoot lived on the eastern edge of the prairies, in the Red River country near Winnipeg. They still speak the Algonkian language of eastern Canada, just as the Plains Cree and the Gros Ventres do. They had been moving slowly westwards across the plains for some time and when they got horses and guns they moved even more quickly towards the mountains.

The Gros Ventres, who also spoke an Algonkian dialect and had come from the east, were at one time the close allies of the Blackfoot. They used to live just to the east of the Piegans, between the modern cities of Regina and Swift Current, but moved south into the United States before 1800. They got their strange name, which is French for Big Bellies, through a peculiar mistake. In the Indian sign language their tribe was indicated by moving the hand in front of the speaker as though to show he had a big fat belly. The true meaning of this sign was "no matter how much they are given, they want more" or "they must have big bellies for they eat everything given them"; in other words, they were "beggars", always asking for more and never satisfied. They were also called the *atsina,* a Blackfoot word with much the same meaning.

The Plains Cree also spoke an Algonkian dialect and followed the Blackfoot from the eastern woodlands onto the prairies. Their country stretched across the northern fringe of the plains from the country of the Swampy Cree, to whom they are closely related, south of the Churchill River to the eastern edge of Blackfoot territory. They spread out onto the prairies only a short time before they first met white men and still show traces of their original home and customs. It was probably when they got guns and horses that they started to move towards the west. They were active in trapping and fur trading with the Hudson's Bay Company and were allied with the Assiniboines in their frequent war parties.

The Assiniboines, whose name is an Ojibwa word meaning "people who cook with stones", were originally a branch of the Dakota Sioux, and they still speak a Siouan dialect. They once lived south of the Cree, near the Red River and in northern Minnesota, and moved up towards Winnipeg about 1650. Here they became the allies of the Cree and today the two tribes are very much alike in many ways, though they speak entirely different languages. They gradually spread farther west and now occupy all the area south of the Plains Cree, from the eastern plains to the Blackfoot country.

The SIOUX, whose name is an abbreviation of the Ojibwa word *nadouessioux* meaning "adders" in the sense of "enemies", are recent arrivals in Canada, coming here after the Custer Massacre on the Little Bighorn River in Montana on June 24th, 1876, when General Custer and 264 men were defeated and killed by the Sioux. There are only seven or eight hundred Sioux now living in Canada and, as they surrendered no land to the government, they are not paid treaty money as many other Indians are. They well remember their origin in the United States and have never given up their right to get stone from the famous Pipestone Quarry in southwestern Minnesota. They have little to do with the Indians of other tribes and have kept a good many of their own customs.

The SARCEE, whose name comes from a Blackfoot phrase *sa arsi* meaning "not good", are also recent arrivals on the prairies. They live along the upper part of the Athabasca River, northwest of the Blackfoot, and came from the north by way of Lesser Slave Lake, not far away. They speak an Athapascan dialect and their

MAP SHOWING WHERE THE PRAIRIE TRIBES LIVED

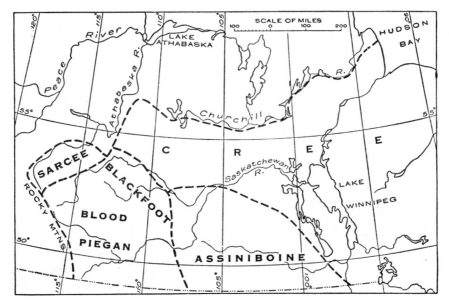

nearest relatives are the Beaver Indians of the Peace River, still farther north. They became the allies of the Blackfoot, and there are both Crees and Blackfoot living with them on their reserve today. They number less than two hundred. They are the only Athapascan people in Canada who moved from the northern forests onto the prairies.

POPULATION

We have no accurate figures to tell us how many Indians there were living on the prairies, and 35,000 is about as close as we can get today. They suffered severely from small-pox, and the great epidemics of 1780-81, 1837-38, 1845, 1857-58, and 1869 took many lives. In 1864 hundreds more died from measles and about six hundred starved to death in Montana when the local herds of buffalo became extinct. Since 1900 they have been increasing slowly in numbers and there are about 15,000 living today.

PHYSICAL APPEARANCE

There is not very much to distinguish the prairie Indians from any others as far as looks are concerned, though they are a little taller than most. The Blackfoot people averaged 5 feet 7½ inches, which would mean that just as many of them measured more than that, as measured less. Actually there are a good many six-footers among them.

The prairie Indians are well-built men, strong and active, and their skin is a little darker and redder than that of other tribes, though the Blackfoot are somewhat lighter in complexion. The hair

MAN IN WOLF SKIN DRIVING BUFFALO

is black and straight and the women were proud of its length, for it often reached the ground. The Blackfoot, Cree, and Assiniboine had rather delicate, soft faces, very different from the Sioux whose high cheek-bones, hawk-like noses, and long faces are often thought to be typical of Indians as a whole, though in fact this type of face is pretty well confined to their tribe. They are at times fine and striking-looking men.

THEIR COUNTRY

Nobody who has lived on the prairies can ever forget them. The vast, seemingly endless expanse of flat, treeless land, the sky like a huge bowl with its edges resting on the far horizon all round, is like no other part of the world. To the stranger it appears empty and monotonous, but those who live there know that, hidden in the folds and dips, are valleys great and small, with groves of green trees and running streams. They know of the countless little lakes, some of sweet water, and others so filled with salt and other chemicals as to be quite unfit to drink, and of the little sloughs that give the ducks a million safe places for their nests.

Here and there are ridges of hills, sometimes with forests on top, sometimes low and sandy. In winter, it can be bitterly cold, and wild blizzards sometimes make travel dangerous if not impossible. The summers are hot and breathless, but the springtime with its multitude of flowers and the autumn with its abundant wild fruits are beautiful indeed.

FOOD

In the old days, there was seldom any long lack of food on the prairies. The buffalo, the principal source of meat, roamed the plains in almost countless thousands. Nobody is sure of the exact figures, of course, but men who have made a careful study of the matter think there must have been about twenty million buffalo left in 1850, which is just over a hundred years ago. In earlier days, they were probably more numerous still and sixty million is thought to be about the number that once lived on the prairies. If you put them in a long procession, ten feet from one head to the next, they would reach almost half way to the moon.

Buffalo meat could be eaten fresh, or it could be smoked and dried, or it could be made into pemmican. If the meat was to be eaten fresh, it could be roasted on a spit over the open fire, or boiled in a skin bag by means of hot stones. This method produced not only boiled meat but also a rich and nourishing soup which was very popular. Sometimes the stomach of the freshly-killed animal itself was used to cook the meat in. Either a small pit was dug in the ground and lined with the stomach, which had been cut open and washed out, or it was hung on a circle of sticks stuck in the ground. Water and meat were added and then hot stones were dropped in to boil the water and cook the meat.

Dried meat, often called jerky, was used almost as much as fresh. Meat that was to be dried was taken from the lean parts and cut into thin slices. These were slit here and there till they looked almost like coarse netting, and then they were hung on racks to dry in the hot sun. If the sky clouded over, the women hurriedly brought the meat into the tipis so that it should not get wet and spoil. When it was thoroughly dry it was stored away in rawhide bags called *parfleches* and then could be kept for a long time. It did not look very tasty but was good and nourishing when softened in hot water, or eaten dry. One of the favorite tricks of the boys was to knock down the drying racks and snitch pieces of meat when their mothers were not watching.

Pemmican was a common prairie Indian food, and even today experts in diets have found nothing so valuable for men going on expeditions to places where there is no food, and everything must be carried in. It was made from dried buffalo meat which was pounded into a powder by the women. They would lay a buffalo skin on the ground and put a flat stone, perhaps ten inches across, down in the middle of the skin. The slice of dried meat to be powdered was held on the flat stone and hammered with another stone till it was broken into tiny bits, almost a powder. When enough of this had been prepared, hot melted buffalo fat was poured over it and the two were mixed together. Then it was stowed away in skin bags, which were sewn up tight. When the pemmican cooled, it hardened, and the powdered meat, soaked with fat, would keep for years. It was a valuable food for men going on the war path, as a small bag of it was no trouble to carry and held enough food to last a man for days. One pound of pemmican was said to be equal in food value to five pounds of meat. It could be eaten cold, or cooked, or made into soup.

An especially nice kind, called berry pemmican, was made by adding crushed choke cherries or berries. The ripe cherries were pounded, just as the meat had been, and the cherry paste, stones and all, was stirred in with the meat and fat. Now and then, as a very special touch, a few crushed leaves of peppermint were added.

Buffalo meat was not the only kind that could be made into pemmican. Elk, moose, deer, and antelope all served equally well

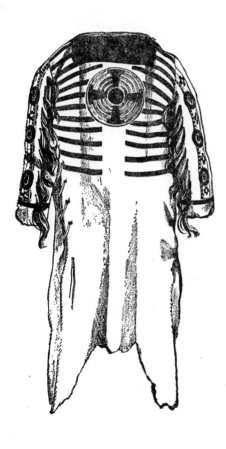

MAN'S TUNIC

WOMAN'S DRESS

and some of the people living in the northwest of Canada even made fish pemmican. Of course, the meat of all these animals was eaten fresh too. There were few animals that the prairie Indians would not eat, though the Blackfoot thought the bear was too sacred and few of the people ate dog meat except in some ceremonies. Many prairie Indians avoided fish.

Vegetable food, when it could be had, was used in large quantities. The Assiniboine used wild rice, just as the Ojibwas did, and the Blackfoot in the west of the plains ate a wild lily bulb called *camas*. The prairie Indians also ate service berries, wild cherries, red willow berries, prairie turnips, bitter root, and wild rose haws. All through the prairies the people moved to places where berries were numerous, as soon as they were ripe, and picked large quantities of them which they stored in skin bags. Often the berries were spread out on skins and dried in the sun, so they would keep longer.

Fire was made with a simple bow drill, using a shaft of oak and a cedar hearth, but, once camp was pitched, it was generally easier to borrow fire than to make it. There were no regular hours for meals, though the family often ate together if it was convenient.

AGRICULTURE

There was nothing like as much agriculture here as among the Iroquois, though the Sioux had gardens and the eastern prairie tribes sometimes grew a little corn. Tobacco was an important crop; one Blackfoot planting has been recorded that was about a hundred yards long by five wide. For smoking, tobacco was often mixed with other things, such as the inner bark of the red willow, and the leaves of the bearberry, called *kinikinik*, meaning "the stuff that is mixed".

HUNTING

Abundant though the buffalo were, they had to be hunted and killed before they could be eaten, and the Indians of the prairie tribes knew several ways of doing this. Because buffalo often grazed in large herds, hunting was generally an organized affair in which many men and even women and children took part. When the people needed fresh meat, which was quite often for they consumed enormous quantities of it, they would send out young men to look for buffalo. Sometimes they were found almost immediately; at other times it might be two or three days or even more before any were sighted. Some believe that, before they had horses, the Indians used to set fire to the prairie all round the buffalo herd and then kill them as they milled about in a terrified mob, for the buffalo had an instinctive dread of fire. Indians say they rather doubt that this method was used often, for the only time at which the prairie grass was dry enough to burn was in the autumn when the buffalo hides were at their best, and fire would have scorched the skins and made them useless.

Another method of hunting the buffalo was to drive a small herd into a corral or pound. To do this, the herd was started moving slowly in the desired direction, taking care not to frighten them and start a stampede. To do this, two or three young men would sometimes go down on their hands and knees with a wolf skin draped over them and move towards the grazing buffaloes. The animals would move off, keeping just ahead of the "wolves", and could easily be steered towards two long lines of people who lay, at some distance from each other, so as to form the sides of a big letter V, sometimes two miles long. As the herd of buffalo passed, the people would stand up and the animals, catching sight of them, would

MOCCASINS

move on a little more quickly. As the sides of the V drew closer together, the buffalo would move faster and faster, now quite alarmed, and then they would break into a run. The people behind them would wave blankets and shout, and soon the whole herd would be stampeded into a circular pound of strong logs at the end of the V. Here the Indians would spear them or shoot them down with arrows.

Sometimes the end of the long V of people was at the top of a steep cliff and the buffalo, running at top speed, those in front pushed on by those behind, had no time to stop even if they realized their danger. Some would be killed when they fell over the cliff, others would be unable to escape because of broken legs and were easily killed.

Places where these buffalo jumps and pounds once were are still to be found on the prairies; there are thick beds of bones from the hundreds of animals that were killed there. Scattered among the bones may be found stone arrowheads and skin-scrapers, used in killing the beasts and preparing their skins.

These methods of hunting, exciting though they must have been, were certainly not without danger, for the herd would sometimes break through the line of people, trampling some of them, and now and then a wounded animal would turn and attack the hunter. The walls of the pounds were made as strong as possible, but even these gave way on occasion.

The use of the pound seems to have been largely dropped when the Indians got rifles and horses, for they then adopted another way of hunting, called the surround. When a herd of buffalo was found, the mounted Indians would form a circle and gallop round and round the bewildered animals shouting and waving, shooting them with either a bow and arrow or a rifle as they passed. The herd had little chance of escaping and before long all of them would be dead. The Indians used the same tactics in attacking the waggon trains of early settlers crossing the plains.

Buffalo hunting was so important to the people that it became almost a religious rite. Everything about it was controlled and ordered by strict ceremonies and any man who tried to get a buffalo on his own was severely punished for he might frighten away a whole herd that the people could otherwise have killed. Even the building of a pound was regulated, and "Poundmaker" was an honored name among the Indians.

Before the days of firearms, the bow was the principal weapon and the bows of the prairie tribes, though short, were very strong. There are true tales of bows able to drive an arrow right through a buffalo, if it was not stopped by hitting a bone. Bows had many advantages and their use continued long after rifles were brought in. Even now there are some old men who get an occasional grouse, rabbit, or duck with their bow.

The Sarcees preferred bows made of wild cherry, with arrows of willow. Other people, such as the Cree, liked bows of willow. A willow of fair size that had been scorched and killed in a fire, but was still standing, made an excellent piece of wood for a bow.

Lances or spears were used too, but they do not seem to have been common and there are but few specimens in museums.

Although the buffalo was easily the most important of the large animals hunted by the plains Indians it was by no means the only one. Next in order came, perhaps, the antelope, or pronghorn, once common but now seldom seen except in a few places. Antelopes are very swift runners, having been timed at as much as thirty-two miles an hour. One of the usual ways of hunting them was by driving them into a corral or pound, much as with the buffalo. The chief difference was that the V-shaped wings leading into the pound turned suddenly so that the animals could not see the enclosure till they were almost in it. Frequently a pit was dug in the pound itself into which they would fall, with greater chances of injuring themselves. They are so active that they could easily have jumped over the walls of any ordinary corral.

The people living on the northern fringe of the prairies, where the plains merged with the forest, hunted more kinds of animals, such as the moose, deer, bear, beaver, and porcupine, which were less abundant on the open prairies. The Blackfoot, to the west, hunted the elk on the lower slopes of the Rocky Mountains and occasionally they killed mountain goats or mountain sheep. Many of the prairie people used snares, made of sinew or babiche, for deer and smaller game.

One unusual form of hunting was eagle trapping. Eagle feathers were used as badges for war deeds, and the catching of an eagle was in reality a religious ceremony, the hunter always praying for help beforehand on top of the highest hill. Here he dug a pit in which he had room to lie down comfortably and carried the dirt he took out a long way off and scattered it about. When he had finished digging the pit, the top of it was covered over with loose sticks on which grass was spread to make the pit invisible and, last of all, the hunter laid a piece of red raw meat on top for bait. A cord was tied to the meat, the loose end to be held by the man in the pit so that the eagle could not fly off with the bait. Sometimes a wolf skin was stuffed and stood up in such a position as to make it look as if the wolf were eating the meat. The hunter took a long thin stick into the pit with him which he would use to drive away smaller birds.

The hunter had to be in the pit before daylight and lie inside, perfectly still for hours as the suspicious eagle circled round and round watching for signs of danger. When at last the eagle did alight, it would always be near the pit, but never actually on it. After waiting for a moment, the big bird would walk over to examine the meat. Finding it could not fly off with it, the eagle would begin to feed, and then the hunter would reach up between the loose sticks covering the pit and grab it by the legs. At once there would be a terrific fight, and few hunters killed their prey without being badly scratched in doing so.

Sometimes the man had to wait for days before he caught even one eagle, and at other times he might be lucky and catch several in a single day. Among the Blackfoot, five eagles were worth one good pony. Only the golden eagle was caught in this way. The bald-headed eagle was too dangerous and its feathers were not valued.

FISHING

Most prairie tribes used but little fish and some of them actually had taboos against eating fish at all. The Blackfoot apparently did not make any fish hooks or fish spears, but after their food supplies had been reduced by the extermination of the buffalo, they did take to eating more fish than they had before. The Cree, who so recently had left the eastern and northern forests, were still accustomed to eating fish. They used traps woven like coarse baskets, as well as circular fish fences into which fish were driven, much as the buffalo were driven into a pound.

DRESS AND ORNAMENTS

Clothing, on the prairies, was made entirely of skins, until cloth was brought in by traders and blankets took the place of the soft robes the people had always worn. The women were wonderfully expert in tanning skins and could make them thick or thin, hard or soft, as they wished. The tanning was a long and tiring process and took up much of the time of almost every woman in the camp. So important was it, indeed, that a woman was judged largely by the quantity and quality of dressed skins she produced.

The hard stiff rawhide used for the soles of moccasins and for parfleches was the easiest to make. When the hide had been taken

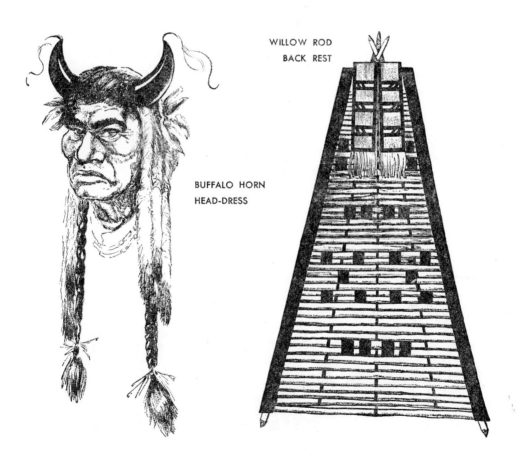

WILLOW ROD
BACK REST

BUFFALO HORN
HEAD-DRESS

off the animal it was staked out flat on the ground, hair side down, and thoroughly scraped with a special fleshing tool which took off all the shreds of fat and meat clinging to the skin. This job took more energy than sense, and was really hard work. Once this was done, the skin was left for a few days and then worked down to an even thickness with a skin-scraper, an adze-like tool with a cutting edge. Generally, this work was done in the shade, the woman standing on the stiff hide and bending at the waist to get at the work.

BUFFALO-
SKIN TIPI

When the inside was finished, the hide was turned over and the hair side was treated in the same way, scraping off the hair till the skin was clean and even. Then the hide was left to dry and harden.

To make a soft skin, the same process was gone through and then the hard rawhide was rubbed thoroughly with a mixture of animal brains, fat, and liver. The exact composition of this varied a good deal and, when hides are treated today, Indian women use a mixture of brains, lard, and even soap. As long as it is an oily, fatty substance, it seems to be satisfactory. The work of rubbing it into the hide was done by hand, sometimes with a smooth stone to help. Then the hide was left to dry in the sun again. When it was thoroughly dry, it was soaked in water, rolled up in a bundle and left for a time to "cure". Then it had to be stretched, to overcome the shrinking that had taken place. It had to be scraped all over again on both sides, this time with a rough and gritty stone, or with a special form of skin-scraper, and then dried and rubbed and worked till it was completely soft and pliable. It took about seven days of fairly steady work to tan a large skin.

For clothing, light skins were preferred such as cow buffalo, antelope, elk, or deer. Heavy robes, with the hair left on, were often worn in cold weather. It might be a single skin, or a robe could be made up of smaller skins sewn together, perhaps beaver. Similar robes, but lighter in weight, were often used as "best clothes" for formal occasions. Later these were replaced by the brightly colored blankets which we think of as typically Indian.

Clothing varied a good deal with the season, with the age and sex of the wearer, and with the work he was doing at the moment. Nobody would wear his best clothes when hard at work skinning and butchering buffaloes. Most people wore as little as possible, especially in fine weather. The men quite often wore only their moccasins and a breech-cloth, and the children nothing at all.

The shape of a tanned skin had a good deal to do with the shape of the garments, and the women cut them as little as possible, to save both work and skins. A certain amount of tailoring was done, but not nearly as much as among the Eskimo.

Men usually wore a breech-cloth, held up by a belt. To this belt were tied the soft leather thongs that supported the long leggings and also, at times, a knife-sheath, firebag, and a little bag for face-paint. The breech-cloth was a strip of soft tanned leather, about four feet long and a foot wide, which passed between the legs, the ends being lapped over the belt, back and front. Moccasins on the feet completed the costume, unless a skin shirt was worn in cool weather. The winter robe was wrapped round the body horizontally with the tail to the right. Often the right arm and shoulder were left bare.

Women wore similar clothes, but the shirt was lengthened into a skirt from the neck to below the knees, usually made of two skins, one for the front and one for the back. The women's leggings were shorter than the men's and tied just above the knees. The moccasins were the same as the men's, but smaller. There were no sleeves on the skirt or dress, but small cape-like extensions were sometimes sewn over the shoulders, which gave much the same effect. As a rule, the sides of the dress were not sewn together, but were laced. Children, when they wore anything at all, dressed much as their parents did.

Moccasins were used by everybody. Two styles were common on the prairies, one cut from a single piece of skin and having a soft sole, and the other, a two-piece style, with an added sole of tough hard rawhide. There were slight differences in cut and decoration and in the old days a good Indian scout could tell what tribe a man belonged to by the shape of his moccasin tracks in the sand or mud. Some moccasins were beautifully decorated with porcupine quills or beads, and Blackfoot moccasins often had a three-pronged design on the instep, the three prongs representing the three tribes, Blackfoot, Blood, and Piegan.

The magnificent feather head-dress which so many people think of as being "really Indian" was originally worn only by a few important men of the Sioux and was certainly not common. It was adopted by the Indians in the famous Wild West Show of Buffalo Bill's, which toured the world many times about fifty years ago, and so millions of people got the idea that these head-dresses were worn by all North American Indians. Today even some of the Indians believe this, and so any Indian who gets dressed up for a parade feels that he must wear one of them too.

As a general rule, prairie Indians wore nothing at all on their heads, except that the men might wear a warm cap in winter. Often these were made from the skin of the head of an animal, such as an antelope, and the ears were left sticking up, giving an amusing effect. Other winter caps were made from warm bird skins.

The various secret and military societies also had special head-dresses, sometimes decorated with buffalo horns. The Blackfoot sometimes made elaborate head-dresses with the white winter skins of the weasel. They were less interested in the eagle feathers used for the big war-bonnets, which were made from the tail feathers of the golden eagle when it was two years old. The younger birds and the older ones too had feathers which lacked the sharp black tips and white body that were especially admired and desired.

The men spent a good deal of time combing and braiding their hair, and putting ornaments in it. Many of these ornaments were worn for their magical value as charms, which were thought to help the wearer in his daily life and to protect him from dangers, rather than merely for ornament. Some men did their hair in two braids, others preferred four, two hanging behind the ears and two in front. The Assiniboine men added lengths of false hair

WOVEN FIBRE BAG

PARFLECHE OF RAWHIDE

to their own, till their long locks actually reached the ground. They often did it up in a big coil which they wore on top of their heads fastened with a strip of otter skin.

Hair brushes were made from the stiff bristly tail of a porcupine. These had wooden handles that had been put inside the skin while it was still moist, so that it would shrink and dry in tight. The women, who were not nearly so careful about having tidy hair as the men were, wore it either loose or braided, but seldom brushed or combed. They sometimes ran a line of vermilion down the parting. The men were careful not to let any hair grow on their faces, which was not difficult, for they seldom had any beards or moustaches. What few hairs did appear, they pulled out with tweezers made from a pair of clam shells or, in later years, of steel.

Many of the men wore face-paint, not only when they were going on a war party, but also at other times. Red, yellow, white, and black paints were carried in little leather bags, and also some grease to mix them with. Sometimes they were simply mixed with water. Red was the favorite color, and the Sarcees often had the whole upper part of the face painted red with ochre or vermilion. The horses were often painted too. Today a few of the old men still use face-paint, but the custom is rapidly dying out.

Many ornaments were worn on the clothing, both as charms and for decoration. Tufts of human hair, including scalp locks, were

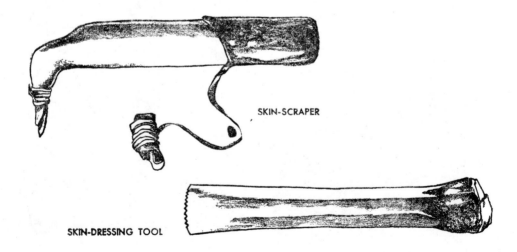

SKIN-SCRAPER

SKIN-DRESSING TOOL

used for trimmings, and necklaces made from beads, shells, claws, teeth, bones, and even bits of scented fungus were worn. Shells brought in from the sea coast were considered very valuable, especially the soft pink ones which were worn at the throat. Some well-to-do women wore dresses heavily covered with elk teeth showing they were the wives of rich and important men.

Quill embroidery was once used by almost everybody on their best clothes, but little of it is to be seen now, beads bought from the traders having taken the place of the quills. Some of the special parade costumes are loaded with glittering beads wherever there is room for them, and these outfits are valued at hundreds of dollars. All the horse trappings, cinches, bridles, cruppers, are heavy with beads and the result is brilliant, if a little gaudy.

The gaily-beaded firebag which most men wore at their belts to carry their tobacco in was almost an ornament in itself, and so were the heavily beaded belts the men used to wear when blankets took the place of the old skin robes. These are seldom seen today and most of the men wear quite ordinary clothes. Men, and women too, pierced their ears so that they might wear ornaments in them, but nose piercing does not seem to have been customary on the prairies.

Tattooing, though not very common, was by no means unknown. The Cree used it a good deal and some of the other people too. It was a very painful process and many a young man found that he did not want to go on with it. Sometimes a boy's girl friends were asked to come and watch the operation so that he would be ashamed to cry out or ask that it be stopped.

DWELLINGS

The Indians of the prairies, as most of us know, lived in tall cone-shaped tents called tipis. Tipi is a Sioux word, in which *ti* means "dwelling" and *pi* means "used for", so *tipi* means "used for a dwelling". In the old days, tipis were made of buffalo skins, and it took twelve or fourteen of them to make an ordinary tipi. Today canvas is used, but the shape has not changed. The great advantage of a tipi was the fact that it could be carried along when the people moved camp and, if made well, would last for a few years. The average Blackfoot tipi was about eighteen feet across.

In summer time, the tipis were put up, usually in a circle, almost anywhere on the prairies. Naturally a place near good water was selected, and if there was a grove of poplars in the river bottom they would be used as a convenient source of firewood. In winter, the people often made a more permanent camp, generally in a sheltered river valley where they were protected from the cold winds. Sometimes they built cabins of logs here, especially the Sarcees who had used log cabins in the northern woods before they moved to the prairies. Today many of the people live in log cabins the year through, though some of them, especially the older people, like to move into a tipi for the summer.

The tipis were made, owned, and set up by the women. When one was to be put up, the first step was to place the poles in position. These varied in number from as few as thirteen to over twenty, the average being about sixteen. They were a good deal longer than seemed necessary, often as much as twenty-five feet. The foundation poles, on which all the others rested might be either three or four in number. The Blackfoot, Blood, Piegan, and Sarcee used a four-pole foundation, and the Assiniboine, Cree, and Gros Ventres used three. When the foundation was up, the other poles were laid in the crotches formed at the top and the pole that went in the middle of the back of the tipi went up last. The top of the tipi cover was tied to this one, so that they went up together. Then the cover was carried round the two sides to the front, and fastened together with a series of pegs above the doorway. At the top were two adjustable ears, each with its separate pole, which could be moved according to the direction of the wind, preventing it from blowing downwards into the tipi and giving a good draught for the fire which was built just behind the middle of the tipi.

The bottom of the tipi might be held down by a number of pegs, but in those parts of the country where there were plenty of sizeable stones, these were used to weigh down the edges. Numbers of rings of stones, still lying where they were left after a tipi was taken down, are still to be seen on the prairies. It took about half an hour to put up a tipi and get it ready for use.

When a tipi was properly put up, the cover fitted tightly over the poles, which were moved outwards towards the edge of the circle to adjust them in position; the back of the tipi sloped up a little more steeply than did the front, and the door faced the east. The Indians often had to go a long way to get a good set of poles. They generally used tall slender pines, called lodge-pole pines because they were so often used for tipis. The old Indians used to say jokingly that a good set of tipi poles was more valuable than a wife.

The door was a sheet of skin, large enough to cover an opening in the front of the tipi. The door was spread flat by wooden rods and sometimes patterns were painted on it. Often, too, a bunch of buffalo dew claws hung on the door so that anyone lifting it to one side to come in would rattle the dew claws, letting the people inside know they had a visitor.

Inside the tipi there was often an inner wall, about six feet high, of painted skins, fastened to the tipi poles on the inside. Today they use canvas walls. The purpose of the inner wall was to prevent a draft and at the same time give ventilation inside. A good tipi is a most convenient and comfortable dwelling. On the floor at each side of the door was a space, which was generally kept clear for putting down such things as saddles and bundles that might be needed at any minute. Farther back, on the ground by the walls, were the beds, which were skins laid down with a pole along the outer side to keep things in place. At the head of the bed, and perhaps at the foot too, was a back rest to lean against and at the very back of the tipi was a tripod on which were hung the family medicine bundle and other sacred things.

FURNITURE

The back rests were triangular mats of willow wands, tapering to a point at the top and woven together with three rows of cord. Sometimes strips of color were added as a decoration. The back rest was supported on a tripod of decorated sticks. Sometimes a rack made of rods was fastened to the tipi poles high enough to be above the heads of people when they stood up. This was useful for keeping things on and also as a place for hanging up meat so that it might dry in the heat and smoke of the fire.

At least some of the prairie tribes used to make pottery but they seem to have given up its use as soon as they got horses, perhaps because the pots got broken so easily. Now they use bags, usually made of skin, to carry things in, or did until a few years ago. Some of them are of soft leather and others of stiff rawhide. One bag of this type, called a *parfleche,* was made from a sheet of folded rawhide, something like a big envelope, and was often used for carrying dried meat. The word *parfleche* is French and means "(shield) against arrows". In the old days the Indians made shields of the same hard leather. The parfleches were often decorated with paint and so were some other skin bags.

Very few baskets were used, but they had some flat bags woven of vegetable fibres, chiefly nettle and milkweed. Apart from these, weaving was almost unknown, though they did make a few bags from woven buffalo hair. Firebags, for carrying tobacco, flint and steel, and paint bags for holding face-paint were carried by nearly all men. Old parfleches were not thrown away but were cut up to make hard soles for moccasins.

TOOLS

There was but little work in wood or bone, though some bowls for use at meal times were carved from wood. Bone was used for the handles of some tools and so was elk antler. Spoons were made from buffalo or sheep horn, and sewing awls from small bones. Sinew was used for thread. Cord was made from tough vegetable fibres and from rawhide thongs.

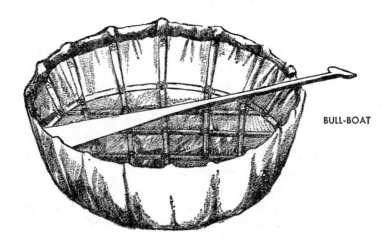

BULL-BOAT

Stone hammers were used for a good many purposes. Some of them had grooves round them for fastening the handle on and there would be several of these hammers to be found in most camps. They are still to be seen lying about on the prairies and it is said that the people didn't often bother to carry any with them for they could nearly always find one or more on an old camp site. They were used for breaking up fire wood, crushing bones to get the marrow, driving tent pegs and horse pickets, and for pounding up choke cherries to mix with pemmican.

Knives were originally made of stone, but these were replaced by steel knives as soon as they could be had. A few knives were made of bone, which can be made sharp enough for many purposes. Skin-scrapers were of stone or of bone, and in recent times of steel. Every woman had several of them in her kit for they were used almost daily. Her sewing awls she kept in a special case, which was often carefully decorated.

Arrow shafts had to be smooth and straight, and the Indians had special tools for ensuring that they were. Arrow-shaft smoothers were pairs of stones, grooved to the size of the shaft, and gritty in texture so that they would smooth and polish as sandpaper would. Arrow straighteners were made from bone or stone, shaped something like a wrench, and used with a levering motion that bent the shaft till it was no longer crooked but quite straight. Arrow tips were sometimes used as drills and, for deeper holes than could be drilled with arrowheads, they had special stone drills. These were used for hollowing out the bowls of tobacco pipes, which were of a soft black stone or of a bright red stone which they got from a special pipestone quarry in Minnesota. This quarry was open to all the tribes allowed to use it and here fighting was forbidden by old custom.

Another tool was the digging stick, a heavy curved rod, sometimes with a handle, that the women used for digging up edible roots, which were sometimes hard to get from below the dry sun-baked prairie soil.

TRANSPORTATION

Before the horse was introduced to the Canadian prairies, about 1775, the people travelled on foot, carrying their possessions on their

backs or making use of their dogs as beasts of burden. When they
came to a river that had to be crossed they built bull-boats, which
were circular craft like deep floating saucers made of willow saplings
covered with buffalo hides. Some tribes, such as the Cree, preferred
to build rafts. At times rafts were made from the poles and tipi
covers. In winter, the people still moved about on foot though the
Cree made some use of the dog sled. Even on the northern fringe
of the prairies, snowshoes were not used.

Dogs were used to pull a curious contrivance called a *travois*,
which is a French word meaning "shaft". The travois consisted of
two long poles, one on each side of the dog, which made him look
as if he were standing between the shafts of a carriage. A rack
was fastened between the shafts behind the dog, and on this rack
various things could be carried, the dog dragging the poles along
the ground behind him. Some dogs could pull as much as seventy
pounds in this way. There was a good deal of variation in travois
design but the general idea was always the same.

When the horse came along, everything was changed. Men
need no longer walk, they could ride and they took to it with great
enthusiasm, soon becoming daring and skilful horsemen, and a man
or a boy who had a horse wouldn't even walk down to the river bank

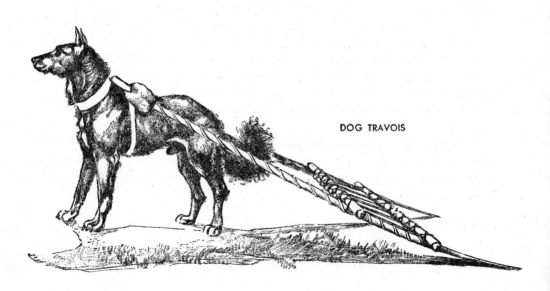

DOG TRAVOIS

close by for a drink of water, he would ride instead. Horses became of first importance in war, and their capture by stealth or by an open raid was a great adventure.

Horses were used for transportation too and the dog travois was soon adapted to the horse, merely using longer poles. Now they had a rack big enough and an animal strong enough for heavier loads; such things as tipi covers, children, old people, and so on, were all carried on the travois. Sometimes the rack was square-cornered, and sometimes oval. The Assiniboine used an oval rack, and the Sarcees and Gros Ventres used a square one. The Blackfoot used both.

Soon it became fashionable to decorate horse saddlery and harness and today the horse trappings used in parades are bright and glittering with beadwork. Sometimes one can hardly see the horse itself.

Children were tied to special cradle boards that could be carried on a woman's back, hung from the horn of the saddle, or stood up against the side of a tipi as the mother found convenient.

SOCIAL ORGANIZATION

Because the different tribes of the prairies are of various origins, their social organization differs somewhat from tribe to tribe, though there is a fairly general pattern running through them all. Some of them we know but little about, and others such as the Blackfoot have been thoroughly studied.

A tribe was made up of a number of smaller units, called bands, each of which had a chief and perhaps also a number of counsellors. Membership might be inherited through the mother, in which case the band was called a clan; if the inheritance was through the father, we call the band a gens. Usually one had to marry outside one's clan or gens.

When all the bands of a tribe met together their tipis were pitched in a circle, not just one row deep, but perhaps two or three. When the tribe moved to a new camp site, the leaders picked out a spot and marked off a sort of entrance, generally facing east. The bands moved in through this entrance and then turned to the right or left to take their usual position in the circle, and put up their tipis with all the doorways facing east. In the middle of the circle was the council tipi, and the tipis of the "police", the members of the military societies, stood here and there in convenient positions.

The members of the military societies acted as camp police and regulated the behavior of the people in hunting and in other things. Some tribes, such as the Blackfoot, had several of these societies; others, the Assiniboine for instance, had only one. One of the best known societies, found with a similar organization in most of the prairie tribes, was called the Crazy Dogs. There were also the Kit Foxes, the Horns, and the Bulls, as well as several others.

These societies were so arranged that a man could progress from one to the other, in a regular order, with other men of about the same age, much as do the pupils in our schools. Each of these societies had special rituals and regalia and resembled in some ways our own lodges and secret societies. There were also women's societies, patterned after the men's. Membership was by purchase, that is to say a man had to pay the society a fee in order to join it. This might be so many horses, or other things of value.

Each tribe had its own council, consisting of the chiefs of the separate bands and some of the older and wiser men. They talked over matters which concerned the tribe as a whole and looked after such things as treaties with the whites, but they had not nearly the detailed organization of the Iroquois.

DOMESTIC ANIMALS

Horses and dogs were the only domestic animals known to the prairie Indians. The dogs were the descendants of animals the Indians had had with them from very early days and were used chiefly as pack animals, either carrying packs slung on each side or dragging a travois. The dog travois is very little used now, but it is still well remembered.

The prairie Indians already had horses when first they were visited by Europeans. These they had obtained (generally by stealing) from tribes to the south who, in their turn, got them, not from bands of wild horses, the offspring of animals that had escaped from the Spanish Conquistadores, but by purchase from Indians or Mexican settlers. The Indians of the plains were excellent horsemen and spent a lot of time in caring for their herds and in making saddles and other riding gear. A man's importance depended largely on the number of horses that he had, and they were used almost as money in paying for admission to military societies, in buying a medicine bundle, or as presents to the parents of a girl who was desired in marriage by a young man. Women owned horses too, especially their own saddle and pack horses, but they seldom built up large herds as the men did. In most of the prairie Indian dialects, the word for a horse means "big dog".

WARFARE

There is little doubt that there was some warfare on the prairies, even before the Indians got horses, but once they were

CRADLE,
KOOTENAY
TYPE

SCALP AND
SCALP LOCK

armed with guns and on horseback the fighting became more
intense. Horses brought once distant enemies much closer in a sense,
for a man on a horse could cover several times as much ground in
a day as a man on foot could. No people can spend all their time
fighting, of course, so there were periods both of peace and of war.
Then, too, some tribes, such as the Blackfoot, did a lot more fighting
than some of the peaceful tribes, such as the Sarcee.

Warfare and horse stealing blended into each other. A band of
young men might go out with the intention of stealing some horses
from another tribe, creep up on the camp at night, make off with a
dozen horses and be half way home before the theft was noticed.
On another occasion though, they might be seen before they even
got close to the camp, or they might be caught while actually taking
the horses, and then there would be a fight, perhaps big enough to
start actual warfare between the tribes.

Horse stealing was not only the recognized way of acquiring
wealth, it was the way to fame too, and the more horses one had
stolen, the more raids one had been on, the greater was one's
reputation as a brave man and a famous warrior. Any group of
young men who wanted some excitement might organize a horse
stealing raid, generally with the consent of the chief of the tribe or
band, and anybody who wished to do so might go along, but nobody
who didn't feel like going was expected to.

Strangely enough, killing the enemy was not considered nearly
as brave an action as touching him with some weapon, such as a
bow or a lance or the muzzle of a gun. This was called counting
coup, from the French word meaning a blow. If a man was near
enough to the enemy to strike him a blow, he must be near enough
to be in real danger and counting coup was therefore thought more
highly of than was killing and scalping an enemy who might be shot
with a bow or a rifle at a safe distance.

Scalping was fairly common among the prairie tribes, though
the custom apparently did not start there but in the valley of the
St. Lawrence, and it seems to have been the white people who
carried the idea west and introduced it to the people of the prairies.
It was because bounties were paid for dead Indians that the white
men valued scalps; the Indians on the other hand valued them as
proof of triumph over an enemy. Scalping was the act of taking a

square or round patch of skin, often with a scalp lock of hair attached, from just behind the crown of a man's head. It was painful, of course, but by no means fatal, and many a man has been scalped and then let go, even white men. Much more frequently the man was killed first and then scalped. Many Indians used to grow a

"OLD SARCEE'S" WAR DEEDS PAINTED ON CALF SKIN

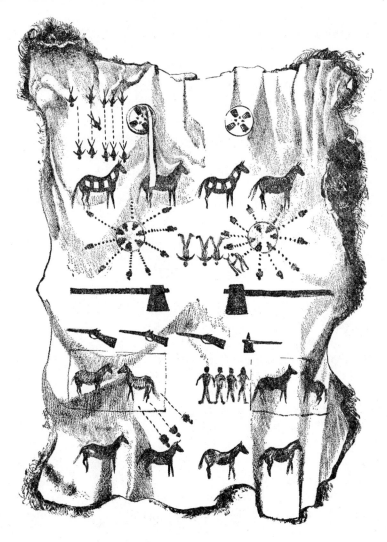

special lock of hair, which they wore braided and decorated with beads, for the convenience of the enemy as a sort of act of defiance. Sometimes quite a large piece of the scalp might be taken, which was later cut up into smaller pieces for decorating a war shirt or for some other purpose.

A warrior's bravery was not measured by the number of scalps he had taken, but by the number of coups he had counted, and scalps were not, in reality, specially valued; once they had served their purpose in the scalp dance, which was performed by the women after the return of a victorious war party, they were often thrown away.

To a prairie Indian, the list of his war deeds was as important as are a college athlete's records. Feathers were worn in special ways to show what a man had accomplished, and when he drew near the end of his days he might draw on a buffalo skin a series of sketches recording his war deeds. Once he had made the outlines, he would get somebody else, probably a nephew, to fill in the colors and, having drawn his war deeds once, he was not allowed to do so again.

War, therefore, with its accompanying raids and horse stealing, was almost a game, with definite rules and ways of keeping score. It wasn't a matter of increasing the size of the tribe or gaining larger territories, or accumulating wealth except in the form of horses, and there was less of the deliberate cruelty that went with Iroquois warfare. Torture was more rare, though not unknown, but sometimes white men who were taken prisoner were cruelly tortured and mutilated, even after death.

The weapons used in war were the bow and arrow, spears, clubs, knives, and guns in later years. Ash was a favorite bow wood and the arrows were of saskatoon or of willow. They often had shallow wavy grooves down the shaft, the purpose of which is not known, though some people think it was to let the blood run out more easily. Some bows were made of willow and there was a good deal of variation in the style of them, though most were short so as to be convenient for use from horseback. Arrowheads were of bone or antler and some were chipped from stone. Thousands of chipped stone arrowheads are still to be found on the prairies, but the Indians of today all insist that their forefathers

did not make them and that they found the arrowheads there
when they first came into the country, so we think that there were
other kinds of Indians living here before the present ones.

Arrowheads for use in war were sometimes fastened rather
loosely so that they would come off in a wound and make it more
difficult for a man to get well. The common idea that arrowheads
were so fastened that they would lie flat and slip easily between a
man's ribs is all wrong, for an arrow spins as it flies and there would
be no way of telling what the position of the arrowhead would be
when it struck its target. Quivers for carrying the arrows were often
made of the whole skin of an otter or of cougar skin.

Some men wore heavy jackets of several thicknesses of leather
when they knew they would be in for a fight, but armor of this
kind was not common. It might stop an arrow but not a bullet.
Shields were much more popular. They were generally round, less
than two feet across, and made from the heavy skin on the chest
of an old bull buffalo. These too would stop an arrow, and their
use continued long after guns were brought in, for at least half
their value was in the magic that was believed to be in them. They
were decorated with eagle feathers, kept in special soft leather
cases when not in use, and painted with sacred designs and symbols
seen in dreams.

Magic had a lot to do with keeping a man safe in battle. In
addition to the shields, whose value was half real and half magical,
they had in later years such things as magic shirts filled with little
slits and covered with flat brass buttons. The slits were supposed
to be holes made by bullets and the brass buttons represented

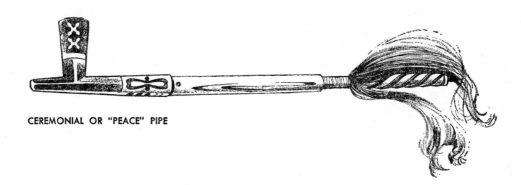

CEREMONIAL OR "PEACE" PIPE

bullets that had flattened themselves out on hitting the magic shirt. Surely, argued the medicine maker, a shirt that had been cut and hit so often must be safe from now on. Such a magic shirt was, of course, quite useless except that it probably gave the man who wore it more confidence and courage. They even had shirts which, they thought, would make the man who wore one invisible. Poundmaker put on such a shirt, made of quite ordinary white cotton, at the battle of Cut Knife Hill in 1885.

Every warrior wore charms as a matter of course, generally skins or skulls of birds or animals seen in a vision. A man could make such charms for himself or he could buy them from a medicine man. Special prayers had to be said and songs sung when putting them on before a raid or a battle.

While horses might be stolen from almost anybody who had them, some tribes thought of each other as friends and allies and not as enemies. These would join together for self-defence or to attack a larger group, but small affairs such as raids for horse stealing were usually strictly band business. The Blackfoot joined with the Bloods and the Piegans to form a group of three allied tribes who spoke the same language and the Sarcee were in with them, but they were often at war with the Cree, Assiniboine, Sioux, Crows, Flatheads, and Kootenays. They fought, too, with the whites in the United States and barely tolerated the Hudson's Bay Company people from whom they bought their guns, powder, and shot.

Warfare was well organized, with scouts sent ahead of a war party, systems of signals with smoke or, later, the flashing of mirrors, ambushes, and surprises. The method of surrounding an enemy and galloping round them again and again, shooting as they drew ever closer and closer, was the same as they somtimes used in buffalo hunting and just as effective. They also dug trenches or fox-holes large enough to shelter a man, but they seldom charged in a group as European soldiers often did.

The vanishing of the buffalo saw the end of the Indian way of life. No longer could they roam the plains following the herds, killing them for food and clothing, but they must settle down on the reservations marked out for them by the white man. That meant the end of the horse stealing raids and the end of war. It happened as recently as about 1885 and there are still men living who were boys at the time and often heard their fathers tell of the old days before the white man killed off all the buffalo and left the Indians to starve, as they put it.

SOCIAL LIFE

People think of the Indians, especially those of the prairies, as being very solemn and silent. This was true when they were on their best behavior, with important white strangers present, but when they were by themselves they were very different, and fond of fun and laughter. They were among the happiest of all the native tribes of Canada, living a good and easy life, full of the excitement of war and the pleasures of feasting and dancing.

Most of the bands were made up of several families who hunted and travelled together, and their daily life followed pretty much the same pattern all over the plains. At dawn the women made up the fires and began to get the first meal ready, while the men and children went down to the edge of the water for their morning plunge, summer or winter. After eating, the men would saddle up and go off hunting by twos or threes, perhaps taking a little dried meat or pemmican with them. Some women followed them with a travois to help in the butchering and to bring back the meat and hides. Other women spent the day in household duties, tanning skins, making clothes, and caring for the children. Towards noon the hunters straggled back, some with meat and some with none.

Another meal would follow, and the men loved to call out invitations to others to eat with them. From then till evening they wandered from one tipi to another eating and smoking. Later, when the sun had set, social dances were held, the women, dressed in their best, dancing opposite the men, with drummers providing the music. Such was a normal day in a Blackfoot camp.

In the springtime, the scattered bands would gather and the whole tribe might be re-united, camped in a large circle of tipis. Now the dances and the ceremonies were more serious, and sometimes hundreds of Indians would gather for such important occasions as the Sun Dance. This was held in midsummer, generally following a vow by some man or woman to give a Sun Dance as thanks for delivery from some danger or difficulty. The Sun Dance is still performed now and then, but it is nothing like such a big event as it once was.

A large pole is cut for the centre of the Sun Dance Lodge and put in place with ceremony. Then the men pretend to attack it, count coup by striking it as if it were an enemy, and make offerings which they fasten to it. In the old days, young men, to prove their bravery, would force sharp wooden skewers through the skin of their backs or chests and fasten these to rawhide lines which were tied to the top of the Sun Dance Lodge pole. Then they would dance and struggle at the ends of the ropes till their skin gave way and they were free. Others would cut two slits in the skin of their backs, pass a line through, and drag heavy buffalo skulls at the end of it till they managed to tear themselves loose.

There were other dances and ceremonies, some of them purely social and others largely religious, some given by the military societies and others by private people. Some of the dances that are best remembered are the Ghost Dance, the Medicine Pipe Dance, the Horse Dance, and the Chicken Dance.

Among the men of each band there were always some of more importance than the others, not only the chiefs but the leaders of the military societies, the medicine man, the leaders of the dance societies, and those men who, as the result of a dream or vision, were allowed to paint designs on their tipis. These would be also the men with the most horses, whose advice would be asked for and followed, and whose children would be expected to marry the children of men of similar rank. There were outstanding women too but the position of women varied from tribe to tribe. The Assiniboine, for instance, treated their women better than the Blackfoot did. Sometimes a chief would announce that one of his boys was his "favorite son", which meant that all honor would be paid to the boy by his parents, he would have the best horses they could find (or steal) for him, and marry the most important girl in the band or tribe.

Boys were given names at birth and these names, which were only baby names, would be changed at the next Sun Dance or other suitable ceremony. The new name might well be kept till the boy went on his first war party. After that, he might change it again, possibly several times. An Indian, especially a Blackfoot, would not tell anybody his name if he could help it, but would ask somebody standing by to give the information when it was wanted. He felt that he was giving away part of himself if he gave away his name. Among the Plains Cree, when a child had to be given a name, four old men would be called together and asked to suggest one that was suitable. Naturally they would be invited to a feast after they had come to their decision, as a reward for their work. Almost the only time a man could freely use his own name was when he recounted his war deeds, and then he would proudly shout, "My name is Kimistihow, and this is the way I do things!" Girls seldom changed their names, not even when they were married.

The education of children was not at all like that of our schools. Little boys were not expected to do very much, but they were always so keen to be grown up like their fathers and big

LEATHER SHIELD

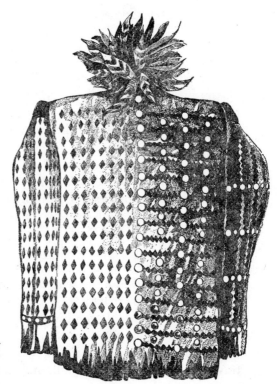

MAGICAL
WAR SHIRT

brothers that they tried in every way they could to imitate them. They organized miniature hunts of their own and, as soon as they were nearly old enough, learned to ride and to shoot. They would follow war parties as soon as they were able to, often without permission, so that they could see how to behave themselves later on, when they were really allowed to go.

Little girls had a busier life and were expected to help their mothers by gathering fuel, sewing moccasins, carrying water, and doing whatever else they could. Both boys and girls would be told tales in the evenings, but only after the sun had set, for the Old One doesn't like the ancient stories to be told in the daylight. Many of these old tales were meant to show the children what was right and good and what was wrong and shameful.

Marriage did not need any special ceremony, but the young man's parents would give presents to the girl's parents and, if they thought the match a good one and the presents were valuable enough, they would give their consent. Many men had three wives, and a few even more, for there was no limit to the number of wives a man might have. As the prairie Indian people had no slaves, a man who was a skilful and active hunter needed several women in his household to tan all the hides he brought in and dry all the meat. Men usually married women who were sisters if they could, saying there was less quarrelling then. The first wife was the head one and the others did as she told them to.

GAMES

Naturally, a people as interested in dancing and feasting as these were had numbers of games too. War came first, as we have already seen, and with war we may include horse stealing raids. Then there were contests, such as races, or archery trials with arrows for prizes, and group games like lacrosse and shinny.

Gambling was most important, and there were various games at which men could lose, or win, large stakes in horses, or even their clothes. The women had their own games too, and many of them were just as fond of gambling as were the men. Children had games such as ring and pin and snow snakes and whipping tops which they spun on the ice in winter. They had toys, too, small travois for the puppies to pull, and dolls for the girls.

Smoking was a favorite recreation of the men and, while it had a religious meaning, people smoked for pleasure, too. It was made into quite an elaborate ceremony and a man could easily show his ignorance of good manners if he was invited to share a pipe and did not observe the fine points of etiquette.

Prairie Indian pipes were most elaborate at times, though those used for everyday were plain enough. The really good ones were carved from catlinite, a smooth bright red stone, and these often had most complicated and highly decorated stems. We have often heard of the peace pipe, but there are many misunderstandings about it. In the first place, it was not the pipe bowl but the pipe stem that was important in the peace pipe ceremony, and actually any pipe at all could be used, for pipe bowls were not specially made for that purpose. Even now we don't know very much about the actual ritual, or where the ceremony started or when.

MUSIC

The musical instruments known to these people were a drum of a simple tambourine type, a whistle, and a rattle. The drum head was a sheet of rawhide shrunk, while still wet, onto a round frame. It had to be warmed to tighten up the drum head before it would give a good tone. The whistles were made from the long hollow bones of eagles or cranes. Some of them could be played from either end, giving two notes. The rattle was made by filling a wet

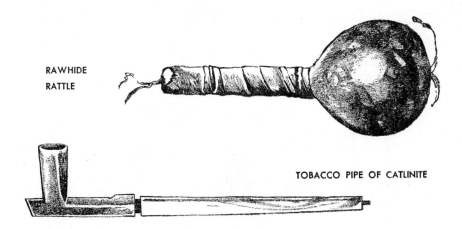

RAWHIDE
RATTLE

TOBACCO PIPE OF CATLINITE

rawhide bag with wet sand and moulding it into the shape wanted. Then it would be set aside. After it was quite dry, the sand was poured out and the hardened rawhide would then keep its shape. A few pebbles were put inside and the neck of the rattle was then closed and plugged tight.

They had many songs, for all sorts of purposes, war songs, society songs, love songs, dancing songs, and gambling songs. In all of these the melodies were more important than the words and many of them actually had few words that made sense, all the rest of the song being nonsense syllables, like our hey nonny nonny.

ART

While it is true that art was not highly advanced on the prairies, the designs they did have were very distinctive and are not likely to be mistaken for those of any other people. Most of their patterns were made up of what we call geometrical designs, that is to say, of squares, triangles, lozenges, and sometimes circles.

The men painted designs on tipis, parfleches, and rawhide bags; the women embroidered moccasins with quill work and later with beads, and painted some very fine designs on the soft hides they wore as robes in cold weather. They did not use the paint brushes we know, but wedge-shaped pieces of porous bone which

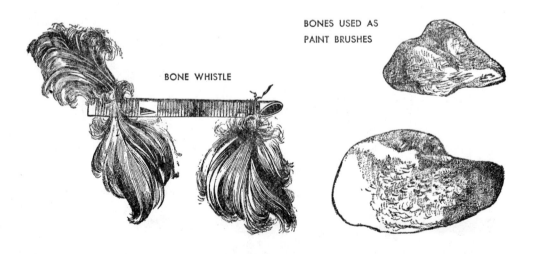

BONES USED AS
PAINT BRUSHES

BONE WHISTLE

held a good deal of color. The sharp edges of the bone were used for drawing thin lines and the flat sides for filling in the larger spaces. Their colors were mostly minerals mixed with grease or water and sometimes with the sticky juice from the leaves of the prickly pear cactus, which is common on many parts of the prairie. White, yellow, red, and black were the usual colors, but they have many more today, for they buy them at the store.

Some of the prairie Indians used to arrange stones in patterns on the tops of hills, making wheels and circles, the figures of men and animals, all laid out with boulders. We are not sure what the purpose of these was. It may have been done just for the fun of it. They also painted designs on big rocks, generally in red paint, drawing the figures of men and animals and geometrical designs as well as some we can not identify. The purpose of these, too, is not quite certain, though we know that some of them were done by people who went out alone to fast and pray in the hope of seeing visions and of finding a supernatural helper. Others seem to have been drawn just for fun.

LITERATURE

Like the other native tribes of Canada, the prairie Indians had no way of writing but they knew hundreds of legends. Many of them are about Napiwa, the Old Man of the Dawn, who puts wrong things right, and fights evil wherever he finds it, and even helps in the creation of hills and rivers. Powerful as he is, yet he does all sorts of silly and stupid things too, so that one does not know whether they worshipped him or laughed at him, or a bit of both. One day he tried to pull the Lynx in half and that, they say, is why Lynx has such a long body and awkward legs. There are stories too to explain where the various tribes came from, and others in which animals grant favors to human beings. Still others are about imaginary animals such as the water monster and the thunderbird, a huge bird like an eagle that causes the thunder and lightning.

Also to be counted as a kind of literature are the hundreds of songs and prayers they knew, some of them very beautiful.

There was a strange kind of language used on the prairies, which we call the sign language. All the tribes used and understood it, for it was not based on any one tribal language but on signs made with the fingers and hands which could be learned by anybody. Some of them were quite easy to understand, such as the sign for a travois made by spreading two fingers and drawing them along the palm of the other hand like travois poles dragging along the prairie. Some tribes, the Blackfoot for instance, were very good at the sign language, and people who knew it well could talk for hours about all sorts of things without ever speaking a word.

SCIENCE

Science, as we understand it, was quite unknown. They did use a few herbal remedies, but these were based on magic rather than on certain knowledge. The one subject on which they did seem to have some clear thoughts was that of raising and caring for horses, even though they had known them for only a couple of hundred years at the most.

RELIGION

Nearly all the prairie tribes shared the same general religious beliefs. The great spirits were the Sun and the Thunderbird and Napiwa, the Old Man of the Dawn. The Sioux called these the *wakan tanka*, which means something like "the greatest sacred ones". Among these the Sun stood first, and almost equal in rank were the Sky, the Earth, and the Rock. Next came the Moon, and the Winds, and the Buffalo, and so on down to the commonest spirits with little power. Nearly all the great powers, and the lesser ones too, could be controlled more or less by wearing amulets which had been shown to one in a dream. Some of these would work for one person only, but more elaborate amulets or collections of them, might be important to a whole family, or band, or even tribe. Such collections of charms were known as "medicine bundles" and were very important indeed. The man who was charged with the care of the tribal medicine bundle had bought the privilege from the previous guardian for many horses, and its care was a continual nuisance: it had to hang out-of-doors in the sun in fine weather and be brought inside in bad weather; nobody must pass behind it; and every time it was moved the right prayers had to be said. When the bundle was opened there were special prayers which must be said for every article in it, and there might be many of them.

When a man bought a medicine bundle he had to learn all these prayers by heart and remember them too, for if the prayers were said with mistakes in them, all the magic was washed out, "like so much blood from a wound" as they put it. In spite of all the trouble of being responsible for a medicine bundle, it was still a great honor and the man who had it in his care was highly respected and very proud of his sacred duty. When the people were on the move, the medicine bundle was wrapped up and carried in a special decorated rawhide case. In the bundle itself might be found the skins and skulls of various birds and animals, strangely-shaped stones, braids of scented grass, a tobacco pipe, some tobacco, and a wooden food bowl. Hardly any two bundles had exactly the same contents, but the general sort of things was always the same.

Stones with holes in them, or with curious markings on them, were considered important and nearly all prairie Indians would pick them up and, sometimes, keep them as amulets. This some of them do even today. One curious kind of stone, still thought to have great power, is really part of a fossil shell. It looks something like a very crude buffalo. Such stones were highly valued in the old days. They were painted red and kept in a special little leather case with a hole in it so that the "buffalo" could see out. The custom was to throw them up in the air and their position when they fell to the ground told the hunter in which direction he should go to find buffalo. A man who had one of these stones was believed to be able to call buffalo to him just by carrying it with him.

The peace pipe ceremonies and ritual smoking, which have already been mentioned, had a large place in religion too. Many prayers included the smoking of sacred tobacco and blowing puffs of the smoke to the four quarters of the horizon, to the sky above and the earth below. When a group smoked together there were special prayers to be said while the bowl was being filled, and the tobacco lighted, and the pipe passed in a certain order from one to the other.

An important part of the training of many, but not all, boys was the time when they went out alone into lonely parts of the country where people seldom came. Here they would, if they could manage it, go for four days with no food or water, praying for a vision and hoping to meet some animal or other being who would tell them what the things seen in their dreams meant, and teach them sacred songs to sing. Many of the boys who tried, and grown men too, came back without having heard or seen anything, but others felt that they had been quite successful. Naturally, they would never tell what they had seen or heard for if they did they would lose its power.

Dreams were thought most important, whether they were dreamed when seeking for a vision or at any time. If a man started out on the warpath, and he was warned in a dream that things looked bad for him, he would turn back and nobody would blame him. Dreams, they said, were sent by the spirits to warn people and

CONTENTS OF A MEDICINE BUNDLE

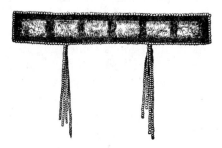

DECORATED HEAD-BAND

DRUM

MEDICINE BUNDLE WRAPPED IN LEATHER

help them avoid danger, and a vivid dream was nearly always acted on.

Magic was firmly believed in by everybody, and if one person wanted to harm another, magic would nearly always be the means chosen. The one wishing to work the magic would try to get hold of some bit of the other person's hair, or nail parings, or some intimate bit of clothing, and say charms over it to injure the original owner. One way was to place things like this in a little bag and tie it to the tip-top twig of a high tree and then, the more dizzily the tree top danced in the wind, the more dizzily the poor victim's brain danced until he became completely mad and died.

The medicine men were the specialists in magic, both good and bad. When somebody fell sick and was thought to have been bewitched, the medicine man tried to use a still stronger magic to drive out the sickness.

Burial on the prairies took several different forms. The Assiniboine sometimes burnt the bodies of the dead, and at other times they buried them in a grave lined with bark or skins, and then

MORE CONTENTS OF A MEDICINE BUNDLE

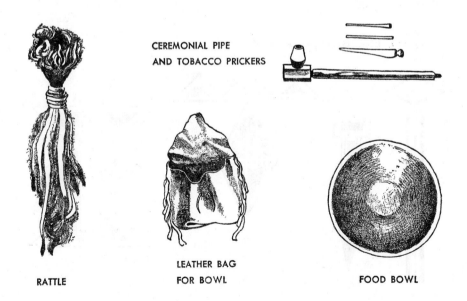

CEREMONIAL PIPE
AND TOBACCO PRICKERS

LEATHER BAG
FOR BOWL

FOOD BOWL

RATTLE

covered them over with logs and earth. Among the Sarcee the warrior's horse was shot and left, with food and clothing, on the grave. Many bodies were wrapped in their robes and placed on a scaffold of poles, there to stay till it all fell down and disappeared. In the case of important people, the bodies were sometimes put in small tipis on the brow of a hill or knoll and left there. In some places the rings of stones that held the burial tipi down are still to be seen on hilltops. When the Blackfoot dead were placed on scaffolds or in trees, their feet were turned to the west, and in some instances the body was painted and carefully dressed before being disposed of.

PRESENT CONDITIONS

The good old days, and in the case of the prairie Indians they really do seem to have been "good" old days, are gone and will eventually be forgotten. There are no more buffalo to hunt, no more wars to fight, no more horses to be stolen. Instead the people live on their reservations and grow wheat and raise cows, the White Man's Buffalo as they call them with a smile of mixed amusement and contempt. The old men remember the tales their fathers told them, and the Calgary Stampede, the Indian Days at Banff, and the

GEOMETRICAL DESIGNS TYPICAL OF PRAIRIES

occasional country fair and rodeo revive those dear, warm memories. Most of them are happy enough; many of them are quite well to do. They are generous, intelligent, friendly people. There can be no going back, and therefore they are going forward and making a better job of it than some tribes whose change to the new conditions has been even less easy.

The river of whispering ghosts

A Legend of the

Western Prairies

Not far to the west of Calgary, almost in the shadow of the Rocky Mountains, runs the River of Whispering Ghosts. It's not a big stream, but it has a history that will stick in your mind long after the memory of the river itself has faded.

The story runs like this. In the old days, before the white man came, there were two tribes of Indians in this district, the Sarcees and the Blackfoot. They are firm friends and allies now, but this was many years ago and they fought each other bitterly for the right to hunt elk in the foothills and buffalo on the prairies. They had been at war for generations and the chiefs of both tribes knew that it was time to stop all this and come to an agreement before more of the best warriors were killed off. There seemed no way to peace without a loss of dignity on one side or the other.

One summer, the chief of the Sarcees gave a great feast to which he invited everybody from far around, including the chief of the Blackfoot people, enemies though they were. The feast was to give the Sarcee chief an opportunity of announcing that his only boy child, Lipoto, was to become his "favorite son", which meant that every possible right, privilege, and honor would be heaped on him from then on.

The chief of the Blackfoot people was puzzled. This was something new indeed! An invitation to a feast, and from the chief of the Sarcees, who had been on the war path against the Blackfoot for so long. What was he to do?

He determined to call all the older men in council — men who were famous for their war deeds, the many horses they had stolen, the many coups they had counted, and the scalps they had brought home for the women to dance and sing around in the scalp dance.

For a long time they debated, the old men speaking loudly and insistently, the younger ones sitting quietly by and listening. Was this just a trap? It was an old familiar scheme, to invite people to a feast and then give them so much to eat and drink that they grew careless. Then, what was easier than to kill them as they slept?

But then, there was the boy, Lipoto. Surely they would never plan such a thing right after an important ceremony, nor would they risk a fight in which Lipoto might be killed. No, it was better to accept the invitation in the hope that it might be the beginning of a better understanding and lead to peace.

So the Blackfoot chief attended the feast and brought with him his wife and his only daughter, Winona, a beautiful and accomplished girl of sixteen. Naturally, the two young people fell deeply and incurably in love with each other or there would be no legend about them.

They had little or no chance of speaking to each other and, while the ceremonies were still going on, there were so many people about that it was quite impossible to arrange a secret meeting.

When all was over, the Blackfoot chief moved his camp to the far side of the river and stayed there overnight. This was the chance that Lipoto had been waiting for. On the pretext of taking his horse to drink, he rode down to the ford to where he could see Winona when she came down to the river to get water for her mother.

In the sign language, known to all prairie Indians, Lipoto signalled that he would meet her on the river bank shortly after moonrise, and to this she agreed.

That night, when all were asleep, Lipoto stole down to the river. Was that Winona he could dimly see on the other side of the swift water?

"Winona?" he whispered, as loudly as he dared. He could hear no answer, though she had heard him and called softly back, "Lipoto!"

The noise of the wind in the willows and the lapping of the water prevented him from hearing her answer and so, feeling certain that each was waiting on the other side of the stream, they both advanced into the black and icy waters.

"Winona?"

"Lipoto?"

Each sought the other desperately, struggling, looking, calling, at each moment more distraught, till both were swept away and never heard of again.

Even today, if you go down to the River of Whispering Ghosts, you may hear them, still whispering for fear that they may be heard, pleading, sobbing. Or is it only the wind in the willows calling "Winona", and the lapping of the waves that answers softly, "Lipoto"?

CHAPTER 5

THE ESKIMO

MACKENZIE RIVER ESKIMOS

Mackenzie Eskimo
Copper Eskimo
Central Eskimo
Labrador Eskimo

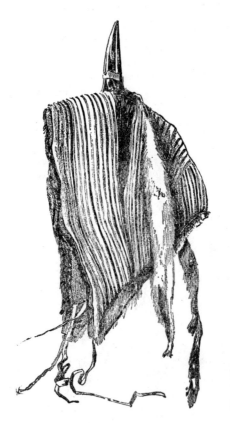

DANCING CAP
WITH LOON'S
BEAK ORNAMENT

THE ESKIMO

L ONG BEFORE NORTH AMERICA was discovered, the people of western Europe had heard tales of mysterious men living across the Atlantic Ocean. Canoes had been washed up on the coasts of Spain, France, and Ireland, clearly not of local make, sometimes even carrying the bodies of dead men. Fishermen on the west coast of Scotland told of finding slender boats covered with skins, and now and then a whale or a seal would be killed that bore in its flesh an ivory harpoon head.

Men decided that there must be a land to the west from which these things had come, but it was not until Columbus discovered the West Indies in 1492 and saw Indian canoes there that this conclusion was proved to be true. In 1576, when Martin Frobisher reached the southern part of Baffin Island and met the Eskimo, who paddled out to meet his ship in their kayaks, the mystery of the slender skin-covered boats was explained.

Frobisher's account and those of later explorers led European scientists to an investigation of these people whose life was so different from their own, and there have since been many studies of the Eskimo, till we now have a better knowledge of them than of almost any other people in the New World.

One would suppose that the question so often asked, "Where did the Eskimos come from?" could be answered simply and briefly, but actually it is extremely complicated. To begin with, we must divide it into two parts: "What is the origin of the Eskimo people?" and "What is the origin of the Eskimo way of life?"

As for the Eskimo people, they are Mongolians, that is to say they are of the same stock as the Chinese, Japanese, and some other tribes of eastern Asia, as we shall see when talking about their physical appearance.

The origin of the Eskimo way of life is a subject to which a great deal of attention has been paid in recent years. It is probable that these people once lived in eastern Siberia and crossed to Alaska by way of Bering Straits. Recent explorations in central Alaska have shown that some of the Eskimos of those early days, if not all of them, may have lived inland rather than on the coast as they do

153

now and were perhaps driven out of their homes there by a new
wave of people coming from the east, quite likely Athapascans.
Once having taken to living on the coast, the Eskimo invented special
methods of hunting sea animals, such as seals and walrus, and
found it much easier to live here than in the barren interior.

Gradually they moved eastwards along the coast, crossing to
the numerous islands when they had an opportunity, until eventually
they travelled as far as the east coast of Greenland and as far south
as Newfoundland. We are now certain that they met Norse settlers
in Greenland and possibly on the Labrador coast too and perhaps
even farther to the south about 1000 A.D.

Some Eskimos, the Caribou or Barren Ground people, continued
to live inland and, falling back before the advancing Athapascans,
were driven eastwards till they reached their present position in
the lake-strewn country west of Hudson Bay. These people number
only a few hundreds and some of them live entirely inland, seldom
if ever coming down to the sea coast.

PRINCIPAL ESKIMO GROUPS

The Eskimo of today live almost entirely north of the timber
line, along the Arctic coast, and in the southern rank of Arctic islands.
They are mainly a beach-dwelling people and may, for convenience,
be divided into several principal groups. In Canada, the most
important of these are: the Mackenzie Eskimo, who live near the
mouth of the Mackenzie River; the Copper Eskimo, round about
Coronation Gulf; the Central Eskimo, including those of Baffin
Island, Southampton Island, and the mainland to the west; and
the Labrador Eskimo, who occupy the coast of Labrador and the
Ungava Peninsula. Differences in local conditions cause slight variations in the habits of these groups of people, but in the main they
depend upon sea animals for their food during the winter months
and on the caribou in summer, with the addition of other food
whenever it is obtainable.

They do not always stay on the coast, but make frequent trips
inland to hunt caribou, or to fish in the lakes, to cut timber in those
districts where the trees are not too far away to be reached con-
veniently, or to quarry soapstone for lamps and pots, returning
always to the coast as their real home.

At one time, people lived on the more northerly Arctic islands, as we can see from the remains of their houses which were built of stone, wood, and whale bones. It is probable that these homes were deserted only a few hundred years ago. The ruined dwellings are largely on the south coasts of the islands or in places where it is comparatively warm and sunny.

Though the Eskimo live along the whole Arctic coast line, they are scattered very thinly. Settlements are established where food is easily obtained, either all through the year or at certain seasons. The presence of driftwood and fresh water (which seldom presents any difficulty) has a good deal to do with deciding where the bands will settle.

POPULATION

Taking a census in an area as remote and inhospitable as the Canadian Arctic must be difficult, and estimates of the total number of Eskimos have varied greatly. Not long ago it was said that they were dying out and that a few more generations would bring them to their end. Now we know that they are rather increasing in number, for each fresh count gives us a larger population. Even today

MAP SHOWING WHERE THE ESKIMO LIVED

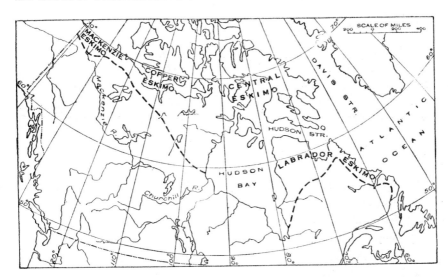

accurate figures are hard to get but the total number of 50,000, which includes all known Eskimos from eastern Siberia to the east coast of Greenland, is probably right to within about five per cent.

This is made up of 3,500 in Siberia; 19,028 in Alaska; 9,493 in Canada (including the Northwest Territories and Yukon, Manitoba, and Quebec); and 17,400 in Greenland. Not many years ago the total Eskimo population of Canada was put at less than 6,000; some of the increase may be owing to better methods of census-taking but there seems to be little doubt that improved medical services and better sanitation have also reduced the death rate among the babies and lengthened the life of the adults.

There used to be a good deal of difficulty in counting the Eskimos because many of them had the same name. Then, too, they have a way of changing their names and this, added to their wandering habits, made for further confusion. In 1941, metal disks, each stamped with a serial letter and a number, were issued to all Eskimos in Canada, so now a man may be identified as being himself no matter how many others have the same name, or how often he changes his name, or where he moves to. This has greatly simplified the work of recording family allowance payments, marriages, births, and deaths, as well as accounts at the trading posts. Whether the Eskimos will go on increasing or not is still in doubt. It depends on many things, over some of which we have no control.

PHYSICAL APPEARANCE

The Eskimos are, on the whole, below average height. They are heavily built, with comparatively short legs, and are unusually well-muscled. Many of them are very strong and will tackle a load or a task that most white men would consider impossible. In color, they vary from a light olive-tan to a much darker brownish yellow. Their faces and hands which are not protected from the weather are well tanned. Many of them are as light in coloring as Europeans on those parts of the body that are seldom exposed to the sunlight. Hands and feet, particularly in the women, are usually small, and many Eskimo tools are not big enough to fit our hands.

Their faces are broad and round, sometimes looking quite fat. The people tend to be long-headed, often with a clearly visible ridge on the crown of the skull from back to front. The eyelids, especially among women and children, show the "slant eye" of the Chinese which helps to prove their Mongolian origin, and the iris of the eye is generally dark brown. Both men and women are active and energetic when in good health and they have great powers of endurance.

NATURE OF THEIR COUNTRY

Some people say, and they may be right, that the Eskimo live in the hardest climate in the world. At any rate, it is true that long cold winters, fierce storms, and a barren treeless land, rocky and forbidding, are part of their daily life.

Just the same, it would be wrong to think of the Arctic as a land of ice and snow, with a winter twelve months long. The summer, short as it is, from the beginning of July to the first week of September perhaps, can be most pleasant. The sun is high in the heavens, not setting at all for several weeks, flowers are out in uncounted hundreds, and the air is loud with birds. The worst plague of summer is the mosquito, which swarms in thousands tormenting men and beasts. In summer, the temperature may occasionally go up to 70° Fahrenheit, and the Eskimos consider that uncomfortably hot.

Winter is much longer than summer, all the rest of the year in a sense, for the first heavy snow storms often come in September and the ground may not be bare again till well on in May. Fog settles in dense clouds and, when the sun has set not to appear again for a few weeks, there are only a few hours of twilight in the middle of the day.

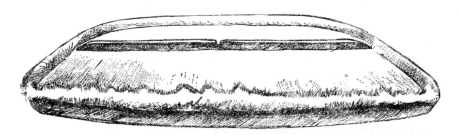

SEAL-OIL LAMP MADE OF SOAPSTONE

Very strong winds are not common, but blizzards do occur every winter when low temperatures and a raw dampness in the air make even a moderate wind seem unbearably cold. Nearly everybody gets frost-bitten now and then, Eskimos and whites too.

The coast line, where the natives spend most of their time, varies from high cliffs to low beaches, with bays and inlets, fiords and river mouths scattered along its length. Usually it is bleak and rocky, and only in the most sheltered valleys do the willows grow more than a couple of feet high. Most of the plants are dwarfed and low to the ground, often only a few inches in height, and practically invisible in winter.

FOOD

There have been many stupid things said about Eskimo foods. Some authors appear to take a strange delight in showing them as eating rotten meat or other unpleasant things, or even such inedible objects as candles. While it is true that the Eskimos do not share our tastes in food, and so do eat meat that has been kept a good deal longer than we would keep it, we must remember that among ourselves less than a hundred years ago, game was often "hung" till it fell from the cord and even today many people eat cheeses which are disgusting to others.

Most Eskimo food was clean, wholesome, and straightforward. It was nearly always cooked, and raw meat was eaten only when

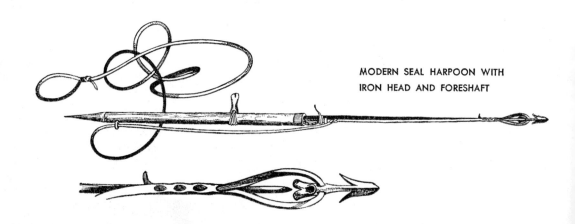

MODERN SEAL HARPOON WITH
IRON HEAD AND FORESHAFT

cooking was not convenient or when the meat was frozen hard. Then it can be sliced very thin and is most delicious.

Eskimo food was almost entirely animal and their ability to get along well with very little or no vegetable food has been of great interest to specialists who study diet. Unlike ourselves, who eat principally lean meat and only a little fat, the Eskimo eats also the various glands, such as the sweetbread, as well as the brains, the intestines, and sometimes the semi-digested contents of the stomach, which would be vegetable in the case of the caribou and probably clams in the walrus, all of which were a source of vitamins and hormones essential to good health.

Simmering was the usual way of cooking. A pot of soapstone, rectangular in shape, hung most of the time over the seal-oil lamp. In this pot meat bubbled almost constantly, and any member of the household could help himself to hot meat and hot soup when he came in. Water was the only liquid used for drinking, except the soup just mentioned. Today a great many foods from the trading post are used and they have not all resulted in an improvement in the health of the Eskimo. Their teeth which, in the early people, were strong and free from disease, are now often riddled with holes, for refined flour, refined sugar, lard, tea, and coffee are not nearly as good for them as is strong nourishing meat.

Fire was usually made by striking two lumps of iron pyrites together and catching the resulting spark in a tinder of dry moss roots, of the down of willow catkins, or of Arctic cotton. The usual fuel was the oil extracted from the blubber of the seal, which was burnt in a long narrow lamp of soapstone. A wick, composed of the

LUMPS OF IRON PYRITES

TINDER OF WILLOW CATKINS
IN LEATHER POUCH

same materials as were used for tinder, was laid along one edge of the lamp, and the flame was controlled by pricking the wick with short rods of wood or stone. In summer a good deal of the cooking was done out-of-doors and the second-rate fuels of the Arctic, such as driftwood, dwarf willow, or heather, were used. They were seldom abundant and often so damp that they produced only a smoky and half-hearted fire.

HUNTING AND FISHING

There is, in the North, a sharp division into summer and winter seasons which greatly affects hunting and fishing. In summer the

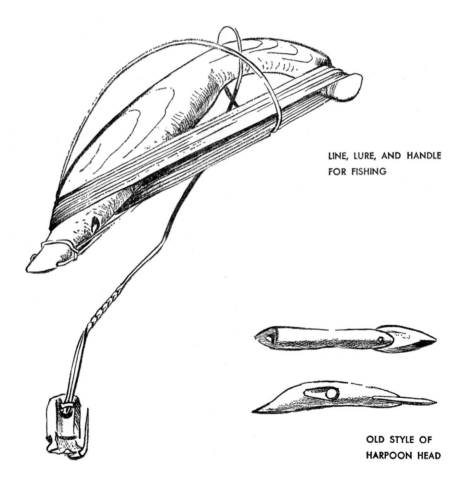

LINE, LURE, AND HANDLE
FOR FISHING

OLD STYLE OF
HARPOON HEAD

people go inland to hunt caribou, sometimes making long journeys for this purpose during which they travel on foot, sleeping out-of-doors or in tents, and dressed in lighter clothing than in the winter. The sled and other heavy winter equipment and clothes are all laid aside and protected by stone caches. If the inland lakes are still frozen in the spring, some people fish through the ice, while others collect birds' eggs and fledgling birds, living entirely off the land. A little later in the season they gather a few berries and occasionally chew leaves of sorrel for their sour taste, and nibble a few pieces of seaweed when they get down to the beach. This is almost the only vegetable food they use.

At that season, caribou is their most important source of meat and in the old days musk-oxen were killed too. Now these animals are so rare that there is danger of their becoming extinct, and so killing them is forbidden. Ducks and ptarmigan and any other small game they can find all add to the larder.

In winter, the scene is completely different. Hunting now is done along the outer edge of the sea-ice and the people build their winter snow houses miles from the land. There are various ways of seal hunting, depending on the ice conditions and the time of year. A common method is for the Eskimo to wait patiently at one of the seal's breathing holes, first found for him by his dog, standing till the seal comes for air and then darting the harpoon into its neck or skull as it rises above the water to breathe. In early spring, when the sun has come back to the Arctic, the seals lie basking on top of

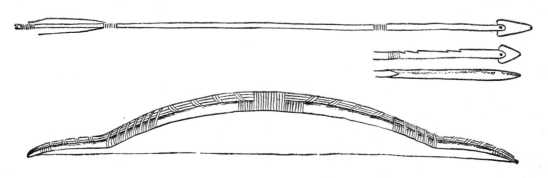

COMPOUND BOW AND ARROWS

the ice, ready to dive into their holes at the least alarm. The hunter approaches warily, advancing only when the seal is napping, until he gets close enough for a rifle shot. The seal must be killed instantly, or else it dives and is lost even though mortally wounded. Before they had rifles, the hunters had to come close enough to harpoon the sleeping seal, which required great skill in stalking. Some seal hunting is done in summer, using the kayak and a special harpoon, but this is not the custom of all Eskimo groups. In summer, too, the walrus and the narwhal are all taken with harpoons, as was the whale in previous years.

A common method of fishing is with the jig. This is a barbless hook attached to a plaited sinew cord, wound up on a sharply bent "fishing rod", only about a foot long. Just above the hook, a flashing white lure is fastened. Sometimes this is carved to look like a small

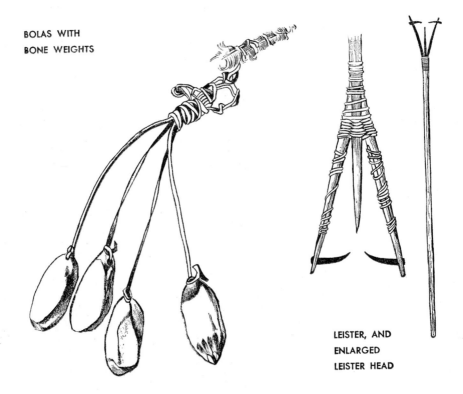

BOLAS WITH
BONE WEIGHTS

LEISTER, AND
ENLARGED
LEISTER HEAD

fish, but even more often it is only a thin plate of walrus ivory. No
bait is used, unless the fisherman prefers to do so. The hook is let
down till it is felt to touch the bottom and is then drawn up a few
inches and jigged steadily up and down till some luckless fish,
attracted by the fluttering lure, is hooked. Then the line must be
held taut and drawn in quickly and steadily, for the fish will wriggle
free if given a chance to do so. After it is landed the fish is killed
by hitting it on the head with a club, or by biting through its back-
bone near the skull. In winter, the fish, as they are caught, are
arranged in a circle with their heads towards the hole from which
they were drawn, possibly in the hope that the fish below the ice
will behave like those above it and head for the hole. This method
of fishing is used inland, on the frozen lakes, and also for catching
tom-cod at sea. Nets do not seem to have been used much, but fragments of them have been found in long-abandoned villages, so they
were at least known. Since white traders brought nets in, they have
been used for catching fish and also for seals.

Harpoons of various types and the bow were the chief weapons
used in Eskimo hunting. The detachable head, with its locking
action, is the essential thing about the harpoon. The shaft and foreshaft serve only to thrust the sharp head through the animal's hide
and into the muscle beneath. The shaft and foreshaft then drop
away, leaving the line, which is fastened to the harpoon head, in the
hands of the hunter. As soon as any strain is put on the line, the
harpoon head takes a cross-ways position below the skin and usually
becomes firmly embedded. A harpoon head, once solidly placed
under the skin of a seal or walrus, will stand the steady pull of half
a dozen men without tearing free. This toggle enables the hunter to
hold his prey until he can stun or kill it.

When using the harpoon in sealing from a kayak, a blown-up
sealskin is tied to the far end of the harpoon line, serving both to
show its position and to hold the harpooned animal.

The bolas, made of half a dozen stone or bone weights tied to
a string, was used for hunting ducks and other birds. The bolas was
whirled round and round and then let fly towards the birds. Turning
as it flew, it would wrap itself round any duck or other bird it hit
and pinion the bird's wings so that it could no longer fly and must
fall to the ground.

Two types of bow were in use. One, a self-bow, which means one made from a single piece of wood, was usually of spruce because the Eskimos could get no better wood. The other was a compound bow, generally made in three sections and more complicated than the self-bow. It might be entirely of wood, or caribou antler, or musk-ox horn might be used. Bows of both types were sometimes strengthened by a strip of leather glued along the back. This not only made the bow itself stronger but added to the distance it could shoot. The bow was further re-inforced by an intricate lashing of braided sinew. The only purpose of this lashing was to strengthen the bow itself, and reduce the chances of its breaking under strain; it did not add to the distance the bow could shoot an arrow.

The arrows were generally of spruce wood, sometimes carefully spliced together to make them long enough. Some arrowheads were only an expansion of the wooden shaft but more often separate heads of stone, bone, ivory, or antler were used. In the Coronation Gulf district, copper, picked up on the ground in nuggets, was used for making arrowheads and many other articles.

Fish dams were made by piling boulders across a narrow stream or in some convenient part of a shallow lake and the fish trapped in these dams were caught with leisters. A leister is a special kind of fish spear with elastic jaws that spring apart and then close their barbs on the sides of the fish, opening to grasp it, and closing to hold it firmly.

Today the trapping of foxes and a few other fur-bearing animals is an important part of Eskimo hunting. Steel traps are used and occasionally the old native traps, such as deadfalls. Another kind was a circular stone wall about waist high. Bait was put in the bottom of this trap and the fox, which had no difficulty in getting in, found itself quite unable to jump out again, because there was no room to take a run at it.

Most hunters wore charms of one sort or another to increase their good fortune in hunting. These were often bits of skin or the bones of the animals hunted, or sometimes of other animals, such as the weasel, which was admired for its courage and skill as a hunter. Live bees were sometimes shut up in little boxes, for their buzzing and stinging made them ferocious little hunters too. Even tiny children often had charms sewn to their clothes.

DRESS AND ORNAMENTS

Adequate clothing has always been a serious problem in the
far north. Garments must be warm enough for people to stay out-
of-doors in temperatures many degrees below zero, they must have
the strength required for use by people who lead a very active life,
and they must be made of materials that are at least reasonably
easy to get.

The best solution of this problem is the use of the skins of
animals, principally the caribou and the seal. At times other skins
were used, such as polar bear, fox, hare, ground squirrel, and some
bird skins.

Eskimo clothing is tailored, a process rare among the native
people of the world. The skins are handled much as we handle
cloth; the woman cuts out the necessary pieces, following the intricate pattern she keeps in her head, altering the proportions so that
the garment will fit the person for whom it is being made, and then

SKIN CLOTHING

sews the edges together with a fine needle or an awl, using sinew
for thread. Caribou sinew was generally preferred. Seal sinew was
not used because it was too short and, the Eskimos say with a smile,
"that would make the seals feel ashamed". Some Eskimo women
are very clever at sewing and would be greatly upset if a garment
they made did not fit well.

Clothes have to be kept carefully mended, especially in bad
weather, for a torn legging can easily let in enough cold air to freeze
the skin near the rent and cause serious trouble. It is for this reason
that a woman, good at sewing and mending, nearly always goes
with a man on a long journey. A man travelling alone will always
carry a sewing kit with him.

For very cold weather, caribou skin makes the best clothing.
It is light and warm and, when it is made from the long-haired
winter coat of the caribou, the wearer can stand very low temperatures. In the bitterest weather, two suits are worn at the same time,
the inner one with the hair turned inwards against the body and
the outer suit with the hair outwards so as to break the wind and
reduce the loss of bodily heat. In milder weather, clothing made
from the summer coat of the caribou is used. The hair is much
shorter and lies close against the skin. Garments of this material are
made also for inner suits and for "best clothes".

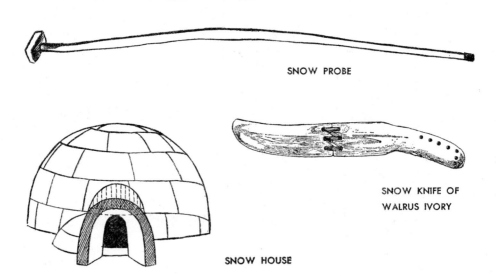

SNOW PROBE

SNOW KNIFE OF
WALRUS IVORY

SNOW HOUSE

Caribou skin has the disadvantage that the hair sheds readily if the skins get wet. For this reason, it is not used on rainy days, sealskin taking its place. In snowy weather, caribou skins are carefully brushed and shaken free of snow when brought into the igloo so that they may not become wet when the snow on them melts.

In summer, the need is not for warmth as much as for clothes that will stand a lot of hard use. For this purpose the skin of the common harbor seal, light in weight and very durable, is preferred. Other sealskin garments, scraped thin and made water-tight, are used by the Greenland Eskimo for wearing in the kayak. In the western Arctic, waterproof clothes are made by scraping and slitting the intestines of sea animals and then sewing the flat strips of tissue together. It looks almost like cellophane.

Clothes vary somewhat from one part of the Arctic to another but the standard dress consists of a tunic reaching from the neck to the top of the thighs and a long pair of leggings which may or may not end in foot gear. As well as these, short trousers from the waist to a foot above the knees are frequently worn, especially by women. The rest of the leg is covered by the long leggings. No hats or caps are worn, but the outer tunic often has a peaked hood which can be pulled up over the head. Recent fashions, especially in the western Arctic, insist that the hood must have a large ornamental fringe of long fur. Special dancing caps, ending in a loon's beak and intricately decorated, were used by the Eskimos around Coronation Gulf.

Boots are of various kinds depending on the season and the conditions under which they are to be worn. In cold weather, inner socks, often of hare skin, are worn with outer boots of seal or caribou hide. In summer, when the tundra is wet and there are many occasions to walk in shallow water, boots of sealskin, reaching to just below the knees and completely waterproof, are an essential. They are most carefully made with a tight double seam of blind sewing which lets in no water at all.

The women of Greenland are noted for their long and handsome boots of bleached sealskin reaching high up the thighs. The women of the central Arctic make shorter boots, also of white sealskin. Mittens of various types, suitable for different kinds of weather and work, are also used.

Clothing was often decorated with patterns made with strips of black, red, brown, and white skin or fur. Some of the strips were no more than a quarter of an inch wide and a number of them would be sewn side by side to make up a broad and colorful band of decoration. Boots, tunics, and dancing caps were often ornamented in this way. These are seldom seen now.

Today clothes from the trading post are preferred. They require less work in tanning and sewing and, then too, it is the fashion. Woollen clothing is reasonably satisfactory, but cotton and the new synthetic materials are less useful, especially in very cold weather. Thick, tightly-woven cloth, such as "moleskin" and "duffel", is used for making clothes, bought by the yard and cut and sewn as it would have been if fur had been used. Many Eskimo women own sewing machines and are expert in their use.

In the early days fashions differed a good deal from one district to another. The women of the west coast of Hudson Bay were noted for the huge hoods they wore and also for the pouches at the knees of their leggings, often used for smuggling small articles off the ships, by the way. In this district, too, decoration of the clothes was extreme and the old patterns, once made with strips of fur have been replaced by similar designs in glass beads, not nearly as attractive.

In Coronation Gulf, the tunic worn by the men had a close-fitting, rounded shoulder, but the women's coat was cut to form a square shoulder. In many parts of the Arctic both the back and the front of the tunic ended in tails, about a foot wide and three feet long, varying in cut in different districts. These tails were largely for decoration, but they were useful too when one sat on a snow bank or on a cold boulder.

Children's clothes were like those of the grown-ups in material and cut, and skins of lighter weight were often used. Very small children wore no clothes, except perhaps in recent years a little cap, but were carried naked against their mother's back, a special enlargement being made in the back of her tunic to hold the baby. A belt round her waist enabled the child to get a foothold so that it could stand upright and peer out over the mother's shoulder and, when a year or more old, solemnly stick out a grimy little paw to shake hands as the white men do. The common belief that

Eskimo women carry babies in the hoods of their tunics is just one of the many false ideas about these people.

DWELLINGS

Housing, because of the harsh climate, was also a serious problem. During the milder weather of summer, tents were good enough and they were used till sufficient snow had fallen to make it possible to build a snow house. The tents were made of sealskin or caribou hide, and though bulky and heavy, made comfortable shelters and were fairly easy to carry when travelling. Some of the skins were scraped so thin that they were almost transparent, and made the tents less gloomy inside. Tents varied in shape. One was like our "A" tent with a horizontal ridge pole. Another kind had poles spread in a fan, sloping from a high point in front to the ground

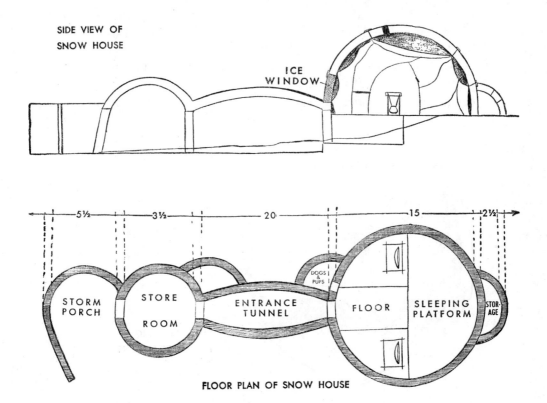

SIDE VIEW OF
SNOW HOUSE

ICE WINDOW

STORM PORCH STORE ROOM ENTRANCE TUNNEL DOGS & PUPS FLOOR SLEEPING PLATFORM STORAGE

FLOOR PLAN OF SNOW HOUSE

at the back. The front of this tent could be closed or left open as the occupants desired. This type was more common in Greenland than in the central and western Arctic.

Tent poles were difficult to get. Generally, pieces of driftwood were used, and at times short bits had to be joined together to make them long enough. Long straight pieces of bone were used, or even a narwhal tusk might serve as a tent pole. The poles, of course, were always carried along with the tent, for there was little chance of replacing them.

Hunters who went on short trips inland for caribou would often not bother with a tent but slept in the open wherever they happened to be when they felt tired.

In winter, warmer and more permanent dwellings were necessary. In the east and west of the Arctic where driftwood was to be had, semi-underground houses were built with the lower part dug into a gravel bank. Stone walls were built up, sometimes with large pieces of bone from whales worked in, and the roof was of driftwood covered with skins or turf. Such houses are seldom used now, but their ruins are common along the coast. The inside was dark and stuffy. The floor was paved with large flat stones and the sleeping platform took up the back of the house, standing eighteen inches or so above the floor, at least six feet from back to front and as

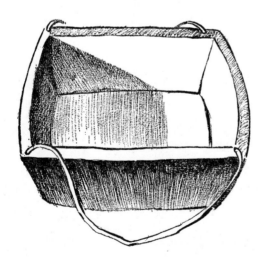

SMALL COOKING
POT OF SOAPSTONE

wide as the house. Smaller platforms were built at convenient points along the other walls to put the lamps on or to serve as tables. Small niches in the walls or under the edge of the sleeping platform served as cupboards in which small articles were kept.

The snow house, often thought of as typical of the Eskimo, is generally referred to as an igloo. Actually *igloo* simply means a house, as contrasted with a tent, whether it is built of stone or of snow. The snow house was not used all through the Arctic as many people suppose. In the east it was built only when on a journey, and in the west it was seldom used at all. It is only in the central Arctic that it was the usual winter house. Today there are not many Eskimos who can build a snow house and many hundreds of them have never seen one in their lives.

The building of a snow house requires a good deal of skill and experience. The first need is a bank of snow, hard packed by the wind and laid down in a single storm. The builder tests it with a slender rod tipped with ivory, hoping that the resistance to his probing will be the same all the way down. A snow bank that is uneven in hardness, or that is made up from the snow of several storms produces snow blocks with a tendency to split up into layers.

Having found suitable snow, the builder marks out on the surface a circle about fourteen feet in diameter, using a snow knife or his heels. Then he cuts blocks, about the size and shape of an ordinary suit-case, from one half of the inside of this circle. He

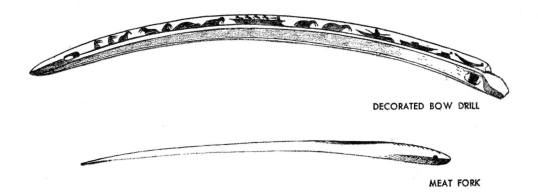

DECORATED BOW DRILL

MEAT FORK

arranges the first blocks in a low circular wall, all standing on their edges, following the line he has marked out. When this row is complete, he cuts a large notch in it, with one side straight up and down and the other sloping gently upwards. The first block of the second tier fits into this notch and then the building continues round and round. The blocks are so cut as to fit closely where they meet and to slope inwards so that the wall begins to slant in. The edges of the last block, the key-stone as it might be called, are bevelled, so that it fits neatly into the opening and locks the whole dome solidly together.

The builder works from the inside and can generally build his igloo from the blocks cut from one half of his floor space. This gives him two levels, the lower one becoming the floor and the upper one, which is the original surface of the snow bank, becoming the sleeping platform. Opposite this platform, the builder now cuts a doorway and climbs out. In the meantime, the woman has been working on the outside of the building, filling in crevices between the blocks of snow. She now goes into the house and her husband passes all the household equipment in to her. She arranges the mattresses of willow twigs and the caribou-skin sleeping bags, puts up the broad plank used as a table, and places her lamp and the cooking pot with the drying rack above it, lights the lamp and starts to get the evening meal. Very soon the house is cosy and bright, giving complete protection from the Arctic storms.

The ordinary traveller's snow house could be built in an hour or so, but in the more permanent villages larger buildings were put up, sometimes two or three of them connected to a single entrance passage, also built of snow blocks and with a right-angle turn in it to cut down the draft. Some larger buildings were used for dancing and community festivities.

Small lobes were sometimes added at the sides of the entrance passage as storage places or as shelter for the pups. The sled, harpoons, and any gear with rawhide on it, usually went up on top of the igloo out of reach of the hungry dogs. Sometimes a sheet of clear ice was set high in the wall to give more light, and a snow block might be stood on edge near the window to reflect still more light into the house. In some districts, a ventilating hole was poked through the roof but this was not always done.

FURNITURE

The average Eskimo was a good deal better equipped with furniture than were the Indians to the south. The sleeping platform in the house was generally covered with mattresses of willow twigs on which caribou or other skins were laid and the sleeping bags, also of skins, were put on top of these. In the day time, the sleeping bags were rolled up and pushed to the back out of the way. The lamp stood on the wooden plank table, one end of which was thrust into the wall of the snow house and the other supported on a special leg. An oval hoop of wood laced with braided sinew cord served as a drying rack and hung above the lamp. In addition to her soapstone bowls and pots, the woman had a number of others made from wood, and a series of smaller articles, such as meat forks, knives, and ladles, to use in her cooking. Spare clothes were kept in large skin bags which, with the sleeping bags and robes, formed the top part of the load on a sled when travelling.

In addition to these things, most households had one or more beaters of wood or antler for brushing the snow from one's clothes on entering the house, the wing of an owl or of a sea-gull for a whisk, and a bird skin for use as a hand towel. Other articles about the place would be a snow shovel, water buckets made of skin, leather bags for oil and blubber, and blubber pounders of musk-ox horn. A few coiled baskets were made by the Eskimos of the eastern Arctic.

TOOLS

Both men and women use many different tools, which is only to be expected considering the great mechanical ability of these people. An Eskimo man, instead of having one stone knife in his kit

SNOW BEATER OF WOOD

as an Indian might, will have several special knives: one for whittling, one for skinning and butchering, and another to cut snow blocks for building with. The woman, too, will have an *ulu*, which is the half-moon shaped knife she uses for most purposes, but she will probably have another knife in her sewing kit, as well as awls and lacing needles. Men have drills and scrapers of various sizes, whetstones, and antler flaking tools for making stone arrowheads and knives. A man might also have a mattock for digging turf, a pick for cutting holes in ice, adzes, various hammers of different sizes, and a special set of tools to keep his archery tackle in order.

The bow drill consists of three parts: a mouthpiece in which the wooden drill shaft rotates, a short bow of wood or bone, the string of which is wrapped round the drill shaft and sawn quickly back and forth to make the drill spin, and the drill shaft and bit. The drill bit used to be of stone but steel is generally used now.

Men usually kept their tools in special wooden tool boxes or skin bags and the women kept theirs and their sewing kits in skin bags. Near the Coppermine River, many tools and weapons were made from native copper. Nuggets of this metal were picked up on the ground and hammered into shape, apparently without heating the copper. Many of the smaller tools had holes drilled through their handles so they could all be strung together on a leather thong, which helped to keep them all together and thus prevent their loss in the snow.

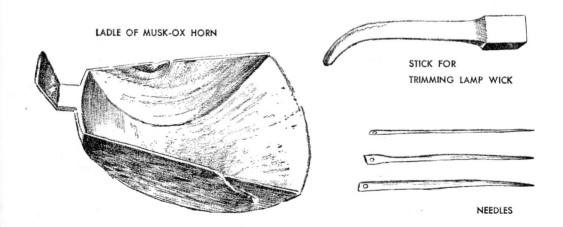

LADLE OF MUSK-OX HORN

STICK FOR TRIMMING LAMP WICK

NEEDLES

TRANSPORTATION

The contrast between summer and winter had a marked effect on transportation. In summer, travel might be over land or water. There was no special equipment for travelling across country in summer and everything needed on a journey, short or long, had to be carried on the backs of dogs or of human beings. Dog-packs were simple sheets of skin with slits cut in the edges so that they could be laced up into pouches, one hanging on each side of the dog. These could hold only small articles, weighing up to thirty or forty pounds altogether for each dog. Anything that was bulkier or heavier had to be carried by the people themselves. Usually goods that were to be back-packed were rolled up in a caribou skin from the sleeping platform and the bundle lashed tight with the ends of a tump line. In summer, naturally, the least equipment was needed and every effort was made to travel as lightly loaded as possible.

Summer travel by water was much more organized. Two kinds of boat were in use, the *umiak* or woman's boat, and the *kayak* or man's hunting canoe.

The umiak was an open boat large enough to carry thirty or forty people together with their dogs and all their belongings. It was used for moving from one camp site to another and also, in some districts, for whale hunting. The framework was of driftwood, lashed together with sealskin thongs, and covered with hides sewn with a waterproof stitch. Umiaks were rowed with round-bladed oars, usually by the women, hence the expression "women's boat". Few of these are to be seen today; they have been replaced by Peterhead boats, which have been popular with the Eskimos since the whaling days of a hundred years ago.

The kayak is one of the most familiar of Eskimo objects. It is a very light framework of wood or bone, covered with sealskins and built in much the same way as the umiak, but it has finer lines and is completely decked over, except for the small cockpit in which the hunter sits, his legs stuck straight out before him. He uses a double-bladed paddle, and an experienced kayak man is amazingly clever in handling his craft. In Greenland, some of the young men are so expert that they can turn the kayak completely over (upside-down) and come up again on the other side, repeating the feat as often as they feel like doing it. In some other areas, kayaks are not so common and their owners are not particularly skilful.

The deck of the kayak is fitted with various thongs, loops, and stops which are used to hold the hunting gear securely and close at hand on deck. Normally the hunter carries with him his harpoon, with its line and float, a killing lance, and a boat hook. In modern times, he has a rifle too.

Today some Eskimos own motor boats and take a keen delight in running them. Their mechanical skill stands them in good stead and they are quite able to strip a motor, make the necessary repairs, and re-assemble it. Now and then a broken or missing part may be replaced with complete success by one like it carved out of walrus ivory. The motor boat is used to take a group of people to the trading post or to a good sealing ground and the kayak is often towed behind or carried on board the motor boat, for it is a more efficient craft in the actual seal hunting, being easily managed and almost silent.

The Eskimos are thoroughly familiar with the waters in their own neighborhood, taking advantage of currents, tides, winds, and short cuts through the many islands off the coast. They are usually weather-wise and one does well to take their advice when travelling.

In winter, the lakes and coastal waters are frozen over. The kayak and the umiak have been turned upside down and put on

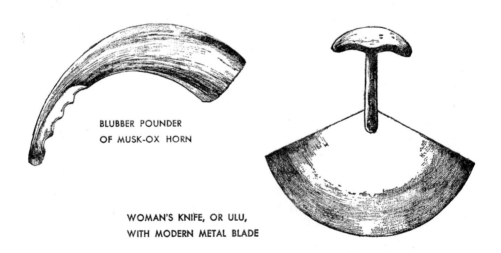

BLUBBER POUNDER
OF MUSK-OX HORN

WOMAN'S KNIFE, OR ULU,
WITH MODERN METAL BLADE

stone pillars out of reach of the dogs, to be left there till the following summer. At times, the skin covers are taken off too. Travel is
now almost entirely by dog-team over the snow-covered landscape.
The sleds, unlike the toboggans of the Indians, have separate
runners which are lashed by thongs to a series of cross-pieces. They
differ in length and width, depending on local custom and the purpose for which the sled is intended. Fifteen feet is a fairly normal
length, with a width of about two feet. The runners may be eight
or ten inches high and a couple of inches thick, with a two-inch
shoeing of mud and ice bringing the total height up to about a
foot.

The runners curve up in front and the cross-bars, each three or
four inches wide, are spaced roughly a foot apart. In front, a stout
thong is fastened to a toggle of ivory or musk-ox horn and to this
the traces of the dogs are hitched by an end-loop. In the eastern
Arctic the fan hitch is used, the lead dog having the longest trace
and running out in front of the others; they, on shorter traces, fan
out on each side. In other districts, in the west particularly, a different hitch is used and the traces are fastened, not directly to the
sled, but in pairs to the main trace, with the leader at the front.

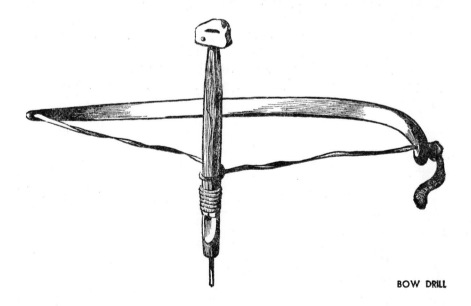

BOW DRILL

The dogs are guided by the driver's voice, and a good lead dog understands, and sometimes obeys, simple shouted commands. The driver has, as well as his voice, a whip with a short handle and a murderous long thong with which he can stimulate any dog that seems to need it. The dogs are all well aware of their duties and, when well-treated and not overworked, appear to enjoy them. Each dog knows his position in the team and will fight for his right to it if he has to. When the snow is unusually crusty and hard on the dogs' feet, special leather moccasins are made for them and the dogs soon learn to appreciate them, lying down on their backs or holding up their paws before they start off in the morning, to have their boots put on, sometimes even when there is no need for them.

Young dogs are broken to the sled when about a year old and the behavior of each dog is carefully noted so that the most intelligent ones may be trained for the post of leader. A good lead dog has trail sense, will pick out the best way, will not dash off after every animal it sees, and can often be depended on to find the way to camp, even when the driver himself is lost. In working, especially with the fan hitch, the dogs are continually jumping over each other's traces, so that the driver must stop every now and then to untangle them, and a cold and tiresome job it is, with a bitter wind blowing and naked fingers struggling with a stubborn tangle of knots.

The dogs are fed on fish and meat, seal or walrus or whitefish as a rule, and finding food for a team of six or more hungry dogs is one of the problems of Eskimo life. Caches of reserve dog food are kept at convenient places, but it is not always possible to keep

SLED, OR
KOMATIK

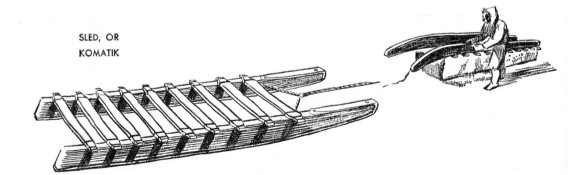

them full and at times the dogs have to go hungry for several days together.

DOMESTIC ANIMALS

Dogs are the only domestic animal known to the Eskimo. They are a part of everyday life in the north, and it would be easy to fill quite a large book with stories of them.

They are the descendants of native dogs which the Eskimos brought with them when they first came to North America, but white men have brought in their own dogs now and there has been some cross-breeding. Frobisher said that they had two different breeds when he was in Baffin Island, one for pulling sleds and the other for food.

Dogs are, on the whole, well treated, for the Eskimo knows that he is dependent on them and that he must feed them well if he is to get any work out of them. Dogs have their own names, often being called after dead members of the family they belong to, and they know their names perfectly well. Pups too small to run are carried on the sleds or by the people and a special place for them to sleep in, where they will not be too cold, is provided. When they are very young a nest for them and their mother is made in the igloo or in a lobe off the entrance passage. Grown dogs sleep out-of-doors even in the worst weather and are quite used to it. They curl up in tight balls, tails over noses, and are often drifted deep in snow by morning.

In summer, when they have but little work to do, they are given less to eat, but they manage to scrounge food for themselves along

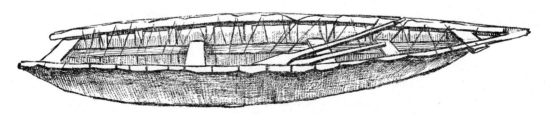

UMIAK, OR "WOMAN'S BOAT"

the beach, being eternally on the look-out for whatever they can pick up. Few of them are actually vicious, but they are not pets and they are not used to being fondled as our dogs are. There have been occasions when dogs have pulled down a child and devoured him before help could come. Even grown men have been killed by dogs, when they happened to fall down among them and could not get up again quickly.

SOCIAL ORGANIZATION

The social organization of the Eskimo is extremely simple. Government, as we know it, is totally unknown to them. They are not grouped in tribes under "chiefs" like the Indians to the south of them, but bands made up of numbers of people related by blood or marriage who hunt and fish in a certain area. The larger bands are sometimes called by the name of their biggest settlement with " miut" added, meaning "the people of" such and such a place. Thus the Padleimiut would be the people of Padlei and so on.

The bands were not governed by chiefs, but were under the unofficial leadership of some outstanding man who had no actual authority but whose advice and suggestions were taken by most of the members of the group. There were no formal laws, but the people believed the breaking of any of the taboos they observed might be very dangerous. If a woman should be so careless as to cook caribou meat, which comes from the land, together with seal meat, which comes from the sea, trouble of some sort for herself or for her family might be expected. This was not because she had broken any law, but because she had offended the spirits who control the caribou and the seals. Usually a public confession of her mistake was enough to set everything right again. Now and then somebody disturbed the peace of the community by murder, by repeated thefts, or by trouble-making; such people might be put to death if the group as a whole agreed that it was necessary. The person chosen to execute the unwanted member of the group would not be blamed. On the other hand, murders not approved by the village sometimes started blood feuds which might go on for generations.

The influence of the white man on Eskimo social organization has been strong. These people are expected to obey our laws, and things that were permitted in the old days are now forbidden. The

Eskimo himself is easily led and, when the white man becomes better understood and more familiar, there will be fewer offences against, and misunderstandings of, the white man's laws.

The primitive Eskimo, before the days of the whites, used a number of well-established trade routes. Along these flowed much business in such goods as wood, soapstone, copper, and nephrite or jade, a very hard tough stone used for making tools. These raw materials were collected in the various places where they were to be found and were then traded to people of other districts. A man who went inland to the timber line to cut wood for a table top or for making a pair of sled runners, or to get soapstone for pots and lamps, would bring back with him more than he actually needed, trading the extra for things he himself was short of. Other goods, such as skins, sinew, and foodstuffs, were probably exchanged among neighbors but few traces of this commerce are left. Some manufactured goods were traded too, wooden bowls, horn spoons, articles of clothing, bows and arrows, and soapstone pots and lamps.

Today these old native trade routes are almost unused and the only commerce is barter between the natives and the white traders, with skins as the medium of exchange instead of money. The most important skin is that of the Arctic fox which is of little use to the Eskimo, and fox meat is not used for food. The price of fox skins changes from year to year and the welfare of the Eskimo is much affected by these changes. In a bad year he can do no more than supply himself with the things he really needs; a good fox year, on

MAN'S HUNTING
CANOE, OR KAYAK

the other hand, enables him to buy the usual things and some luxuries as well. In a good fox year, too, it is possible for an Eskimo to have money to his credit at the trading post, but this he is seldom willing to allow, preferring to trade in his catch of skins immediately. There are some men, especially in the western Arctic, who have built up credits of several thousand dollars and are perfectly able to look after their own interests.

Commerce between the Eskimos and the Whites has been going on since the days of the whaling ships. Trading posts have been built all through the Arctic, except in the most northerly islands, and there are few Eskimo bands today who do not send some of their people to the trading post at least once a year. Many Eskimos live quite close to the post and, as long as they can get along there, they don't much want to go out on hunting and sealing expeditions.

WARFARE

Actual warfare, as we know it, was quite unfamiliar to the Eskimos. It was not possible for them to raise an army and there was seldom anybody with whom they wished to fight. It is true that they did not get along well with the Indians and both sides kept away

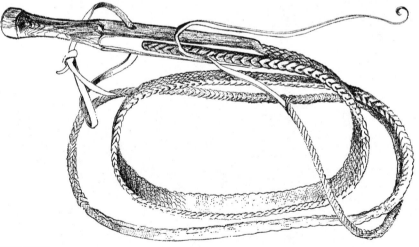

DOG WHIP

from each other as much as possible. There was a fairly broad stretch of No Man's Land between the two people in some places, where the Indians never ventured because they were afraid to, and the Eskimo kept out of it because they had no good reason for going there. When the two did meet there was likely to be a fight. One such incident was recorded by Samuel Hearne when his Indians fell on a camp of Eskimos at Bloody Falls on the Coppermine River, surprising them when they were asleep and killing every one of them.

In the Labrador and in Alaska the Indians and Eskimos lived closer together and there was a good deal of trading between them and even an occasional marriage. It was only where they were comparative strangers that they were enemies. When the first Europeans visited the Eskimos there was sometimes conflict and Martin Frobisher in 1576 even lost some of his men. He went ashore at one place and saw where a fire had been lit. Then he climbed to the top of a hill and "perceived a number of small things fleeting in the sea afar off, which he supposed to be porpoises or seals, or some strange kind of fish; But coming nearer, he discovered them to be men in small boats made of leather. Afterwards he had sundry conferences with them, and they came aboard his ship, and brought him salmon and raw flesh and fish, and greedily devoured the same before our men's faces. They exchanged coats of seals' and bears' skins, and such like, with our men, and received bells, looking-glasses, and other toys in recompense thereof again. After great courtesy and many meetings, our mariners, contrary to their captain's direction, began more easily to trust them, and five of our men going ashore, were by them intercepted with their boat, and were never since heard of to this day again."

SOCIAL LIFE

The Eskimo knew nothing of the hour by hour organization of time that we are accustomed to, for they had no clocks or watches. Such regularity would be out of the question in a land where the sun does not set for days on end in summer and where winter nights last all day.

In the Arctic, people do what they have to do when it suits them. If a man feels like working or hunting, he does so either alone

or in company with some others. When he is tired, he lies down
for a short nap or goes to bed, taking off all his clothes and wrapping
himself up in his sleeping bag. Often the rest of the family will go
to bed at the same time as a matter of common convenience, but if
the children are outside nobody would think of calling them in, and
they would play until tired and then come home to sleep.

A man returning from out-of-doors would be given something
to eat from the soapstone pot that simmered almost constantly over
the seal-oil lamp, but there were no set meal hours. People in a
family often did all take a meal at the same time, but as there was
no tablecloth to lay and no dishes to wash this was by no means
important. As a result, everybody had much more personal freedom
of action than we have.

All but the youngest and the oldest had their tasks and duties
in an Eskimo community. The head of the family was expected to
fish and hunt to provide food for them and to obtain skins from
which their clothes could be made. He was responsible also for
making and keeping in repair the sled, kayak, tools, and articles of
furniture needed by the family. He built snow houses in winter in
those parts of the Arctic where they were used, and he did the heavy
work of building the stone and sod houses or log cabins in the
eastern and western parts of the country.

The woman's task was cooking, making clothes for the whole
family and keeping them mended, sewing hides to make a tent or
cover a kayak, the care of the children, and the thousand and one
little jobs which a woman does almost anywhere.

The children had fewer responsibilities than their parents had,
but even when they were small they helped in every way they
could. The little girls were useful in the house, carrying water,
collecting wood, and helping their mothers with the cooking. The
small boys did what they could and often brought in birds and
other small game to swell the family larder. Elderly people who
were no longer active enough to go hunting often spent their time
in preparing skins and in other forms of "light duty".

The aged and infirm, the sick and mentally unsound, were
usually looked after by the rest of the community unless their support and care proved too much of a burden, and then they might be
left to die alone of cold or starvation. Very old people, knowing

themselves to be a trouble to the others and unable or unwilling to keep up with the people on their frequent journeys, sometimes asked to be put to death or left behind to die. In winter, a small snow house would be built and the old person left there with very little food or perhaps none at all. Sometimes old people were strangled at their own request.

Children were well cared for and much loved. They were treated with great kindness and were left to do much as they pleased. They were seldom punished but might be scolded if they annoyed others. They knew many games and were usually very happy little people.

Marriage was performed without ceremony, though the young husband might attach himself to the household of his father-in-law and live with them for some time before he and his bride got a separate igloo of their own. Women were not in the lowly position they occupied in some Indian tribes. Their advice was asked and considered and their influence on group affairs was often as strong as that of the men.

Family relationships on the whole were happy and pleasant. Jealousy is not common among the Eskimos and in a small community, where everybody's actions were visible to all, there was seldom cause for jealousy to arise. Divorce was unusual; when a couple who had been married decided to separate, there was no ceremony to make it official. Many men had more than one wife and

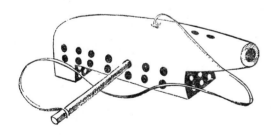

RING AND
PIN GAME

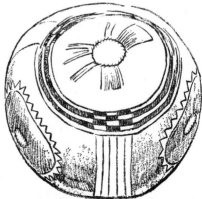

LEATHER FOOTBALL,
STUFFED WITH
CARIBOU HAIR

few had none. The custom of wife-lending, which so interested the white man, was largely a matter of convenience and necessity. If a man wished to start out on a journey, he needed a woman to go with him to do the cooking and to keep his clothes mended. If his own wife was not a good traveller or was not expert at mending or at cooking on the trail, the man might borrow, from some other man, a woman who had the necessary ability.

Travellers in the North agree that the Eskimo people as a whole are remarkably intelligent, friendly, honest, and cheerful. Now that they are getting used to the white man and his peculiar ways they have become invaluable friends and companions. They are quick to understand, and take a great delight in, such things as motor boats, sewing machines, and gramophones. Some of them own cameras and take good pictures. They insist that they could build the same things themselves if they had the tools and equipment, in which perhaps they are right. In these matters they admit the white man is superior to them, but in other respects, such as travelling and living off the land, they regard the white man as a strange and rather pathetic fool, who doesn't know the first thing about hunting or driving a dog team. They are slow to get angry and rather fear the fighting type of white man, with his violent temper, who is always ready to use his fists to settle a dispute.

GAMES

Amusements were few or at least lacking in variety. Sometimes the men held wrestling or archery contests or would run races. A strong skin rope, stretched tight between two solid supports, made a sort of horizontal bar for gymnastics. Sometimes they stretched a rope from one side of an igloo to the other, reinforcing the building so that they wouldn't pull the walls down. They played a primitive game of football using a skin stuffed with caribou hair for a ball and, as far as one could see, there were no goals and no rules.

There were simpler games played indoors, one of the favorites being the making of string figures like our cat's cradles. They knew dozens of different patterns and could make them very quickly. Some of them could be made to move and there were little stories that went with them. Another game was very like the ring and pin game of the Algonkians.

Now and then the children had silence competitions, and when one of them unexpectedly shouted "Ika" all the rest had to keep perfectly quiet. The first one to break the silence was laughed at by everybody. Little girls had dolls and made clothes for them and small boys played at building snow houses and driving puppies in a toy sled.

During the winter, dancing with singing and drumming accompaniments were, and still are, popular. Not infrequently the medicine man kept people interested while he went into a trance to ask the spirits about a lost article, or something that had been stolen, or the chances for a successful hunt.

MUSIC

In spite of the fact that the drum was the only musical instrument known to the Eskimos before the days of white contact, music was surprisingly well advanced. Singing was greatly appreciated. Many of the people made up their own songs, both words and melody, and sang them at the dance festivals or for their own

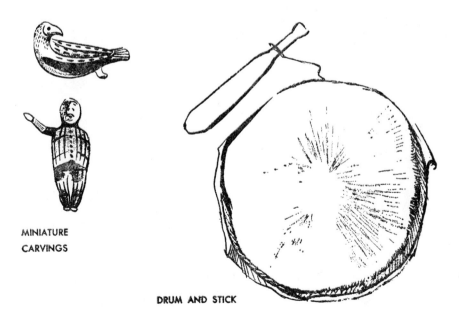

MINIATURE
CARVINGS

DRUM AND STICK

pleasure when out hunting or fishing. Men and women also sang in chorus, the voices of the women pitched an octave higher than those of the men.

The drums were large flat sheets of skin stretched on a narrow wooden hoop and provided with a short handle. The drum-stick

GIRL DOLL   BOY DOLL

was used to strike, not the drum head itself, but the wooden rim of the drum.

ART

The Eskimo, though often a fine artist, has but little chance of showing it. Painting is not seen often even now, though white man's paints are easy to get. It is in carving that the Eskimo is at his best. Miniature figures of men and animals are carved with realism and true beauty in ivory and stone. Digging in the deserted villages has shown that sculpture is not new to Eskimo art, the old people having produced some very fine pieces of carving hundreds of years ago.

Bone and ivory objects were sometimes decorated with shallow cuts, arranged in patterns, or representing a scene, such as hunting or dancing. The cuts were then filled with a mixture of black soot and heavy grease or wax which made the designs stand out from the white background. This form of art was better known in the west than in the east.

In the west, too, was developed an amazing form of art, the carving of grotesque wooden masks. The twisted features, the soft coloring, and the design of the whole mask were so blended as to produce an effect between terror and comedy. Few of these masks are found in modern museums, but they are outstanding examples of Eskimo art.

LITERATURE

The only kind of literature the Eskimo had was unwritten, but they knew hundreds of stories of the kind we call "fairy tales", about how the world was made; how the seals and walrus came into being; the origin of the Eskimos, the Indians, and the white men; stories of giants and dwarfs; and so on. Some groups of Eskimos such as those in Alaska are much interested in these stories and the older people can tell dozens, if not hundreds, of them. Other Eskimos, like those around Coronation Gulf, know only a few and don't care much about them. There are also children's rigmaroles, chanted while playing games, there are weather charms, and many kinds of songs. Some of these have been published in books, but they are rather dull reading even for people who make a special study of such things.

SCIENCE

In spite of his undoubted ability as a mechanic, in which he stands head and shoulders above most of the native tribes of Canada, the Eskimo seems to have had no idea of scientific knowledge, in such things as medicine for example, or arithmetic. Many of them find it difficult to count as high as four. After that, they simply say "Many!" Though they have words for the higher numbers, few people know or use them.

Some of them are clever at drawing maps, while others are not only unable to draw one, but can make nothing out of them. Those who can draw maps seldom get them in proper proportion. A long straight stretch of coast line may be shown in an inch or so, while a difficult bit of the trail, only a few hundred yards long, may take up a lot more room on the "map".

In medicine, most illnesses are thought to be caused by witchcraft and so they try to cure them in the same way, knowing almost nothing of real medicine. Surgery is a little further advanced, and they can set a broken arm or leg, lance a boil, or even amputate frozen fingers or toes.

RELIGION

While it is true that the Eskimo believed, rather vaguely, in a life after death, and in legions of supernatural beings, there was little in the way of formal religion. They believed that all animals and many other objects had inner spirits which might sometimes be dangerous. Medicine men, and a few medicine women, pretended to control these spirits and would appear to talk to them while in a trance. Quite possibly, some of them were sincere in believing that they could do this.

Sometimes they tried to foretell the future by a curious form of fortune telling, known as head-lifting. The person who wanted to know what was in store for him was made to lie down on the sleeping platform, his head supported by a leather strap, perhaps a tump line, which was held by the medicine man. As the spirits

were asked questions, the medicine man would lift the strap slightly
and the enquirer's head would lift easily or remain quite motion-
less, apparently without his will, to say yes or no.

Some of the more important nature spirits have names and
their position in the world of supernatural beings is well known and
explained in legends. Sheela, for instance, controls the weather and
can bring on storms or hold back winds as she wills. Sedna, another
feminine being, is in charge of all the seals and other sea animals
and it is she the hunter must thank or blame for his success or
failure. The medicine men say that they know of many other spirits
and, given a pencil and paper, some of them can draw pictures of
these beings, horrible in appearance, and again balanced halfway
between terror and laughter.

That a life after death was expected is shown by the offerings
they placed in or near graves for the use of the spirit in the land
beyond death. The graves of men might have real or model kayaks

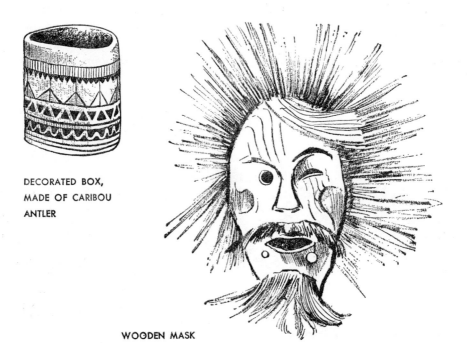

DECORATED BOX,
MADE OF CARIBOU
ANTLER

WOODEN MASK

and hunting gear left on them or hidden near them, and the graves of women were often marked by cooking pots and sewing kits. Burial was difficult in this frozen rocky land and the bodies of the dead were often laid on the ground, wrapped perhaps in a caribou skin, and covered more or less carefully with a mound of stones to protect them from animals.

A new-born child was thought often to be the spirit of a recently dead member of the family who had come back to earth and would be called by the name of this person and treated to some extent as if he actually were the same person born again.

PRESENT CONDITIONS

The Arctic is changing rapidly. The trading posts have brought new ways to the Eskimo and now the aeroplane has made it possible to establish bases in still more remote places. These people no longer live in the Stone Age as they did only a few years ago. They have proved themselves quick to adopt the white man's ways and today the rifle is used instead of the bow and arrow, the motor boat takes the place of the umiak, and the aeroplane often is chosen rather than the dog-team. It is true that in far settlements life goes on much as it did and there are many Eskimos who can still make a bow and a quiverful of arrows, build a kayak, or harpoon a seal in

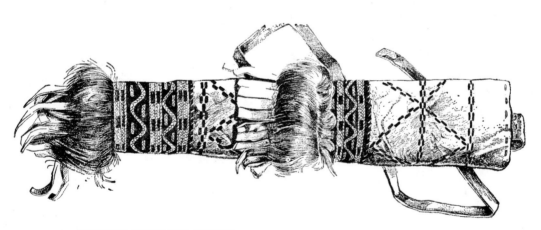

DECORATED QUIVER FOR ARROWS

the old way. Many of them still wear clothes of caribou fur or seal skin, but others prefer the white man's clothes. It will probably not be very long before the old arts and crafts have gone completely.

Quite possibly the Eskimos will adapt themselves to the new way of life better than many of the Indian tribes have done, and in this their undoubted skill in the use of modern machinery will be of great value. They learn easily and with pleasure and are quick to take to new ways of doing things. They soon become most useful and efficient assistants.

The girl who broke all the taboos

A Legend of the Eastern Arctic

Once, long ago, in the old, old days, when all the men were good kayak paddlers and all the women clever with their needles, there lived a strong man who had many sons and one small daughter. She was the youngest of his children and he and his wife and all her brothers were very fond of her and spoilt her completely.

If any of the boys brought in fresh cod fish they gave the eyes to Nauya, the Seagull, for that was her name, and when her mother cut up a seal the choice little bits went to Nauya as a matter of course. In spite of all this, she grew strong and beautiful. Also she was a very good runner, much faster than anybody else in the village.

Now it happened that the strong man, her father, and her mother, and all of her brothers were a bit old-fashioned and very careful to observe all the taboos and never do anything that might offend the spirits. They went to great lengths to avoid irritating even the weakest and least important of the strange beings that were thought to exist invisibly all round them, watching people while they travelled, or hunted, or fished, or even while they were asleep. It was a nuisance, of course, but it all had to be done.

Nauya didn't believe in all these spirits at all and she laughed at the strong man, her father, and her mother and her many brothers for being so easily fooled.

"When have you ever seen a spirit?" she would ask scornfully. "Never, of course."

"Well, perhaps not," her brothers would answer. "But old Anory, the medicine man, has and he can describe them in every feature."

"Describe them!" scoffed Nauya. "So could I describe them, and make up much more horrible ones than he has ever imagined. What about the one that sucks the brains from the weasels' skulls?"

"Oh, stop! Stop!" they shouted at her. "There's no such spirit. You just made it up."

"Of course I did. Just as old Anory makes them up," she admitted. "There's no truth to any of it."

"Don't be so sure of that," they answered. "One of these days you'll do something really bad, and then the spirits will be after you and there will be nothing we can do to save you."

Nauya paid no attention to their warnings. In fact, she seemed to go out of her way to get into trouble and to do things that were taboo. People didn't know about it at first, for her father, the strong man, and her mother and her many brothers tried to keep from the rest of the village the fact that she was always breaking taboos because they were sure the people would be very angry if they knew, and force her to confess what she had done.

One day her brothers were cutting up some seal meat, using small knives, in the way it is supposed to be done and, because the meat was hard and frozen, they were having a lot of trouble with it. Nauya watched them for a little while and then picked up a stone axe that was lying near, elbowed her way to the seal meat, and chopped it all up quickly with a few blows.

"Stop! Stop!" they all shouted. "You know very well you must not cut frozen seal meat with an axe."

"Of course I know it!" she laughed. "And I see that the meat is now all cut up, and nobody is any the worse for it."

One hot summer day she went for a walk with her brothers and they scrambled up a low iceberg that was stranded on the beach. Right up on top they found a pool of sweet fresh water formed by the melting ice.

"Oh, good!" shouted Nauya. "Water! Just what I wanted."

She lay down to drink from the pool before any one of her brothers could stop her.

"Don't!" they shouted. "You know you shouldn't drink fresh water from an iceberg."

"Of course I know it!" she agreed. "It won't kill me!"

And so she went on, doing all sorts of things she knew she shouldn't, breaking all the taboos she could think of.

Now every well-educated Eskimo of those days knew that the spirits noted every taboo that was broken and that, sooner or later, trouble would follow. Therefore it was not difficult for Nauya's family to understand the cause of the accidents and disasters of all sorts that began to afflict the village. Anory, the old medicine man, slipped while hunting a polar bear and broke his leg, and it was just by good luck that the bear didn't kill him. One of the younger men was drowned when he cut the skin of his kayak on a piece of floating ice, several of the dogs in the village fell sick, seals became scarce, and then, to cap it all, the caribou, usually numerous a few miles inland, seemed to have disappeared for ever.

Nauya's family knew very well what the trouble was, and did everything they could think of to make her stop these foolish pranks. She would just laugh and insist that she had nothing at all to do with any of these calamities.

Generally, it was easy to make peace with the spirits after a taboo had been broken. All that was necessary was for the guilty man or woman to admit the breaking of the taboo, whether by accident or by carelessness, to make a public confession, and all was well again. But this, of course, Nauya refused to do.

"Confess, indeed," she raged. "And have every young man in the village laugh at me or scorn me. And now, of all times, just when I hope to get married!"

True enough, Nauya was now the most lovely girl in all the village and young men had come from miles away to see if she was really as beautiful as they had heard she was and to see if they could persuade her to marry them. So far, she had refused every one.

One day, when her mother left the igloo for a few minutes, Nauya did one of the worst things possible. She had often thought of it, but had never quite dared, because she knew just how furious her mother would be. Hanging over the seal-oil lamp was a stone pot of good seal meat simmering in a thick rich broth. It smelt delicious, and good round islands of fat floated on its surface. The meat fork lay on the table and Nauya selected a little bit of the well-boiled meat and nibbled it with relish.

Then she felt quickly in a skin bag her mother had tucked away under the edge of the sleeping platform in which she still had a good piece of caribou meat from the last one they had killed. Nauya picked out a piece about the size of her fist and plopped it into the simmering seal broth.

Now that was very wrong indeed, for it is most strictly forbidden to cook seal meat, which comes from the sea, in the same pot with caribou meat, which comes from the land. Both Sedna, who looks after the seals, and the powerful spirits who have charge of the land animals would be greatly offended.

Even Nauya herself was a little bit frightened, but she knew the meat would be cooked in a few minutes and nobody would know the difference.

Then her father, the strong man, came in from his hunting. He sat down on the edge of the sleeping platform and stuck out his legs so that Nauya could pull off his boots for him.

"My, that meat smells good," he said. "Give me some of the broth."

So Nauya took the musk-ox horn dipper, filled it, and handed it to her father.

"Really good!" he said approvingly. "Best seal meat I've ever tasted. Give me a little more and a bit — just a minute. I'll get some myself."

He held out his hand for the meat fork and moved over to the cooking pot. He poked about in it with the meat fork and soon came up with a nice firm bit of meat. This he put in the dipper along with another helping of the good hot broth.

Nauya could not help seeing that this was the piece of caribou meat she had put in.

Just then her mother came back and she, too, took a dipper of musk-ox horn and helped herself to some of the hot broth and a piece of meat.

"Oh, you have some meat too?" she asked her husband. "I thought there was only one piece left in the pot. I was just going to cut up some more, but I see Nauya has already done so."

Nauya said nothing.

Her father had now finished the soup with its strong taste of seal and turned to the piece of meat.

Just as he raised it to his mouth, he paused, looking at it curiously.

"This smells different," he remarked. "Not a bit like seal meat, now all the soup is gone."

"Oh?" said his wife. "Let me smell."

She leaned over to smell better, and just at that moment Nauya slipped out of the igloo.

Her mother stifled an exclamation, her hand clapped over her mouth.

"That's not seal, it's caribou!" she whispered, her voice trembling with horror. "And they were both cooking in the same pot. Whatever will happen now!"

"It must have been Nauya," her husband said. "Nobody else would do such a terrible thing. Something awful is going to happen, you may be sure of that."

"We've got to stop it before it does!" exclaimed his wife. "This time she must confess, confess to the whole village, marriage or no marriage."

Jumping to their feet, the strong man and his wife rushed out of the igloo and called to the many sons to help them catch Nauya.

"Why?" they asked. "What has she done now?"

Almost breathless with worry and shame, they told them of her last and most awful sin. By now the other people of the village were gathering round and it was only a short time till everybody knew.

"Nauya cooked seal and caribou together!"

The people all turned and looked at the strong man and his wife in silence, unable to believe anything so shameful.

They stood quietly with bowed heads and said nothing.

"We'll have to catch her," somebody said. "If she doesn't confess and appease the spirits, there's no knowing what may happen."

They looked round to see where Nauya might be. Almost at once, somebody saw her, nearly out of sight dashing along the hard flat sands of the beach. Then they all saw her and started off in pursuit.

Now they knew that Nauya was easily the best runner of them all and that the only way to catch her would be to keep her running day and night till she was tired out. This they did, using dogs to follow her trail, and trotted steadily along behind her.

Soon she was miles ahead and, thinking to put them off the trail, she turned inland. Still they ran after her, hour after hour, and when she paused to rest for a moment she could see them far behind but still pursuing her.

On she fled, panting now, and the cold air of the inland hills froze her breath as she ran. Mile after mile she toiled, panting and gasping for air now, clouds of vapor floating behind her.

The people pounded along behind, no longer bothering to follow her trail but guided by the great clouds of her frozen breath. Bigger and bigger the clouds grew, thick and choking, till the people lost all sight of Nauya in the fog she left all over the landscape.

And ever since that day, there have been great fogs in which the people lose themselves and sometimes even their lives, all because a bad girl offended the spirits by cooking seal meat and caribou meat in the same pot.

CHAPTER 6

THE NORTHWEST TERRITORIES

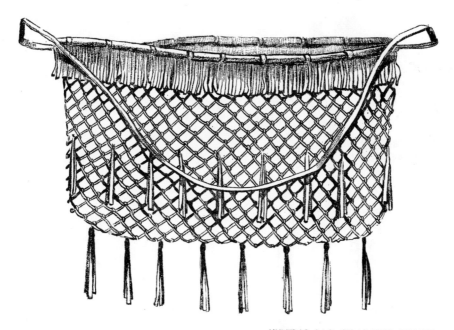

HUNTING BAG OF LOOPED BABICHE

Chipewyan
Beavers
Slaves
Yellowknives
Dogribs
Hares
Sekani
Nahani
Kutchin

CARIBOU-SKIN CLOTHING
WITH PORCUPINE-
QUILL DECORATION

THE NORTHWEST TERRITORIES

FROM CENTRAL ALASKA, right through to Newfoundland, a distance of about four thousand five hundred miles, Canada is covered by a wide belt of dense forest, mostly spruce. Scattered through this vast distance are a few thousand Indians, the remnants of the tribes that once occupied it.

That part of this vast forest that lies between Alaska and Hudson Bay is inhabited by Indians who all speak dialects of the same language, Athapascan. Their speech varies from one tribe to another, sometimes so much so that the people can not understand each other. These natives all call themselves Déné or Tinneh, which means "people", and it is thought by those who have made a study of them that they may be the latest group of people to come from northeastern Siberia to North America, pushing other tribes aside to the north and south as they moved through Alaska and the Yukon into the open country east of the Rockies.

There are little groups of them, such as the Navaho and Apache, scattered all down the west coast of the United States, even as far south as Mexico, but these were never as large or as well established as the tribes in the Northwest Territories. Apparently they were still moving southwards when the whites first came in touch with them.

In Canada, their southern neighbors were the Cree and the Blackfoot, and the Interior Salish tribes of British Columbia. To the north, along the coast, were the Eskimo, whom the Indians held in great dread and avoided whenever possible. We have seen that the prairie Indian people led a most happy and enjoyable life, but this was far from being the case with the Athapascans, for it was difficult to make a living in the dense forests; and on the open tundra to the north and east, food was not as plentiful as it was in other districts, and the winters were long and severe.

The CHIPEWYAN are the biggest group, having a larger population and occupying more territory than any other Athapascan tribe. Their name means "pointed skins" and refers to the cut of their tunics, which had a long dangling tail behind and sometimes in front too. Early travellers told of a people living in the far north who had tails and were half way between men and animals but it was really only a misunderstanding of descriptions of the Chipewyans.

They lived on the edge of the forest, spending the winters in the shelter of the trees and hunting the caribou on the open Barrens in summer. We believe that there used to be about 3500 of them in the old days, but they suffered a terrific scourge of smallpox in 1781 and almost nine out of every ten died from it. Today there are thought to be about a thousand of them still living. They were noted for the harsh way in which they treated their women, making them but little better than slaves and beasts of burden.

The Chipewyans occupied all the territory north of the Churchill River as far west as Great Slave Lake including the southwest corner of the District of Keewatin and the southeast part of the District of Mackenzie.

The BEAVERS got their name from the fact that they depended largely upon this animal for their living. They dwelt in the basin of the Peace River, southwest of the Chipewyan. These people were so close to the prairies that some of them had obtained horses, probably from the Cree or perhaps from the Sarcee, their close neighbors. In customs, they resembled the Sekani who lived to the west of them. They used snares a great deal in their hunting and did but little fishing.

The SLAVES, or Slaveys as they are often called, are spread over a big stretch of country to the west of Great Slave Lake as far as the Mackenzie River. The Crees called them *awokanak*, which means "slaves" and the name, put into English, has stuck. These people were a good deal milder and more restrained than the Crees and the Chipewyans; they were much kinder to their women-folk, and did not abandon sick and old people to starve. The men did most of the hard work. They seldom left the forests for the Barrens and used fish a good deal more than their neighbors did. They were sometimes taken captive by other tribes and made to work as slaves, but at the same time they were feared because of their reputation as skilful magicians.

The YELLOWKNIVES lived in the area of lake-strewn land from the east end of Great Bear Lake to the east end of Great Slave

Lake. They were very much like the Chipewyans, their neighbors to the southeast. In parts of their country nuggets of native copper are to be found lying on the ground and these they hammered into tools and weapons, from which custom they got their name. Other names for the same people were Copper Indians and Red Knives. They lived on the edge of the forests, staying there in winter and venturing on to the Barrens in summer to hunt caribou. They sold copper tools to their neighbors at good prices, but there is no market for them now that steel is available.

The Dogribs lived round about Great Bear Lake and southwards to Great Slave Lake, to the southwest of the Yellowknives. Like the Hares and the Slaves, they treated their women comparatively well, though there was still lots of hard work for everybody. Like most of the other tribes of the Northwest Territories, they lived largely on caribou and a few fish.

MAP SHOWING WHERE THE INDIANS OF THE NORTHWEST TERRITORIES LIVED

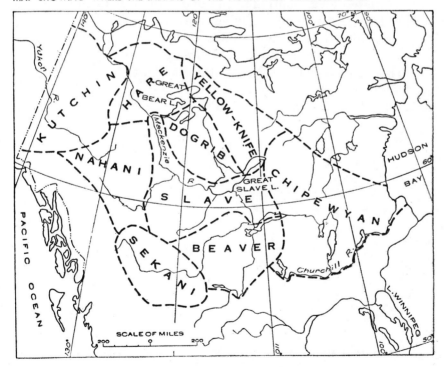

The HARES lived to the west and northwest of Great Bear
Lake and got their name from the fact that they lived largely
on hares (or rabbits as they are called in the North), using the
skins for clothing and the meat for food. Of course, they ate
anything else they could get too. They were a timid people who
always ran away and hid in the bush if they saw or heard strangers
coming, sometimes making their camps under fallen trees well back
from the rivers so that they would not be discovered. As in many
of the tribes of the north of Canada, the men would wrestle with
each other to settle any dispute; among the Hares men seized their
opponents by the hair and twisted till one of them fell down.

The SEKANI, whose name means "dwellers on the rocks", that
is the Rocky Mountains, lived on the eastern slopes of the mountains
in what is now northern Alberta, and in the basins of the Finlay
and Parsnip Rivers, round about the present towns of Peace
River and Fort McLeod. They are somewhat shorter and lighter
in build than are the people farther to the east. They lived entirely
in the forested area, hunting moose and caribou both summer and
winter. They seldom used fish, unless they were obliged to. Strangely
enough, many tribes of mountaineers who depend on hunting for
a living do not care for fish and think rather poorly of fishermen.

The NAHANI lived to the northwest of the Sekani along the
Rocky Mountains. They were divided into three sub-tribes, the
Kaska, the Mountain Indians, and the Goats. They lived on caribou,

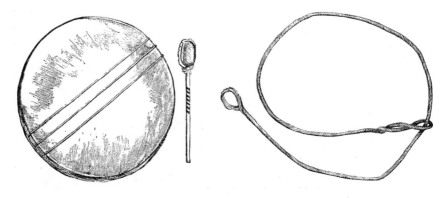

SNARE DRUM AND STICK   SNARE OF BABICHE

mountain goats and, in earlier days, on the wood buffalo which were more numerous in their country then than they are now. They closely resemble the Sekani in their habits.

The KUTCHIN occupied the basins of the Pelly and Porcupine Rivers from the mountains westwards to the Alaska border, taking up much of the interior of the Yukon. They are divided into several smaller tribes, of which the most important are the Loucheux, the Han, and the Tutchone. The Loucheux (which means "squinters") live in the northern Yukon and are much influenced by the Eskimo, their neighbors to the north. The southern Kutchin, on the other hand, were influenced by the Tlingit to the south of them and so these people, though certainly Athapascans, are not so typical as those to the east. The Kutchin fished in summer and hunted in winter, caribou and moose being important, as well as any other game they could get. These people, unlike other Athapascan groups, had a system of chiefs who, though not particularly strong or influential, were admitted to be the leaders, and the chiefs admitted no superiors except the medicine men of whose magic they were much afraid. The Loucheux were divided into three separate groups, something like clans, and nobody was allowed to marry anyone of his own clan. They were most hospitable people, entertaining guests even for months and always feasting as long as there was food. The women always ate after the men had finished, and the children came last. One curious

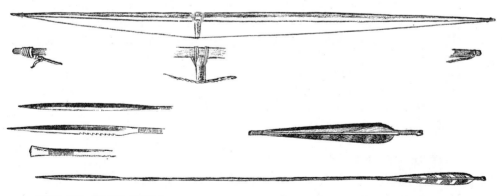

BOW AND ARROW DETAILS

custom of the Kutchin was a wrestling match, started by the two smallest boys in the camp. The winner of the first match took on the next oldest till the contest had worked its way up to the strongest and best wrestlers present, and always the winner of a match had to challenge the next man in order. When all the men had finished, the little girls and the women might go through the same thing for themselves.

POPULATION

It is not possible to say how many Athapascans lived in the northwest before the days of white exploration. Several people have made a guess, and the figure of about 14,000 to 15,000 seems the most likely. Today there are from 5500 to 6000 left, somewhat less than half. The population was never large, and there were great ranges of country with no inhabitants at all. If we divide the number of people into the number of square miles in their vast territories, we find that there was about one person for every 180 square miles, a very thin population indeed and by far the thinnest in Canada. The comparative scarcity of game accounted for this, and it is very probable that the country could not have supported a larger number of people.

PHYSICAL APPEARANCE

As these people all spoke a similar language and, we may suppose, all descended from a common source, they had a certain family resemblance about them. They were more like the Indians of eastern Canada than like those of the west coast, being tall and slight in build. They had the typical Indian straight black hair, the dark brown eyes, and high cheek bones. The women and children particularly showed the slant eye that we think of as being Chinese, and most of the people had a coppery-red tinge to their skin. They are not particularly handsome people, though some of them are better looking than others.

NATURE OF TERRITORY

As we have already seen, the land these people live in is covered for the most part, especially in the west, by a dense forest of spruce. There are also pine trees, poplars, birch, and willows. As the land gets higher or stretches farther north, the forest thins out and gradually gives way to open tundra, soaking wet and covered with dense mats of mosses and lichens. At times even these disappear and there are dreary miles of stony ground with little vegetation. Between the forest and the tundra is a broad strip of land with small trees growing in suitable places, larger trees in the sheltered valleys, and this area is known as "the land of little sticks". There are parts of the Yukon, above the tree line, where wide open prairies or grasslands are found and it is here that good grazing makes good caribou hunting too.

The northern and eastern parts of this country are sprinkled with thousands of little lakes and not a few very large ones. They are almost as numerous in the forested parts too, but there they are more difficult to see and so one is not so conscious of their number.

It is an enormous area, taking up nearly a million square miles, over a quarter of all Canada. Much of it is empty for there

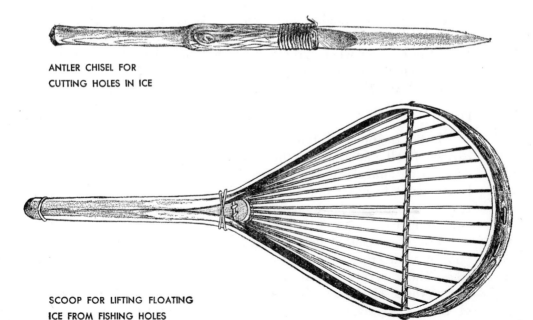

ANTLER CHISEL FOR
CUTTING HOLES IN ICE

SCOOP FOR LIFTING FLOATING
ICE FROM FISHING HOLES

are many parts of it in which game is so scarce that people could not find enough to live on.

The climate is severe, being cold for months on end in winter with plagues of mosquitoes in summer. In 1947, the thermometer at Snag, in the southwestern Yukon, registered 81 degrees below zero and there are claims for even lower temperatures at Fort Selkirk on the Yukon River. Of course, such extremes are rare but 50 below is not at all unusual and many places see 60 below at least once each winter. Most of the Indians stay in the forests then, because here they are sheltered by the trees which protect them from the wind and there is always an abundance of fuel at hand. The Barrens, at this time of the year, are practically deserted, except for the wretched Caribou Eskimo of central Keewatin.

The summer, with its long days and hours of sunlight, is delightful. Flowers bloom in thousands and the calls of the birds and chattering of the streams are most welcome sounds after the long silence of winter. People who were born and brought up in the northwest love it just as any other people love their homeland. There is a tale of an old Dogrib Indian who was told by a missionary of the joys of Paradise and then he asked, "Are the hills there covered with flowers? Do the great musk-oxen roam there? Shall I see the caribou wherever I look? Can I feel the wind, and be like the wind? Does the mist rise from the little lakes in the early mornings? And there, does the loon call, very often?"

FOOD

Just as the buffalo is the chief source of food on the prairies, the caribou is all important in the Northwest Territories. There are other large animals, too, of course, such as the moose, musk-ox, bear, mountain goat, and mountain sheep in the west; buffalo in the western forests; and smaller animals all through the country, but the caribou come first.

Fish were caught by some of the people but they were not popular with others, though they were abundant in many of the lakes. There were whitefish, salmon in the Yukon River basin, and many others. Hares, or rabbits, were important and formed a sort of reserve supply, for game must be scarce indeed when one cannot get even rabbits. There are years, however, when there is hardly a single rabbit to be seen, for they have periods of great abundance and then drop rapidly in numbers. A poor rabbit year can mean great hardship for the people if other game is scarce too. Birds are eaten, as well, chiefly waterfowl such as ducks and geese, and ptarmigan, and grouse.

Vegetable foods were chiefly berries, and the tender shoots of various plants were chewed in the spring. Some bulbs that are good to eat were gathered also.

Food supplies were irregular. One district might be rich in game and another, not very far away, might have none. Then again, one might hunt for days and find nothing only to have more

ONE TYPE OF
WINTER HOUSE

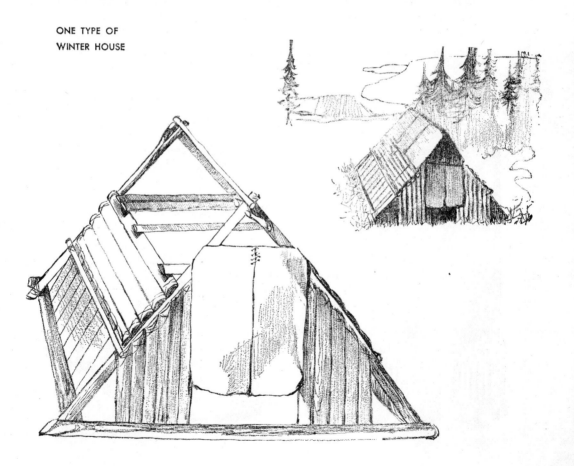

meat than could be eaten a little later. One way of overcoming this irregularity was the building of caches. *Cache* is from a French word which means a hiding place, and food was stored or hidden in caches where it would keep well and be safe. If a man killed several caribou, he might dry or freeze the meat and put it up in a cache till he could come back for it. A cache was a platform of poles built high up in the trees above the reach of animals. The trunks of the trees that supported it might have the bark taken off so as to make them too slippery for the wolverine to climb. Today the Indians nail sheets of smooth tin round the trunks of the trees for the same purpose.

A quick and easy way of caching things was to tie them in a bundle, fasten this to the top of a long pole and then stand the pole up against a tree trunk, so that no animal could get at it.

Meat and fat were dried and made into pemmican, and fish pemmican was made too. This could be put in the caches and kept

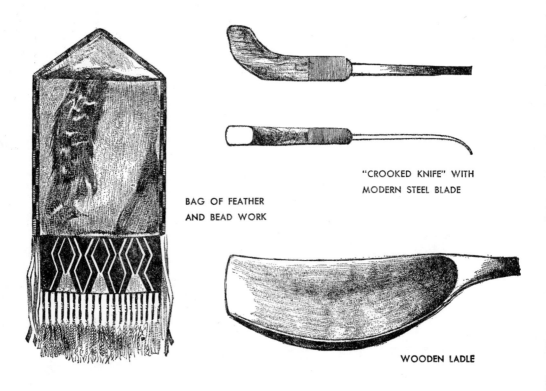

BAG OF FEATHER
AND BEAD WORK

"CROOKED KNIFE" WITH
MODERN STEEL BLADE

WOODEN LADLE

for a long time, so the risk of famine was not as great as it might have been otherwise, but just the same these people often suffered severely from hunger and there have been cases in which starvation was so extreme as to force the people to become cannibals and eat the flesh of those who had already died of hunger.

Fire was made by striking two lumps of iron pyrites together and most cooking was done by stone boiling.

HUNTING

The methods of hunting used here were much like those of other parts of Canada except perhaps that they used snares rather more than other natives did. Nets and traps were used too, and also the method of driving animals into pounds. Here, especially in the western area, hunting fences were built, which might stretch for a long way through the forest. Caribou or moose could find no way through these fences and were led at last into a circular pound, in the walls of which there were gaps. What the animals did not know was that snares were hidden in these gaps and as soon as the beasts tried to push through them they were caught.

The snares were made of babiche, a tough line of rawhide. If several of these lines were braided together the snare would be so strong that not even a moose or a grizzly bear could break it, and both these animals were caught in snares by the Athapascans. Nets of babiche were used for beaver and they had also a special beaver spear with a toggle head, which was chiefly a Sekani weapon.

On the Barrens, musk-oxen were killed for food till hunting them was forbidden by law. Now they are completely protected but it is impossible to watch the herds all the time and undoubtedly some are killed in spite of the law. Musk-oxen form a half-circle when attacked, facing the enemy, with the calves squeezed in between the larger animals where they will be safest. Now and then one of the bulls makes a charge and then backs into position again, keeping the formation unbroken. Such a way of defending themselves was successful as long as they had only wolves to fight against, but a man with a bow or a rifle can shoot them down one by one till nearly all are dead. The last few may suddenly turn and run, thus saving their lives.

Caribou were often speared in the water from canoes, with a special spear. They might be driven into a lake or the people might find a herd crossing a river. The hunters would paddle out into the middle of them and spear them as they swam. Among the Loucheux of the northern Yukon, the hunters used to run the bow of the canoe right up on the shoulders of a swimming caribou and then picking up the spear, stab to right and left till the animal that was carrying them reached the far side.

The women did their share of the food getting by setting snares for rabbits in the willows near their camps. They were very skilful at this and seldom failed to catch something except in a poor rabbit year, when nobody could get any.

FISHING

Fish were caught in nets, with a hook and line, or with spears. Fish traps and weirs were used too, built in suitable places in the rivers. Nets were woven from the tough inner bark of the willow and took a long time to make. The bark had to be shredded finely and twisted into a string and then woven into nets. Most of this work had to be done with the hands under water or else the willow bark became dry and brittle. Some stronger nets were made with fine babiche. The Sekani are said to have used nettle fibre for their nets, but they did not do much fishing anyway. Some fish were taken at night with jacklights from a canoe or even through the ice, holes being cut for the purpose. Nets were set below the ice too and many fish were caught in this way in winter, in places where the water was too deep to freeze to the bottom.

CLOTHING

Clothes, for the most part, were made of caribou skin which, when it was properly treated, was soft and thin, but quite warm. For winter, some skins were used with the hair left on, which made them even warmer. In winter, too, an extra robe might be worn. The principal garment was a long tunic that came to the thighs in men, and to the knees in women, with leggings for both of them. The men generally wore a breech-cloth too because their tunic was shorter. Moccasins might be separate or attached to the bottom of the leggings. In cold weather caps and mittens were worn, but people did not bother with these in summer. Some tunics had hoods like those of the Eskimo.

The Kutchin decorated their clothes elaborately with shells and painted designs. Other tribes, to the east, were more simple in their tastes and there was not much ornamentation. Some of the people were tattooed and many of them, especially the Kutchin, had the custom of wearing an ornament of quill and shells through the division between their nostrils. They valued these shells very highly and used them almost as we use money. Some men had many hundreds of them and were much annoyed if white traders tried to palm off imitations on them. The Kutchin, too, dressed their hair with a mixture of grease and bird-down, so that it made a huge lump at the back of their necks, so big that their heads were permanently bent forward to take the weight of it.

YUKON TYPE OF CRADLE

CHILD SUPPORTED BY
CARRYING BELT

DWELLINGS

There were few large dwellings in the Indian villages of the Northwest Territories. Their houses were for the most part temporary and portable, often no more than a lean-to made of brush. As a matter of fact, that is not as bad as it sounds for a well-made lean-to can be reasonably comfortable in fine weather. In winter they adopted the system of putting up two open-faced tents right opposite each other and only five or six feet apart. A fire was lit on the ground between them and threw its heat into both. The smoke went straight up, inconveniencing nobody, and both tents were light and warm, a very satisfactory arrangement. In cold weather, one or both ends of the passage between the two tents would be closed.

At other times a framework of poles was covered with sheets of bark or skins. An additional coating of brush might be laid over this and even a layer of mud and caribou hair has been used. In the west, some tribes built log cabins with a gable roof for the

BIRCH-BARK CANOE

winter. The other extreme was the over-night summer camp in which the people slept comfortably under the sheltering branches of a large spruce tree. These come low down to the ground and are quite thick enough to keep off a light shower of rain.

FURNITURE

With such simple houses, the furniture was scanty indeed, as one might suspect. Caribou or bear skins were laid on the ground for a bed, often with a springy layer of spruce boughs under them, but there was nothing resembling a chair or a table. Baskets were made of birch bark or woven roots, and bags were of skin or of loosely looped babiche. The Indians made fine network of this kind for bags and in the lacing of snowshoes. Shallow trays, for food, were made from bark, but there was no pottery at all nor do they seem to have known of it.

TOOLS

People who move frequently and have to carry all their things with them are careful not to own too much. The tribes of the Northwest Territories travelled as lightly laden as possible and, therefore, were not able to carry large sets of tools about with them as the Eskimo did. The women had their awls and needles for sewing, spoons and ladles for their cooking, and skin-scrapers for dressing hides. The men had an unusual sort of knife with a beaver tooth for the cutting part and a few more ordinary knives made of stone or copper. They also had a few adzes of stone. Most of their tools, though, were made of bone, horn, or antler, and work in stone was comparatively undeveloped. The Yellowknives, as we have seen, made tools of the native copper found in their country along the Coppermine River and sold them at high prices to their neighbors. Most of the men had an ice chisel made of antler, for cutting holes through the ice in winter for setting nets.

TRANSPORTATION

Summer travel, when not on foot, was by canoe. Spruce bark was the usual material, for the birch trees in the northwest seldom grow large enough for canoe making. Some canoes consisted of a wooden framework covered with skins, not unlike the Eskimo umiak. These were used for bringing loads of furs out of the woods and, when the Indians reached their destination, they took the skins off the framework to be used again, but left the wooden frames lying on the beach. They sometimes do the same thing today, using sheets of canvas instead of the skins. The Kutchin used some birch-bark canoes, for the birch trees grow bigger in their part of the country, and their canoes were small and narrow.

In winter, people travelled on snowshoes. The kind used here were longer and narrower than those of the eastern woodlands and the front ends were turned up in an unusual way. The Chipewyans, by the way, were the only people who made the right and left snowshoes different from each other. Loads were carried on tobog-gans which were pulled, not by dogs, but by the women. Most of the toboggans were of thin slats of wood but some were made by sewing the skins of moose legs together, the short hairs making a good slippery surface. The snow in the woods was too soft for sleds with runners of the Eskimo type and it was in this part of Canada that the toboggan was used most. Dogs were used for packing too, with simple pack-sacks of skin laced up the sides. A strong dog could carry nearly a hundred pounds but most loads were less than half as heavy.

Children were carried in moss-bags and sometimes on the mother's back, in the Eskimo way. The Kutchin, who had many ways of their own, had a curious cradle of birch bark something like a big sugar scoop in which the child sat, a long tongue of bark coming up between the legs. Such cradles are very rare today and are no longer used. Many women carry the baby on their backs under a shawl, with a belt below the child to support it.

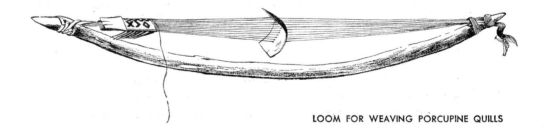

LOOM FOR WEAVING PORCUPINE QUILLS

DOMESTIC ANIMALS

There are two breeds of dogs in the Northwest Territories, apart from the many breeds the white man has brought in. The Indian dogs that are used for packing are probably the descendants of dogs they brought from Siberia with them and so are the much smaller Bear Dogs, or Hare Indian Dogs, as they are sometimes called. These are still to be found in the Yukon and a few nearby places. They are black and white, with a curled tail, friendly and affectionate pets, and do not bark, but only howl or whine. They were used for hunting black bears, their part in the hunt being to find the bears and worry them till they climbed a tree. There they would hold the bear till the hunter could come and kill it.

The Beaver, the most southerly of this group of tribes, had horses as well as dogs when they were first seen by white people, probably having obtained the horses from the prairie Indians to the south.

SOCIAL ORGANIZATION

The Athapascans had even less idea of government than the Eskimos, if that is possible. Small bands of people, who were usually intermarried, travelled and hunted together and acknowledged the leadership only of the more experienced hunters. Even these had no authority at all and the people took their suggestions or ignored them as they wished. The strongest link that joined these bands into tribes was language; all the Dogribs, for instance, could understand each other. Bands who could not speak the Dogrib language were not Dogribs but must be something else. Sometimes there would be differences in the language of a single tribe; among the Kutchin, the Han people speak a language somewhat different from the Loucheux, but they can understand each other fairly well, especially after a little practice.

Some bands laid claim to certain hunting territories but the system was not as well organized and fully accepted as among the eastern woodland tribes. Today the trap lines are registered and each man knows just were he may trap and where he may not.

The Slaves did appoint chiefs if war was expected, but these lost their authority as soon as the emergency was over. The Kutchin, affected perhaps by the solidly organized tribes of the west coast, had chiefs with a little more authority, but they were an exception in this to the other tribes of the northwest.

WARFARE

There was no organized warfare among these people, but constant friction between the different groups made them cautious with strangers, and they might easily decide that it was safer to kill them than to risk being killed themselves. There was occasional trouble with the Eskimos and most of the Indian groups kept well away from those parts of the Barrens where Eskimo might be expected. The Chipewyans bullied the Dogribs and the Yellow-knives; the Crees bullied the Chipewyans; and they all felt it was safe to attack the timid Hares and the Slaves in spite of their reputation as medicine men. These people, the Slaves, made some use of wooden shields and armor of willow twigs lashed together, but armor does not seem to have been used by the other tribes.

SOCIAL LIFE

Everyday life in the northwest saw nothing of the gay feasts and dances of the prairie people. The little wandering bands did not enjoy much in that line and, as a rule, were too busy merely keeping themselves alive to devote time to amusements. There was a small feast when somebody died, and again a year later when a memorial feast was held. A larger feast celebrated an eclipse of the moon, but this was a rare event, and, as the Indians never knew when one was expected, they could make no preparations for it.

Each family lived to itself. There being no chiefs to settle quarrels, only public opinion, the men fought among themselves to get what they wanted by force. The only brake on this way of settling things was that there was always the chance that an apparently weak enemy might prove to be a great medicine man who would take his revenge by magic, or that his family would start a blood feud that could go on for years. Magic, of one sort or another, was constantly in their minds and almost everybody was thought of as a possible magician.

Men wrestled for the wives of other men and the one who was defeated had no way of preventing the stronger man from taking his wife away from him. The women stood quietly watching the contest, apparently not much concerned.

When a young man married he hunted for his wife's family till his first child was born, but from then on he and his wife kept an establishment of their own.

Men were allowed all the wives they could support and it was the strongest man who had the most and the best women to care for his many children and to prepare the skins their husband brought in from his hunting. Men tried to have sisters as their wives, for they agreed with the prairie Indians that there was less chance of quarrelling among sisters.

Children were named at birth, but a man dropped his own name when his first child was born. From then on he was known as "the father of so and so"; if a grown man had no children, he would be called "the father of Blackie, or Spot" or whatever his best dog was named.

The women particularly had a hard life, though it was by no means easy for the men either. Here indeed the women did do all the hard work and were little better than servants, worse indeed, for servants at least get paid. Many women who had girl babies let them die, saying it was better for them to die without having

DESIGNS USED IN PORCUPINE QUILL WORK

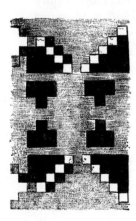

known the hard work, hunger, and pains they would suffer if they were allowed to grow up.

GAMES

Games did not play a large part in the daily life of these people. The men gambled a good deal when they could, their favorite game being one something like "Hide the Button", using two little sticks of wood or bone. Most of the people played the ring and pin game, which was known all over Canada. Dancing was popular whenever enough people got together, and the medicine men sometimes did conjuring tricks to entertain folks.

Archery contests, racing, and wrestling were summer sports, especially among the Kutchin who had more leisure time and showed more interest in games than did the other tribes.

MUSIC

The drum was the only musical instrument and, as usual, it was of the single-headed tambourine type. The only unusual feature was that some of the drums had snares of sinew or babiche stretched across the drum head so that they would vibrate and produce a sort of trembling note. Some of the people sang, but this art was not nearly as highly developed as it was in some other parts of Canada.

ART

The people of the Mackenzie River valley had developed only one form of art that was at all unusual. This was a kind of weaving in which they first made a simple strip of woven vegetable fibres or sinew and worked into it an intricate pattern of dyed porcupine quills. The weaving was so fine that it must have strained the

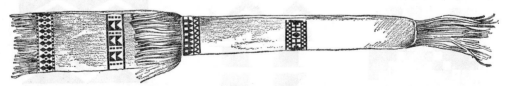

GUN-CASE DECORATED WITH PORCUPINE-QUILL WORK

women's eyes in the poor light of their tents and there is so much work involved that few of them do it now. First the porcupines had to be killed, then the quills had to be pulled from the skin, washed and sorted into different lengths. Next the women would have to go out into the woods to collect dye plants, make the dyes, dye the quills, weave the base on which the work was to be done, and only then would they be able to begin the actual weaving of the pattern.

Some of their clothes, and tools too, were painted but there was very little art of any kind other than the porcupine-quill work. Today they use beads for decorating moccasins and gloves, largely for sale to white men living there or to tourists.

LITERATURE

Legends and fairy tales are known to the Athapascans in hundreds. The old people can tell one story after another for hours on end, and some of their tales are so long that it takes more than one evening to reach the end. They are of the kind usual with the Indians, legends of how the world was made, how the Indians and the white man came into being (often not very complimentary to the white men), what made the Milky Way, why the raven is black, and so on. Some of the same stories are told by the natives living on the other side of the Pacific in Siberia, which strengthens our belief that the Athapascans came from there, probably not very long ago.

SCIENCE

There was nothing resembling science in the minds of the Athapascans. The only people among them who came anywhere near it were the medicine men, part of whose responsibility was the curing of disease and such simple surgery as they could manage.

They pretended to suck pebbles and bits of bone out of a sick person's side, right through the skin, and would blow and suck while the drums beat and other medicine men chanted their magical songs. Some of them said they could foretell the future and among the Kutchin the medicine man was sometimes held off the ground by straps while he did so, for what reason we do not know.

RELIGION

Their thoughts on religion were just as primitive as in other fields. They believed the forests and the Barrens were filled with the spirits of nature. Each waterfall, every mysterious lake, a strangely shaped rock, and dangerous rapids, each had its spirit and the people observed many taboos to avoid giving offence to them. There was no idea of a supreme spirit over these lesser beings.

Many of the Indians had, or professed to have, a guardian spirit, generally an animal or some object, which they had seen in a vision and from whom they had learned a sacred song. These guardians would come to their owner's help in times of difficulty, but not on unimportant occasions. The people felt that there was a strong and intimate relationship between men and animals, and they were usually careful to give no insult to the animals they trapped for food or for furs.

They had some notion of a life after this one, but it was very vague. The Chipewyans believed that the soul of a dead man journeyed in a canoe of stone which moved magically towards a beautiful island on which food was abundant always. If a man had behaved badly in this world the canoe would sink with him before he reached the island, leaving him struggling forever in the water.

Men who thought themselves to be dying would confess their wrongdoing in the hope that this would delay their death. In mourn-

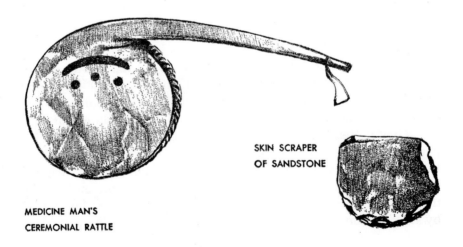

SKIN SCRAPER
OF SANDSTONE

MEDICINE MAN'S
CEREMONIAL RATTLE

ing for the dead, the women cut off their hair and sometimes even joints of their fingers. The dead were cremated as a rule, or their bodies might be put high up in a tree, or laid on the ground and covered with stones in the Eskimo way. Among the Kutchin and many of the other tribes, the clothes and other property of a dead man were burned. The Loucheux used to cut off the huge bunch of hair from the back of a man's head and place it at the top of a stake on the river bank so that everybody who passed by, the river being an important route of travel, might know that he had died.

PRESENT CONDITIONS

The old way of life becomes more difficult every year. Game is scarce and in some parts there is almost none. Trapping is not as profitable as it was, for much of the country is becoming trapped out. The people can now get white man's food and clothes from the trading posts, but these are not always better for them than the food and clothes they were used to. They can get the white man's diseases too, and these have killed off many hundreds of Indians.

A great deal is being done to help them, more than ever before. They get family allowances, and the old age pension. There are more schools and hospitals than there used to be, and the government officials concerned with the Indians are continually on the watch for ways in which they can improve conditions. Large game reserves, in which only natives may hunt or trap, have been set aside for them and these not only provide food for the people but they are also places where the game can thrive and increase with but little disturbance.

The Indians are not on reservations as they are farther south, though they do live in their own villages in many places. Many of them have little gardens and they make what money they can trapping and working for wages. Most of them dress as white people do except for the moccasins which they, and many white men, still think are more comfortable than heavy leather boots.

Why Raven is black

A Legend of the Yukon

Many years ago, when the world was still small, Old Man Coyote decided it was time to do something about the birds.

As things were, all the birds wore the same dull brown clothes and so it was difficult to tell them apart, except by their size and shape, or their voices. Old Man Coyote didn't like this at all but, though he had given the matter a good deal of thought, he hadn't yet decided what to do about it.

One hot morning he was trotting along the banks of the Porcupine River, just about where the village of Old Crow is now, far up north in the Yukon. He paused and stood with his front feet in the water to get a drink, when Raven came flapping along overhead, diving low as he passed.

"Craw!" cried Raven, in his harsh, cracked voice.

Old Man Coyote looked up and grunted.

"There goes another of them," he muttered angrily. "I know it's Raven, because of his awful voice, but it could just as well be any one of half a dozen others."

He bent down again to finish his drink, and, as he did so, his eyes happened to light on the little pebbles at his feet. Some of them were red, some blue; some had a green tinge, and others were a soft gray. As he looked, he saw that hardly two of them were just alike.

"That's it!" he cried. "That's it! Now I know exactly what to do, and I'll do it."

The very next afternoon, because he was busy with other things in the morning, he called all the birds together and explained his plan to them. In soothing, flattering words, he told them that he was going to design new clothes for them all, so that there need never be any confusion among them again.

"Now each one of you will look beautiful," he went on. "The small birds will be brightly colored, like the pretty pebbles on the beach down there, and the big birds will look handsome and important, like those fine cliffs of rock further down stream which I made last week."

All the birds liked the idea very much, and they arranged themselves in orderly rows so that each one could see just what went on. The shore birds sat on the sand and gravel along the river side, and the perching birds found good seats in the row of willows that bordered the water. The grassy banks and the cliffs too were all lined with birds watching and waiting for their new clothes.

The only bird who did not accept the plan in the proper spirit was Raven. He paced up and down, whispering to the other birds out of the corner of his beak, and glancing over his shoulder at Old Man Coyote as though to make sure that he couldn't be overheard, and making a great show of the need for secrecy.

Wise Old Man Coyote paid no attention to him, but set to work at once. The warblers were the first to be done, because they were so small and tricky.

Working carefully, he put a dab of bright red here, and a streak of blue there; here a green wing, and there a neat black cap, using only his smallest brushes.

All the birds were chattering together, full of interest and pleasure, and delighted twitterings greeted each new design. Some of the more impatient ones flew up from their perches and crowded closer to see just how it was done, and Hummingbird hovered so close as to get in Old Man Coyote's way.

"Get away from here, and let me work," he cried, and struck at Hummingbird with his brush, which happened to be loaded with crimson, and Hummingbird has had a ruby throat ever since.

Time was passing, but the crowd of birds waiting to be colored hardly grew less. Old Man Coyote saw he would have to work with broader strokes, so Robin came out part red, and Bluebird (that's the mountain one) all blue.

Still Raven didn't like what was going on. He would stump over and peer into the paint box, picking up a tube of color here and there, and then fly off a short distance to examine it more carefully. Old Man Coyote paid no attention to him, but went on working.

When it came to the larger birds, such as the hawks and eagles, the colors had become so mixed up on the palette as to make brown and gray shades, and so the big birds appeared in those tints, and these were soon used up too. Towards the end, Old Man Coyote found a big tube of Chinese white that Raven had knocked out of the box and the swans and geese had to be satisfied with that.

At last he flung down his brushes, tired but happy. It was the first time he had tried painting and the hot glow of triumph and satisfaction that he felt both surprised and pleased him. His joy was spoilt only by a gentle little tug at his tail and the hoarse voice of Raven.

Old Man Coyote's first feeling was one of anger but he was in a pleasant mood, and so he smiled politely.

"You haven't done me yet," Raven blurted out and then, knowing that he had sounded a little rude, he too smiled politely to cover it up.

"No. So I see," agreed Old Man Coyote, "and I'm *more* than sorry, because I've used up all my paints."

"Well," Raven complained, "I don't like being a dull brown when everybody else has a bright new suit. Isn't there anything you can do about it?"

"Not without paint, there isn't."

Raven thought this over for a minute.

"I've got a few no account odds and ends of paint myself," he said in an off-hand sort of way.

"You have!" cried Old Man Coyote. "*You* have some paint? How does that happen?"

"Well, you see, when you were busy with the other birds I borrowed a dab of this and a dab of that, just to see how they would look, you know . . . ," and his voice trailed off into an awkward silence.

"Oh, you did, eh?" grunted Old Man Coyote at last. "Well, bring 'em along, and we'll see what we can do."

Raven flapped his wings and chuckled hoarsely as he waddled off, immensely pleased at all this special attention.

"I dare say you have some special ideas of your own," said Old Man Coyote drily.

"Well, yes, as a matter of fact I have been doing some thinking," Raven simpered. "You see, I like this brown well enough as a ground color because I'm used to it. I was wondering if I could have a bright red head and neck, something like Woodpecker over there, but bigger and brighter."

Without a word, Old Man Coyote colored Raven's head and shoulders a glowing scarlet.

Eagerly Raven flapped his way down to the water's edge and looked at himself in a smooth little eddy. He turned his head this way and that, trying to see his reflection at its best, now with the sun on him, now in the shade.

"It's not the success I had hoped," he croaked.

"All right, then. What do you suggest?"

"An orange ring round the neck, just below the red to soften the change a little, and then a pair of grass green wings." Raven's answer came out pat and assured.

"Well, well," growled Old Man Coyote. "You're becoming quite an artist." Secretly he was annoyed that Raven should show such a knowledge of art, since Old Man Coyote had only just discovered what it was himself.

"Right you are then," he agreed.

Once more Raven went down to the still water to look at himself, and again he was disappointed with what he saw. He frowned and muttered and peered for a long time.

"I don't like it," he said at last. "I think it's gaudy and ugly. What about a bright blue back, and the underparts just off white? The brown *was* a bit dull after all."

Without a word, but with his lips tight shut, Old Man Coyote made the changes and then Raven flapped off to his mirror.

Terrible! Awful! This would never do. Back he flew.

"It's no good," Raven shouted. "It gets worse and worse. You've made every bird in the woods look beautiful, but you've turned me into a rainbow-ridden idiot!"

Once more he jumped up and down furiously.

Old Man Coyote waited patiently till Raven had cooled off a bit.

"And what would you like me to try next?" he asked in a dangerously quiet voice.

"Do whatever you like," shouted Raven. "You can hardly bungle things any more than you have done."

Still Old Man Coyote kept his temper.

"I've got only one tube of paint left," he pointed out. "Somebody must have spilt the others that you were keeping for me. Would you like me to use that one?"

"Use it? Yes, use it, of course, you fool!"

Raven was quite beside himself now, for never would any bird in his right mind call Old Man Coyote a fool.

"Very well, then. Stand still a minute and stop jumping about. There! Now you're black, all black, and black you shall stay till the cliffs tumble down, and the fish all die, and the Old Man of the Rivers comes striding down the dry bed of the Porcupine, carrying the very last drops of water in a little birch-bark pail."

CHAPTER 7

THE BRITISH COLUMBIA INTERIOR

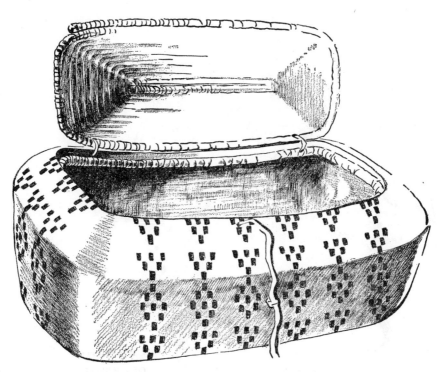

BASKET MADE FROM SPLIT ROOTS AND BARKS

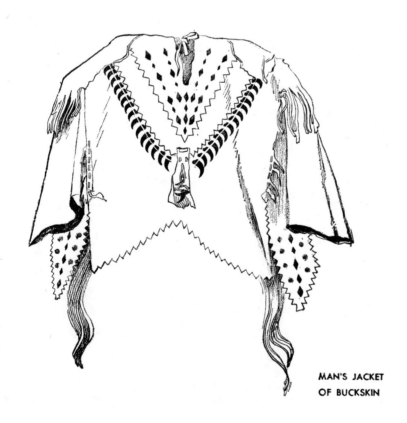

MAN'S JACKET
OF BUCKSKIN

THE BRITISH COLUMBIA INTERIOR

THE INTERIOR OF BRITISH COLUMBIA, from the border of the Yukon in the north to the United States border in the south, lies in a great valley between the Rocky Mountains and the Coast Range. Here live several tribes of Indians who, although they belong to three different language stocks, all made their living in much the same way and so can be treated together.

They ate the same kinds of food and their ways of hunting and fishing were similar as well as their methods of cooking and of preserving food for the winter. Their houses, true enough, did vary in style and there were also some differences in the clothing. Nor were their methods of transportation all the same, and there was a good deal of difference too in their customs and ceremonies. The people they resembled most were the prairie Indians or the Athapascans. In fact, three of these tribes were Athapascan.

The KOOTENAYS once lived on the prairies in the part now occupied by the Blackfoot and it was these fierce warriors who drove the Kootenays across the Rocky Mountains to where they now live, round about Kootenay Lake in southeastern British Columbia. The Kootenays speak a language of their own, Kootenaian, and have kept a good many of their prairie customs. It was probably not much more than two hundred years ago that they crossed the Rockies and, until the buffalo at last were killed off in the 1880's, they used to go back two or three times a year for a big buffalo hunt. Like many of the prairie tribes, they grew their own tobacco, and they were noted too for their own special type of canoe.

The INTERIOR SALISH are a group of tribes or bands who all speak dialects of the same language, Salishan. They were the Lillooet, the Thompson, the Okanagan, and the Shuswap.

The Lillooet, who live in the area round the present town of Lillooet and near Harrison Lake, were strongly influenced by their neighbors and relatives to the west, who lived on the coast. They were great business men and trade was an important part of their life. They shipped dried berries, twine, tanned skins, and mountain goat wool down to the people on the coast in return for slaves, dugout canoes, and sea-shells. So closely were they related that they shared many of the customs of the coast people. The word *lillooet* means "wild onions". These are abundant in parts of their country.

The Thompson River Indians live along the Fraser and Thompson Rivers from Yale through Lytton to Ashcroft, and south up the Nicola Valley. They too traded with the coast people, travelling by canoe up and down the lower part of the Fraser River. One

WHERE THE INDIANS OF THE BRITISH COLUMBIA INTERIOR LIVED

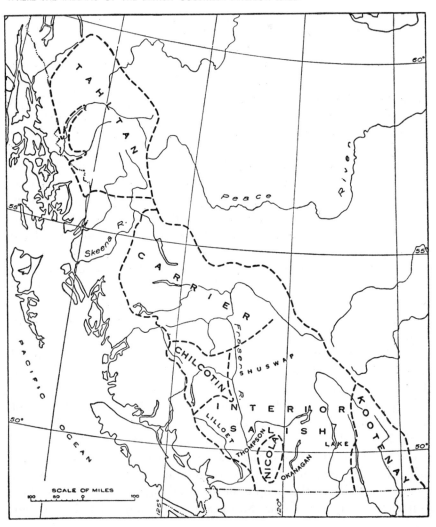

of the chief things they had to sell was jade, a fine-grained tough green stone, very useful for making tools. It is found in the gravels of the Fraser River near Lytton.

The Okanagan Indians live in the valley of the Okanagan River and another small group, known as the Lake Indians, have their home round about the Arrow Lakes and the upper Columbia River.

The Shuswap occupy the land to the north of the other Salish tribes from Lillooet to Alexandria and east to the Rockies. They are the largest Salish tribe and are divided into smaller bands.

The next three tribes, who speak Athapascan dialects, live to the north and west of those already mentioned. They are the Chilcotin, the Carriers, and the Tahltan.

The CHILCOTIN, whose name means "people of young man's river", are closely related to the Carriers, who live to the north and east of them. They, too, had a trade route to the coast down the valley of the Bella Coola River, the stream followed by Alexander Mackenzie when he reached the Pacific from the east in 1793. The Chilcotin people were often at war with the Shuswap. Today they raise cattle and horses and work on the huge cattle ranches of the Chilcotin country.

The CARRIERS are another Athapascan tribe and occupy a large area in central British Columbia, north of the Chilcotin and Shuswap. They include the Babines, a name meaning "big lips" which the French gave them because the women used to use labrets, ornaments worn in the lower lip which stretched it to a surprising size. The Carriers lived so close to the coast, on their western borders, that they adopted many of the customs of the coast Indians.

The TAHLTAN, the last of the three Athapascan tribes, dwell still farther to the north and lived much as did their relatives to the northeast across the Rocky Mountains in the Northwest Territories. Their home was on the upper Stikine River and their route down to the coast followed this stream. They trapped in winter and fished for salmon in summer, but much preferred meat to fish as a diet. Many of them today act as guides for hunters who want to shoot big game.

POPULATION

These tribes of the British Columbia interior lived in a country that was not able to support a large population. There were large areas that were visited only occasionally by hunting parties and never permanently occupied. Villages were built wherever conditions were favorable, and these were often long distances apart. As closely as we can estimate now, the native population may have been about 30,000. There were only 9,000 left at the beginning of this century (1900) but they now number about 14,000 and seem still to be increasing.

PHYSICAL APPEARANCE

Because they came of different stocks, there is some variation in the looks and build of these people. As a whole, they are tall and straight with a good physique, active and alert. The Chilcotins are said to be somewhat shorter and rather like Chinese in appearance, but they have broad shoulders and are stronger than most Chinese. The Carriers tend to be tall and thick-set but not fat, many of them being unusually well-built men, and so are the Interior Salish to the south of them. They all have the black hair, brown eyes, and high cheek bones typical of Canadian Indians. There is a good deal of variation in their skin color, some of them being no darker than many Europeans and others of a deeper brown.

NATURE OF TERRITORY

The inland strip of British Columbia in which these people live is about nine hundred miles long from north to south and from a hundred and fifty to two hundred miles in width, so we may expect a good deal of variation in climate and scenery in such a large area.

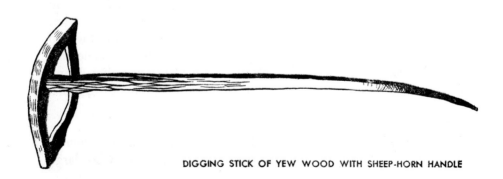

DIGGING STICK OF YEW WOOD WITH SHEEP-HORN HANDLE

In the north it is fairly dry with high mountains and dense forests. A little farther south, between Prince Rupert and Prince George, there is a most beautiful stretch of country of lakes, mountains, and forests, where the Babines and Carriers live. Still more to the south, the country gets drier and drier till we reach what is called the British Columbia Dry Belt, a most unusual part of the province where there is very little rain and it is so dry in some parts of it that it reminds one of a desert. Here cactus grows, and sagebrush, and rattlesnakes are found. It is cattle grazing country with a severe climate, going up to a hundred degrees or more in summer and down to fifty below in winter. In spite of all this, the climate is so dry that neither the heat of summer nor the cold of winter is unpleasant and the people who have the good fortune to live here like it very much.

Salmon is the outstanding food here, but naturally many other things are eaten as well, especially deer meat, as well as roots and berries. There was no agriculture of any kind, except for a little tobacco growing by the Kootenay, the people depending entirely on what they could kill or gather.

The larger animals which were hunted for food were moose, elk, caribou, deer, bear, mountain goat, and mountain sheep. Among the smaller ones were rabbits, beavers, groundhogs, gophers, and porcupines. Birds were used too, ducks, geese, and grouse.

Fish were of great importance, especially the salmon, which came up the streams to spawn every autumn in incredible numbers. At times they were so thick that people felt they could almost walk across the river on the backs of the thronging salmon. There were also trout in the streams, whitefish in the lakes, and several other kinds of fish, such as suckers, pike, and ling. One unusual kind of food was grasshoppers, which are very common in summer in the drier parts of the country. If one walks through grassy places, grasshoppers fly up and settle on one's clothes; the Indians used to pick them off and eat them alive, just as we eat grapes.

Vegetable foods consisted chiefly of roots and berries. Among the roots, camas was the most important. This is a wild lily with a large bulb. There are two kinds of camas, one with a white flower and the other blue. The one with the blue flower is good to eat, but the white flowered kind is poison. As the bulbs of the two kinds look alike, it was safe to dig the bulbs only while the plants were in flower so that one kind could be told from the other.

Camas and other edible roots had to be pried up with a special digging stick, a curved piece of tough wood, often yew, with a handle of mountain sheep horn. The ground where the roots grew was sometimes so hard that it would have been difficult to get them without using a digging stick.

Berry picking time was one of the big occasions of the year. There were saskatoons, salmon berries, raspberries, blueberries, and several other kinds. In early autumn, when these were ripe, the people would start out on a berry picking expedition. They knew where the best places were, often miles away, and might be gone for ten days or more. It was like a long and happy picnic. Most of the actual picking was done by the girls and women, who carried a small basket in front of them and a larger one on their backs to empty the smaller one into when it was full.

When they got back to the village with hundreds of pounds of berries, the first thing was to dry them and press them into cakes for winter use. The berries were laid out on racks made of cedar slats and put in the hot sun. A layer of large leaves covered the racks so that the berries would not fall through between the slats. Often the berries were squeezed first and the juice was saved and poured over the drying berries, helping to make the cakes solid and rich. The cakes were turned now and then so that the sun could get at both sides, and all the children of the village were on hand waiting to lick the sweet and sticky leaves from the rack.

Another vegetable food, often used in spring, was the inner bark of various trees, evergreens and poplars. When the sap is rising, this inner bark is soft and juicy and makes a welcome change from the dried food of winter. It is collected with a special sap scraper of thin bone or antler, and the bark comes off in long white slivers. The Indians say these slivers of bark taste like oranges. Some are hung up to dry and will then keep for months.

In a country with such long and severe winters it was desirable that stores of food be preserved for winter use, when hunting was not successful and fishing or gathering vegetable foods was almost impossible. Roots could be dried and berries pressed into cakes, but meat and fish had to be smoked as well as dried to preserve them. Many thousands of salmon were caught during the autumn runs and only a few of them were eaten fresh. The rest were cleaned and filleted, and then hung up over the smoke of a slow fire to dry. The heads, with the backbones still attached, were dried separately and used for making fish soup. Sometimes dried salmon was powdered and mixed with grease to make fish pemmican, which also would keep for a long time.

In the winter, fresh meat was sometimes frozen and kept in caches, which were little more than small log cabins built high up in the trees beyond the reach of animals. Other supplies of fish and berries were kept in pits dug in the ground near the village; they were lined with birch bark to keep the food clean. Rows of these pits are still to be seen here and there, especially near places where the fishing was good.

Boiling was done by the hot stone method, using baskets of birch bark to cook in. Another method was baking in an underground pit. A shallow pit several feet across was dug in the ground and filled with stones that had been heated in a fire. When the ground surrounding the pit was very hot, the stones were raked out and a layer of camas bulbs was put in the bottom, then came a layer of leaves, more hot stones, and then a covering of earth and skins to keep the heat in. Only old women were allowed to cook in this way, for it took a good deal of experience to know exactly when things were done, and a younger woman might spoil everything and ruin hours of work. When the pit was opened, the bulbs would have all run together into a thick, black, sticky mass which was very good to eat and which would keep for months after it had been cooled and dried. A dark stringy moss that grows on the trees was cooked in the same way.

Fire was made with a hand drill, but care was taken not to let a fire go out if it could be avoided. Fire could be carried in a torch of cedar bark rolled up tight where it would smoulder for hours.

WOODEN SPEAR WITH STONE POINT

Small boys or girls were sometimes entrusted with carrying the fire on the trail, and they would feel most important, blowing on the cedar bark or waving it round and round in the air if it showed any signs of going out.

HUNTING

The hunting methods used in the interior of British Columbia were much the same as in other parts of Canada. The principal weapons were bows and arrows, clubs, spears, and knives. Traps, snares, and pitfalls were used too. Bows were of yew wood or of juniper in the southern part and of willow or of spruce in the north. Arrows were of cedar or of saskatoon. The bow was sometimes backed with rattlesnake skin or with sinew and some of the people fixed a chipped stone point to one end of the bow so that it could be used as a spear too. Quivers were often made of lynx or fawn skin.

Traps and snares were of many kinds. Beavers were caught in nets, and the Carriers used to stretch a net between two canoes and drive flocks of grebe into it. They also caught numbers of ducks and geese in nets when they came down to rest during the spring or autumn migration. The fool hen, a kind of grouse, was so called because it would sit quite still while a hunter came up close with a long thin stick on the end of which was a noose of fine sinew. This noose he would slip gently over the sitting fool hen's neck and pull the bird down.

Hunting fences for deer stretched for long distances through the hills and forests, and the remains of them are still to be seen in some places. Some hunters preferred to follow the deer all by themselves, wearing a skin coat and a deer's-head cap so that, as they crept through the brush, they would look like a deer and could get close enough to one to shoot it. Sometimes pitfalls were dug in a trail that the deer followed. These pits were narrow and steep-sided and could not be seen, as they were roofed over with a light layer of twigs and leaves. The deer would fall in and become so wedged that they could not struggle out.

The people of the interior of British Columbia put great faith in ritual and taboos in hunting, as did hunters in many other parts of the world, and all of them carried charms to increase their chances of success. Good hunters needed not only skill, necessary though that was known to be; the charms and rituals were thought to be just as important.

FISHING

There were many ways of catching fish, some used almost anywhere and others only in suitable places. A special kind of spear with two prongs, each with a detachable harpoon head, was used by some, and a fish gaff, with which the fisherman raked the water, by others. The gaff was used only in dirty water where the fish could not see the man, and be frightened away. The fact that the man couldn't see the fish either did not matter because the gaff was used only when the fish were very numerous.

Many fish were caught in nets, one of the most effective being a dip-net at the end of a long slender handle. The fisherman scooped the net through the water, generally standing on rocks that overhung a swift current. The spawning salmon, swimming upstream would be caught in the net and swung ashore to the women who killed and cleaned them.

Weirs were built across shallow places in swift water, so constructed as to steer the fish into a trap, and at waterfalls cleverly made baskets were so placed that the fish, trying to jump up the

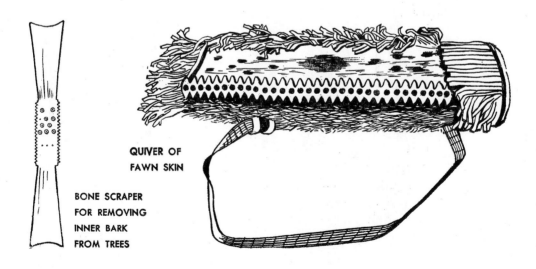

QUIVER OF
FAWN SKIN

BONE SCRAPER
FOR REMOVING
INNER BARK
FROM TREES

fall, were caught. One of the simplest of these was a screen of basketry with a looped-up curve at the bottom. The fish would jump to get over the fall and, if they fell back, would land in the roll at the bottom of the screen. This was tilted so that they would slide sideways and end up in a trap.

In winter, some people fished through the ice. Sometimes a hole was cut with an antler chisel, at other times hot stones were used to melt a hole through it. The fisherman would lie down on the ice at the edge of the hole dangling a lure of white bone from one hand and holding a fish spear in the other. As the fish swam up to see what the lure was, he would spear them. In some lakes, canoe-men with a torch and a spear would catch those fish that came to see what the bright light was.

CARIBOU SKIN
MOSS-BAG

WOMAN'S DRESS
OF BUCKSKIN

In the rivers where the salmon fishing was best, there were specially good places where the current brought the fish close to the rocky shores and where there was a flat place on which the women could build their smoking fires and racks to hang the fish on. All these good spots were owned by separate families and the same family would use them for generation after generation. Everybody knew just who owned each place and people who had no fishing places of their own would have to work for the more fortunate ones to earn their share of fresh fish and winter provisions.

While there were not so many rituals and taboos connected with fishing as there were with hunting, the people saw to it that the salmon, as well as other fish, were treated with proper respect. Special attention was paid to the first salmon caught each season.

DRESS AND ORNAMENTS

Clothing, for the most part, was of skins for both men and women. Usually deer skins were used, soft and well tanned, but the Kootenays made more use of moose hide. In winter additional robes were worn, some of them of woven rabbit skins, others of ground-hog skins sewn together to make a light warm robe. It took about twenty skins to make one. Less expensive clothes were made of woven bark fibres, but only poor people wore these. Among the Athapascans of the interior, very poor people sometimes made themselves moccasins of salmon skins, but most people wore moccasins of buckskin or of moose hide which was tougher. Clothes were often ornamented with painted designs and a line of red ochre along a seam or where a hole had been mended. There were usually fringes on some part of the clothing as a decoration, and the Kootenays, like the prairie people they once were, used to decorate their clothes even more than did the others.

For men, the usual clothes were a buckskin shirt, leggings, and moccasins. Many of them wore a breech-cloth too, as well as the leggings. In winter, they often wore a skin cap. The women wore a longer shirt than the men did and shorter leggings. They, too, had moccasins but did not wear a breech-cloth. Some women wore little caps, of basketry in the south or of skin farther north. The children dressed like their parents, but in the hot summer days they seldom bothered with clothes at all.

Ornaments were very popular and nearly everybody wore necklaces made of seeds, beads, claws, or teeth. Many people had copper bracelets traded in from the west coast. Sea-shells were also used as ornaments, all brought from the sea shore and considered very valuable. Some of the smaller shells were used as beads, and the larger ones made ear and nose ornaments, a few of them quite big and clumsy.

Body painting was common, sometimes for serious purposes, such as a war party, at other times just for fun. Men often painted their faces in designs revealed to them in dreams and visions. The Salish colored their faces red and white to express joy, and sometimes the children would paint themselves all over just for fun. Tattooing was common too. Some of the designs represented their owner's guardian spirits and others seem to have had no special purpose beyond decoration. The men were careful not to allow hair to grow on their faces. Like most Mongolian people they had scanty beards in any case, and the few hairs that did appear were pulled out with tweezers made of clam shells, springy antler, or copper. Hair was combed and tied back or braided.

DWELLINGS

There is a lot of variety in the kinds of house built in this part of Canada. The most remarkable dwelling was the underground winter house that was used in the southern half of the region. This was a round hole in the ground, varying from twenty to forty or even fifty feet across and about six feet deep, though some were shallower. They were generally built on gravelly banks near rivers because the digging was easier in gravel than in other kinds of soil, the drainage would be good, and the river provided water, fish, and transportation. In some places groups of these big round pits are still to be seen where the old houses were. The last one of them to be actually lived in seems to have been in use about 1900, and old people still living in 1954 remember spending the winters in them.

When building one of these houses, the ground was first marked out by tying a rope to a central stake, then drawing a circle by walking round with a stick at the end of the rope to scratch a line with. The earth inside this mark was dug out with root-diggers and by hand, and carried to one side in baskets. When the digging was finished, a framework of logs was put up and the whole thing roofed in with poles, brush, and, on top of it all, the earth taken out in making the pit. An entrance, about four feet square, was left at the very top with a notched log ladder to climb in and out by. The fire was in the middle of the floor below and the smoke went out by the entrance hole above. A large slab of rock stood against the foot of the ladder to prevent its being scorched by the fire. As the cooking was done on this fire and a man coming into the house might knock dirt into the food, it was the proper thing to shout a warning before starting down the ladder so that the women had a chance to put covers on things to protect them.

In a house as big as this there was plenty of room for a lot of people, and sections between the upright logs that supported the roof could be alloted to separate families. In very cold weather, the people might light extra fires in their own sections but as a rule the houses were quite warm enough, too warm in fact according to those who remember them. As you can imagine, they were rather smelly too, though the women made some effort to keep them clean. The central space round the cooking fire was a sort of common room where the people sat and worked when they were not in their own sections.

These underground houses were not used in summer. In the warm weather the Indians moved into conical tents which were a framework of poles covered with rush mats. In the north, the Carriers built log or pole huts with gabled roofs, the doorway being in the end and the fire in the middle. The Kootenays had brought the custom of using a tipi with them and, in the far north, the double lean-to (two open tents facing each other) of the Athapascan tribes was the favorite dwelling for winter.

FURNITURE

There was remarkably little furniture of any kind and what little they had was very simple. Even now many of the people sit on the floor of their houses even when they have chairs that they might use. They made no use at all of pottery, all their cooking, except roasting and baking, being done by the stone-boiling method in birch-bark vessels or tightly-woven baskets. These were so well made that they would hold water, especially after they had been soaked for a while. In the south, among the Interior Salish, some remarkably fine baskets were made, beautifully decorated with colored barks arranged in designs and woven into the fabric of the basket itself.

Many mats were woven from rushes; these were used to sleep on and as a sort of table cloth to eat from at meal times, and were more common in the south than elsewhere. Twine was made from Indian hemp or dogbane and woven into bags, but in the north these were replaced by birch bark. Some of the Athapascan people seldom used baskets or mats at all, preferring bags made of skin. They used large skins to sleep on, instead of the rush mats of the south.

TOOLS

Both men and women used tools of one sort or another, though not to the same extent as the Eskimo did or the people of the west coast. Men had knives, chipped from stone, or made of bone. Some stone was used too for making hammers, pestles, and adzes, but on the whole it was comparatively little used. The Interior Salish were an exceptionally fortunate people, for near Lytton many boulders of jade were found in the river gravels. They cut these blocks of stone into handy shapes and sizes, using a thin slab of sandstone as a saw. Jade is hard and tough, so cutting a block into slices was a tedious job. They generally worked from both sides and broke through the middle piece as soon as it was thin enough. With jade they made knives and chisels as well as adze blades and traded them with other people who had no jade of their own, particularly those on the coast, but also far to the east.

Both bone and antler were used for making tools, beaver teeth for chisels and knives, and antler for wedges. The women had skin-scrapers of stone, awls and sap scrapers of bone, spoons and ladles of wood and horn, and wooden digging sticks. There was almost no work in metal, but copper beads were made as soon as they got the metal from the whites.

Twine was made from Indian hemp, nettle fibres, and the inner bark of the willow.

TRANSPORTATION

Water transport seems to have been rather weak in this area, though some kind of canoe was known almost everywhere. The Thompson River people had at least three kinds, some of birch bark, cedar dug-outs, and wooden frames covered with skins. Farther north, a big cottonwood dug-out was used on the rivers but seems to have been a fairly recent introduction, probably from the sea coast where dug-outs are very well known. The Kootenays had a most peculiar canoe of their own, made of pine bark. The bottom line of the canoe was longer than the gunwale, with a long point fore and aft. One would think they would be difficult to manage but they are said to have been good canoes in swift water and surprisingly easy to handle. The only canoes like them anywhere else in the world came from the Amur River in Siberia but there the canoes, though of the same shape, were covered with skin instead of with bark.

In winter, the people seem to have travelled but little. In the south, they had their warm underground houses and plenty of dried food so travel was not often necessary. In the north, where hunting

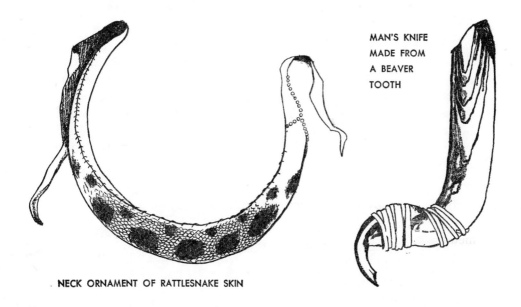

MAN'S KNIFE MADE FROM A BEAVER TOOTH

NECK ORNAMENT OF RATTLESNAKE SKIN

and trapping were winter occupations and men had to travel much of the time, dogs were used to pull a toboggan but snowshoes do not seem to have been made till recently, though the Tahltan may have made use of them in earlier days.

In both summer and winter, back-packing and dog-packing were in use. There was a good system of trails leading from the interior to the coast and many of the lakes were connected by trails, some of them not only still in existence but occasionally in use. These old trails can still be seen quite clearly even though they have not been used for a long time, one reason being that bears and other large animals often take advantage of them and so help to keep them open.

Cradles were of various styles, some made of birch bark and others, in the south, of basketry. The Kootenays have most elaborate cradles, something like those of the prairie tribes, decorated with designs in beads and hung with ornaments and charms for the child to play with. Among the Salish, no cradle is used twice and, when a baby has finished with it, the cradle is thrown away or hidden deep in the forest. In recent years, it has been the custom to hang the discarded cradles on the picket fences round the graves in the cemetery.

DOMESTIC ANIMALS

Dogs were the only domestic animals these people had, and there do not seem to have been many of them before the white man came. Now there is a large number of dogs on nearly every reservation. They were used for running down deer, for treeing bears, for packing, and, in the north, the Tahltans had their own special breed of dogs for bear hunting. Horses were brought in about 1800 and were soon common, especially in the Dry Belt where the wide

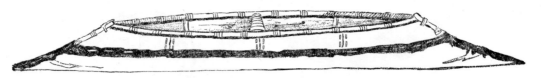

KOOTENAY TYPE OF CANOE

open grasslands made feeding them easy and riding convenient.
Many of the Indians of this part of British Columbia, in the Nicola,
Okanagan, and Chilcotin districts, still use horses a great deal, dress
in chaps and Stetson hats and wear big spurs just like the cowboys
in the moving pictures.

SOCIAL ORGANIZATION

There was very little in the way of government, and the tribes
that did show some signs of it were much influenced by the stronger
organizations of their neighbors. Thus the Lillooet were affected by
the coast people to their west and so were the Fraser and Thompson
River tribes. The Kootenays kept traces of their prairie customs, and
the Tahltan were likely to imitate the Tlingit to the south and west.

For the rest, the people of the various tribes were broken into
little bands, some of which recognized certain men as being more
or less in authority, especially among the Thompson River people
where in each village there was a chief whose position was inherited.
The older men in each band had more to say about how things
were to be run than the others had, because they were likely to be
the heads of the families who owned the best berry-picking grounds,
hunting territories, and fishing stations.

These were the men in whose hands what little wealth the
people had was held, and they based social differences on the
amount of property owned. Just the same, these men could not order
anybody to do anything nor could they punish men who had done
things that were injurious or dangerous to others.

The only people who really could be ordered about were the
prisoners captured in war and kept as slaves, but their slavery
appears to have been of a mild kind and they usually married into
the tribe before very long, unless they were determined to escape
and make their way back to their old homes. The Kootenays once
had a few Blackfoot slaves, captured on their visits to the plains for
buffalo hunting.

WARFARE

There was little systematic warfare, though some tribes fought
against each other more than others did. The Chilcotin, for instance,

were a somewhat warlike people, and often fought with the Shuswap, and the Kootenays had frequent trouble with the Blackfoot.
Many of the tribes occasionally raided other villages, either in
revenge for some insult or injury, or to capture slaves. Now and
then a murder would start a blood feud and the whole band might
be drawn into the quarrel, causing a small war, but more often the
murder was wiped out by heavy payments to the victim's family.

The Thompson River people, more accustomed to the idea of
leaders, selected temporary chiefs to head a war party and it was
they who decided whether to start a fight or not. Scalping was not
usual; the use of war-paint was fairly general, and the Kootenays
used a special kind of face painting as a challenge to a fight.

The weapons used in war were, for the most part, the same as
in hunting, except for special stone war clubs, some of them so long
and slender as to be more like swords. They also made use of a club
with a stone lashed to the end, joined to the handle by a flexible
leather thong. This was an effective weapon when under control,
but an inexperienced man might easily do more damage to himself
than to the enemy.

Poisoned arrows were used by the Interior Salish, quite an
unusual thing for Canadian Indians. Rattlesnake venom and extracts
from poisonous roots were used; the poisoned arrowheads are said
to have been larger than those used for hunting, and they were
carried in a special quiver made of dog skin.

Armor was used to some extent. One kind was a sort of sleeve-
less coat, made of rods or slats of hard wood laced together with
sinew or strong twine. These were good enough to stop an arrow,
but not a bullet. Another type of armor was a long shirt of thick
leather, sometimes double or even four-fold. Some of these were
painted with sturgeon glue and sprinkled with coarse sand before
the glue dried. Magical designs were painted on them, but they
were no more use against bullets than the wooden armor.

War tactics were simple. Ambushes, where a trail ran along
the side of a steep cliff, were common. In such places, logs and big
rocks were piled up on the hillside so that they could be rolled down
on the enemy as they crept slowly along the difficult piece of trail.
Night raids on sleeping villages were popular too; the plan was to
surprise the enemy, steal as many young men and women as

possible, and hurry away. To make it difficult to follow them, Salish war parties travelled fast and, when they did make a fire, would burn only the bark of the yellow pine, because it makes little smoke, it goes out quickly without smouldering, and it is difficult to tell how old its ashes are.

SOCIAL LIFE

Scattered as they were in small bands, and often far apart, these interior people had a much less exciting social life than did the Iroquois, for instance, or the people of the west coast. There were few societies to perform rituals or organize dances and it was only in the winter, when there was little to do and the people lived close together, that they had much in the way of social festivities. Then there was a certain amount of dancing, singing, and story telling to while away the long days of winter.

SUMMER TENT OF
RUSH MATS

The Interior Salish had a First Salmon ceremony in which special honor was paid to the first salmon of the season, and they celebrated also a Feast of Berries and Roots in recognition of the earth's bounty.

Life tended to group itself round the activities of the leading men, who were also the wealthy ones, and who generally had two or more wives and a large family of blood relations, hangers-on, and slaves. There was always a lot to be done, food to be secured, cooked, and preserved, clothes to make, children to look after and, in later years, horses to care for, train, and feed.

The marriage customs that hampered men in so many tribes were less uncomfortable here; in the Thompson River area for instance a man might marry any girl who was agreeable to his proposal, provided that she was not a close blood relative.

The people as a whole were of gentle disposition, kind to their wives and children, and even to their slaves. The children were great favorites and seldom punished, though they were told to listen carefully to the stories the old people told them so that they

SEMI-SUBTERRANEAN
WINTER HOUSE

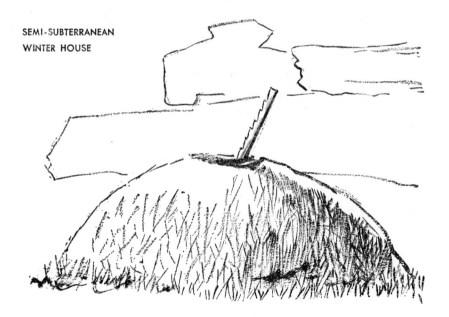

might learn how to behave themselves, for most of these tales had a moral, such as: "We must always feed our visitors", or "We must never laugh at people who are poor and old".

Children were named soon after their birth, but that name was often changed as soon as the child was old enough to go hunting or to marry. Then, there would be a feast for all present and the new name would be announced so that everybody would know it.

Old people generally found some way in which they could be useful and they were not as likely to be left to starve or freeze to death as they were among the Athapascans of the Northwest Territories and the Eskimo. Blind people, though, if unable to help themselves and needing the support of others, were sometimes deliberately taken far off into the hills and there abandoned to die.

GAMES

There was little in the way of organized games, but the children found various ways of amusing themselves. Some of their games, such as snow snakes and ring and pin, were known right across Canada. They also played a rough sort of football, using a large piece of light fungus sewn up in elk skin for a ball. This was in the south, and here too they used to have archery contests, shooting at both standing and moving targets. They also had javelin-throwing matches.

The favorite game for grown-ups was *la-hal*, a game something like "Hide the Button". The players had two bones, one plain one called "the man", and another with a mark around it called "the woman". The player holding the bones would shuffle them from hand to hand and his opponent would order him to stop and then try to guess which hand held "the woman". It is a simple kind of amusement, but they played it with great skill and enthusiasm and would bet large sums on their ability in bluffing and guessing.

Smoking was another form of amusement, shared by men and women alike. There was a wild tobacco to be had and they also smoked the leaves of the bearberry and the inner bark of the red osier dogwood. They thought the white man's tobacco too strong and mixed these things with it, preferring a mild smoke.

MUSIC

The drum was the principal musical instrument here just as it was all over Canada. In addition, whistles were made by the Carriers and Chilcotin, and also wooden clappers. Singing was an important part of any feast or gathering, and many of the songs were the personal property of certain families, having been handed down from generation to generation, just as they were on the coast. Some of these songs were in now forgotten languages.

ART

There was not very much in the way of painting or carving, except simple designs in red ochre on their skin clothing and crude wooden figures that were sometimes placed on graves in the south. Some of the people in the west, in close contact with the highly artistic coast tribes, made wooden masks, but there was little else in the way of art except the beautifully made baskets of the Interior Salish.

Children who had been fasting and praying in the far distant hills in search of a spirit guardian used to paint figures on boulders and flat cliff faces. These were generally done in red ochre or in black and yellow, and represented the things done in their ceremonies or seen in their visions. Grown-up people too used to paint the things that they had seen in important dreams on such places.

LITERATURE

The many stories told in winter were the principal form of literature, together with their songs. Most of their legends were of the "trickster" kind, in which Coyote or Raven or some other creature tricks other animals or human beings into doing foolish or dangerous things. There was no form of writing, but the Carriers were taught by an early missionary a syllabic alphabet, now seldom used if ever. The Kootenays, because of their prairie origin, have some knowledge of the sign language, and their neighbors had picked up a little of it too, but it is not much used today. The Interior Salish learned a form of shorthand from a French missionary and could write and read it easily.

SCIENCE

The medicine man was the only person, except for the occasional medicine woman, who took any interest in what might be considered the beginnings of science. They were expected to cure the sick, to control the weather, to ward off evil spirits, foretell the future, and persuade the salmon to swim up the rivers so that the people might catch them. Some of the medicine men were greatly feared and the people certainly believed firmly in their powers. Probably some of the medicine men themselves really believed in their own powers, but others knew very well that they were trying to impress the people by mere conjuring tricks. Some of them were so much feared that the people said they could kill an enemy by sheer will power, thinking him to death.

The Kootenay medicine men used to practise blood-letting to cure disease. They would open a vein in their patient's arm and draw off quite a lot of blood before stopping the flow by binding up the cut. Another form of curing, used in the south, was the moxa. This was a little cone of inflammable stuff, such as resin mixed with powdered fungus, that was placed on the bare arm or thigh and set alight at the top. As it burnt down it got hotter and hotter till it burnt a deep hole in the skin and muscle. The patient was expected to stand this without showing any sign of feeling pain. The scars remained for life. This treatment was thought to be good for different kinds of sickness, but it is doubtful that it really was of any benefit at all.

RELIGION

The people of the interior had no formal religion in our sense of the word and worshipped no gods. They believed that there must be spirits in the sun and the moon because there was a spirit in everything, but these were far from mankind and in no way interested in his affairs. They did recognize the importance of the sun and, during an eclipse, the Kootenays performed a special dance of healing to cure the sun which, they could see, must be in great danger.

The spirits that lived in dangerous rapids, in waterfalls, in trees and rocks, in animals and birds, were much more important to mankind and some effort was made to gain their assistance or at least to avoid offending them. Here, as almost everywhere in Canada, young boys went off into the hills alone to fast and meditate, hoping for a vision in which some animal would reveal itself as a life-long guardian and helper. Most men, and some women, professed to have such personal guardians and their existence was very real to them and quite sincerely believed in.

The medicine men claimed to be in touch with the spiritual world through their personal guardians, of whom they usually had several, and so were able to know the cause of sickness and, according to their own statements and popular belief, find out who had bewitched the sick person and then take steps to remove the curse.

Among the Interior Salish, graves were usually dug in sandy soil; powdered red ochre was sometimes included in the burial. Tools, some of them of jade, were buried with the dead person, and beautifully chipped knives. It was the custom in some parts of the south to kill a horse at the side of the grave. The skin was hung up in a tree near by and the meat was eaten at the funeral feast. Another form of burial was in steep rock slides. A grave was scooped out in the stones at the bottom of the slide, the body laid in it, and then the rocks were brought rolling and sliding down the hillside till the grave could no longer be seen, except for a long thin pole that was left sticking up from it.

In more recent years it has been their custom to bury the dead as we do, in special cemeteries, often with a little picket fence

CHILD'S CRADLE OF BASKETRY

round the grave. Sometimes a carved wooden figure of a man was placed on the grave, standing upright, but these are seldom seen now. Farther north the picket fences become more elaborate and are sometimes replaced by little houses, only six feet high, but all complete with doors and windows with glass and curtains.

Among the Carriers, the bodies of the dead were burnt on a wooden pyre on the outskirts of the village. It was the custom for the widow to stay near the body till the flames actually drove her off or until the spectators pulled her away; even then she would often try once more to mount the pyre. If she was unpopular or was considered a bad wife, she might be pushed and jostled so much that she really did get burnt, sometimes severely.

Once the cremation was over, a little hut was built nearby and the widow lived in it till her period of mourning was over, which might be two years or even more. The day after the cremation, she picked the unburnt bones of her husband out of the ashes and put them in a skin bag which she then carried about with her till the end of her mourning. It was this custom of carrying the bones of the dead that gave the tribe the name Carriers.

PRESENT CONDITIONS

Few of these people now live as they used to. In the south, they have taken to raising horses and cattle and growing hay to feed them in the winters, and some of the people do well at it. Others prefer to work for wages for white ranchers. They are well able to look after horses properly and make good cowboys.

Farther north more people make a living as guides for hunting parties and by trapping and fishing. Here conditions are more nearly what they used to be, but still the old ways of life become more difficult to follow every year. The people dress like whites, except for moccasins, which many of them still prefer to shoes.

In British Columbia, Indians now have the right to vote in provincial elections and this has done a lot to make them lose their feelings of inferiority and to reassert themselves, which is much to their advantage as well as to that of the white people among whom they must live.

The loon's necklace

A Legend of the Interior Salish

In the Indian village of Shulus, on the banks of the Nicola River, there lived long ago an old blind medicine man, named Kelora. Because of his blindness, he was miserably poor, hardly able to support himself and his wife.

Though he called himself a medicine man, he really did little but dream. In the summer he would sit all day long in the shade of the trees and in winter he would sun himself with his back propped against the house, wrapped in a tattered blanket of groundhog skins to keep out the cold. Now and then his wife would scold him for his idleness.

"After all," she would remind him, "you're not the only blind man there is. Look at Intameen, up there near Quilchena. He finds plenty to do. He gets the spruce roots ready for his wife when she makes baskets, and he makes the most beautiful bone beads, and even spins the twine to thread them on. And all you do is sit here grinning at the sun, and scratching your worthless old hide."

Only once had he tried to excuse himself and remind her that he was, after all, a medicine man and, he would have liked to add, should be shown some respect. Were not medicine men important people?

"A medicine man! You, a medicine man? Nobody ever comes to you unless every other healer he has heard of has failed. 'Fast four days,' you tell everybody the same thing. 'Then take four sweat baths, still fasting, and then chew four juniper berries, taking care to swallow all the juice.' It's four of this, and four of that! Rubbish! Any nitwit could give the same advice and get more for the giving of it."

Old Kelora didn't seem to mind at all. He just sat staring up at the sun as though he had not heard a word of what she had said. There was only one sound that was sure to rouse him and that was the cry of the loon, the strangest and, perhaps, the most lovely of all woodland sounds. Whenever he heard it, a great restlessness seemed to seize him. His blind hands would fumble for his stick and then he would start off, groping his way along the little trail beside the creek that flows out of Mamette Lake. Slowly and painfully he would go, his stick feeling the way, and an upraised elbow shielding his eyes from the twigs and branches that hung over the trail.

Sometimes he was gone for days and, when he returned, tired out, half starved, stained with mud where he had stumbled on the way, he would say nothing of where he had been.

"I have been talking with my father, the Loon," he would explain patiently, and that was all.

After a long wet autumn, it happened that there was a very poor crop of the berries the Indians used to dry for their winter food, and then a very hard, cold season began. Every day the men came home to the village from their hunting with almost no game. There seemed to be no deer, no grouse, no rabbits, but the tracks of wolves were everywhere in the snow. With so little fresh meat, the people were forced to use up their stocks of dried food, and the thousands of salmon which they had smoked during the summer were being eaten much too fast.

The older men met together and wondered whether they should send some young men to nearby villages and even as far away as Kamloops and Lytton, to Tulameen, and even to Lillooet to try to buy food.

One day, after the hunters had come home again empty-handed, old Kelora spoke to the chief.

"Tell your young men and the hunters to be on their guard," he said. "The wolves are hungry too, just as we are, for they have killed all the game in the valley. Soon they will come right into the village and try to steal the children."

The chief, worried and anxious, turned away from the old blind man.

"Go back to your dreaming," he laughed. "I have no time for the chatter of fools. Go back to your medicine making and listen for the call of the loon."

Now hardly a full day had passed, when the women were startled to hear the scream of a child. Running down to the river bank, they caught sight of a large gray wolf, trotting easily towards Warm Springs. They found some blood stains on the snow, a little winter cap of squirrel skins, a toy bow, the tracks of a child, — and of the wolf.

"Old Kelora was right," said the chief. "Even the wolves are starving now."

The wolves grew bolder and bolder. Grown men were no longer safe alone, but had to hunt in pairs. Traps were set and deadfalls built; many wolves were killed, but their numbers hardly seemed to grow less. The people were becoming very much afraid and there was even talk of abandoning the whole village of Shulus and moving somewhere else, an almost unheard of thing to do, especially in the dead of winter.

Old Kelora said this would not be wise, and this time the chief listened to him.

"Do you think we could move more quickly than the wolves could follow us?" he asked, and he was quite plainly right.

"True," the people admitted, "but what are we to do? We are starving, and our children are starving with us."

Old Kelora knew now that the time for which he had waited so long had come at last. If the village could be saved at all, it would be by Kelora's use of his own powers of magic. When he was a boy he had spent many days all alone on the far hilltops, bathing in little lakes, scrubbing himself with harsh hemlock twigs till the blood flowed, starving himself for days on end that he might become a medicine man.

He had not gone through all these hardships for nothing, for in every one of his visions the Loon had appeared to him, and given him powers not known to other men. Nobody had ever guessed that Kelora really had magical powers for he had never proved it to anybody, not even to the most powerful chiefs or important medicine men. Only when there was some serious danger would his guardian spirit allow the singing of his sacred songs, the wearing of his collar of gleaming white dentalium shells, each shaped like a tiny elephant's tusk, or the use of his magical bow. But now, he knew, the right time had come to use the powers that had been given him.

Carefully he felt his way down to the frozen river's edge where the village sweat houses stood on the sandy bank. Four times he steamed himself in the sweat house and four times he plunged into the ice-cold river. Then he made his way home, put on his sacred collar of dentalium shells, and sang aloud his mystical songs. He strung his magical bow and picked out four arrows with their sharp stone tips.

Hardly had he finished getting ready when he heard a shout. Once more the wolves were coming right into the village, hoping to steal some uncared-for child.

In strong, clear tones, Old Kelora told his wife to lead him quickly towards the wolves. She was so surprised that she obeyed without thinking. As soon as they appeared in the village street there were shouts of laughter.

"Are you going to throw him to the wolves?" they asked. "Take him back home. What does he know about shooting wolves?"

"Pay no attention to them," Kelora ordered her, "but point my arrow towards the biggest wolf. Carefully now. As though you yourself were going to shoot."

"All right. Up a little," she said. "A bit more to this side. So. Now. Let fly your arrow."

Old Kelora let fly. Swift and true went the arrow, straight to the flank of a huge wolf hiding in a little patch of brush.

"Look! Look!" cried the people who had been watching. "What a shot! No ordinary man could shoot like that even if he could see properly. Kelora must be a magician. A great magician. We shall all be saved, thanks to Kelora the magician."

The old man said nothing, but turned back to his home.

For the rest of the winter, whenever the wolves were seen he would go out to the edge of the village. Always he made his wife get his aim straight, and always he killed the wolf he shot at. At last they drew off, looking for safer hunting grounds, and once more the village hunters were able to bring back game.

During the next summer, old Kelora decided to go once more to visit his guardian spirit, the Loon. He walked for miles in the distant hills till the day was nearly done. He paused in thought and then he felt the warmth of the setting sun on his left cheek.

"So," he murmured to himself, "then the little lake I once knew so well should lie right ahead of me, just a little way over the top of the sloping ground."

Suddenly, as if to prove that he was right, he heard the long-drawn, quavering cry of the Loon.

Slowly and cautiously he made his way forward, his feet tripped by roots, his face scratched by the underbrush. At last, as the sun sank lower, the rank lush smell of the lake

grew strong and he heard the plop of a frog as it jumped
into the water. Soon he felt the damp earth sink slightly
beneath his moccasins and, bending down, he touched with
his finger tips the cool, still water.

Kelora drew himself to his full height as he stood facing
the lake, his own lake as he always called it. He lifted his
hand to his throat to make sure he still had his sacred collar
of dentalium shells, and he sang once more the sacred songs
he had learned near this very spot so long ago. Then he
called aloud.

"Oh, my Father, the Loon," he cried. "Come to me now.
Help me, my Father."

Close by his feet, a voice answered him.

"What is it that my son desires?"

"I am blind, my Father, and I wish to see."

"Climb then upon my back," said the Loon.

Awkwardly Kelora seated himself on the bird's back.

"Now, clasp me tightly and hold your breath," cried the
Loon and he dived deep into the waters of the lake and
swam swiftly and strongly to the other side.

"Can you see now, my son?" he asked.

"I see, but not as a man should see, for there is still a
thick fog over my eyes."

"Hold tight once more," cried the Loon, and again they
plunged deep into the water. Four times in all they swam
below the surface from side to side of the lake.

"Now I see! I see, and it is as if I had never known
blindness!" cried Kelora.

He turned to give thanks to the one who had made him
see again, but there was nobody there at all, just a loon
swimming quietly on the still water.

None but the dearest of all his treasures would be
enough. Old Kelora took off the collar of little white shells

and, with a wide sweep of his arm, tossed it gently towards the loon.

Spinning slowly as it sailed through the air, the collar wrapped itself round the bird's throat, making the shining white necklace we see there today.

A handful of shells, which broke away from the string, fell scattered on the loon's back.

These, too, you may see on any loon.

CHAPTER 8

THE BRITISH COLUMBIA COAST

CHIEF'S GRAVE BOX FROM NEAR VANCOUVER

Coast Salish
Bella Coola
Nootka
Kwakiutl
Tsimshian
Haida
Tlinkit

TOTEM POLE

THE BRITISH COLUMBIA COAST

THE NATIVE TRIBES of the British Columbia coast had a number of characteristics in common, even though they can be divided into at least four different groups and spoke as many as half a dozen distinct languages. We are not quite sure whether they reached their present homes by canoe, travelling along the coast, or, which is much more likely, whether they moved down from the interior of British Columbia wherever they found a convenient pass through the mountains that would allow them to do so. We are quite sure that the Coast Salish in the south once lived in the interior and the same seems to be true of some of the other coast tribes.

Some of the things they had in common are: the use of large rectangular houses built of cedar planks; the building of fine dugout canoes; their scanty dress; the use of food from the sea; a high regard for their chiefs and nobles and for people who were generous and lavish with gifts; their highly developed art; their intricate social organization, and elaborate mythology.

The first white man to explore their part of the world seems to have been Juan de Fuca in 1592, but we know very little of his voyage and it is not likely that he paid any extensive visits to the Indians. The first actually to set foot on the west coast, as far as we can tell now, was Vitus Bering, a Dane who had become an officer in the Russian navy. In 1741 he landed in what is now Alaska, and died, with many of his crew, after being shipwrecked on an uninhabited island in December of that year.

In 1778, Captain James Cook of the British Navy made a closer examination of the natives and he was followed, between the years 1790 and 1795, by one of his officers, Captain George Vancouver, who charted and surveyed much of the very complicated shore line.

The natives of the tribes of the British Columbia coast are not nearly as familiar to people in the east as are the Iroquois and the Hurons, or the Sioux and the Blackfoot, but many people find them much more interesting, especially because of their curious totem poles and their comparatively high degree of civilization.

The COAST SALISH people speak a dialect of the same language as do the Interior Salish, and are closely related to them. The word

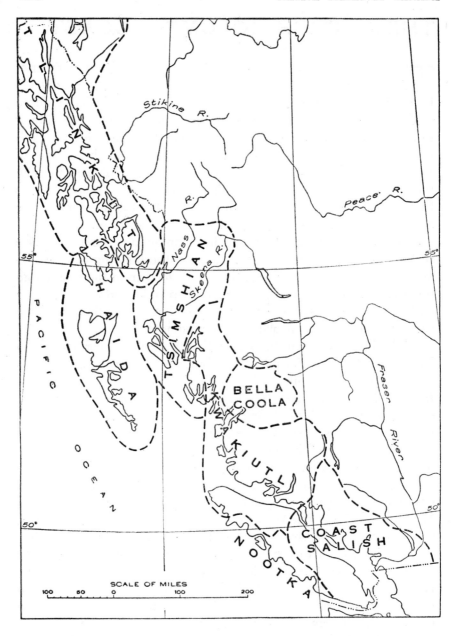

WHERE THE WEST COAST INDIANS LIVED

"Salish", which is one of their own names for themselves, means simply "people". They live in the valley of the Fraser River from Hope down to the sea, and in the southeast part of Vancouver Island as well as up the east side of the island as far as Cape Mudge. At Hope, up the Fraser valley, and at Anderson Lake, just west of Lillooet, they blend with their inland relatives. They still show traces of the old inland culture and depend more on the hunting of land animals, such as deer and mountain goats, than do the coastal tribes farther north, though they use large quantities of fish and shell-fish, especially clams, as well. Large heaps of shells are found near their old villages, made up of thousands upon thousands of shells that were thrown away after the clams had been eaten. In some places these shell heaps are many feet thick and stretch for hundreds of yards along the beach near good clam beds. Scientists, digging in the shell heaps, have found many remains of an ancient people and have learned a good deal about how they lived hundreds of years ago.

The Coast Salish built long, low houses, with an almost flat roof. The framework was carried by large upright house-posts, sometimes carved, but the Coast Salish had no totem poles as did those of the tribes farther north. These people are specially noted for a breed of small white dogs whose wool was woven into blankets.

The BELLA COOLA are another tribe who speak a Salish dialect and once lived in the interior. They moved down to the coast through the valley of the Bella Coola River, which rises in country now occupied by the Chilcotin. The Bella Coola now live on Burke Channel, an inlet of the sea into which the Bella Coola River runs. Another division of them, the Kimsquit, live a little farther north on Dean Inlet. It was down the Bella Coola River that Alexander Mackenzie came when he reached the Pacific Ocean after crossing the continent. He tasted the water and found that it was salt, so he knew that he had reached the sea, but he was still so far inland up the fiord that he could not see the open ocean. He mixed some vermilion with grease and painted his famous message on a flat rock, but no traces of it can be found today: "Alexander Mackenzie, from Canada, by land, the twenty-second day of July, one thousand seven hundred and ninety-three."

Bella Coola is our way of pronouncing the Kwakiutl name of these people, which really sounds more like Bilkoola. They used a great deal of vegetable food, just as the inland people did, and more than the coast people to the north. They spent much of the summer hunting and fishing, storing up food for the winter, which was a sort of holiday season when they spent a good deal of their time in feasts and ceremonies.

The NOOTKA live on the west coast of Vancouver Island from Cape Cook down the coast to near Port Renfrew. They speak a Wakashan language, as do their neighbors to the north, the Kwakiutl. The meaning of Nootka is no longer remembered.

Not only were they expert at building canoes, but they took them on long voyages, often far out of sight of land, when hunting whales. They were the only native whale hunters in all Canada except some of the Eskimo. They depended very largely on fish and other products of the sea for their food, and the Nootka women were noted for their skill in weaving baskets.

The KWAKIUTL speak a dialect of Wakashan as do the Nootka. They live on the north end of Vancouver Island and on the mainland just opposite. The Kwakiutl are divided into three smaller groups, the Haisla, the Heiltsuk, and the true Kwakiutl. Their name probably means "the beach on the north side of the river", perhaps referring to a place where they once lived, but they themselves like to say it means "Smoke of the World", a much more important

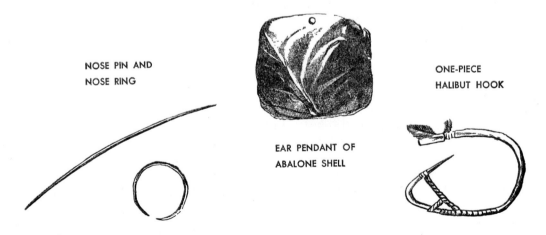

NOSE PIN AND
NOSE RING

EAR PENDANT OF
ABALONE SHELL

ONE-PIECE
HALIBUT HOOK

sounding name. To the north of them live the Bella Bella, another small group also speaking a Wakashan dialect. Their name has no real meaning, for it is an Indian attempt to say the word "Millbank" of Millbank Sound.

It was the Kwakiutl who started the important secret societies that played a large part in the life of the people, especially in winter when the great feasts were held, and valuable gifts were distributed.

The TSIMSHIAN, according to their own tradition, originally lived inland just as the Coast Salish and the Bella Coola did, and they once had close and valuable trading relations with the interior Indians, especially in fish oil, goat wool, goat and sheep horn, seashells, and slaves. They are divided into three groups, the Tsimshian themselves, at the mouth of the Skeena River; the Gitikshan, who lived farther inland along the Skeena; and the Niska, who lived on the banks of the lower Nass River. They all spoke dialects of the same Tsimshian language, and their name means "people on the inside of Skeena". The villages of the two inland groups, the Gitikshan and the Niska, spread right upstream as far as the western edge of the interior Dry Belt.

Though the three Tsimshian groups show slight differences in customs and speech, they all share the same complicated social organization, having four classes of people: chiefs, nobles, commoners, and slaves. The chiefs could marry only in their own class and they saw to it that nobody managed to work himself into their

SEALSKIN FLOAT USED
IN WHALE HUNTING

HARPOON HEAD FOR
HUNTING SEA-OTTERS

select group if they could prevent it. The Tsimshian, both on the coast and inland, depended largely on salmon and oolakan, another kind of fish, for their food supplies. They were noted for their skill in painting and carving, especially for their elaborate totem poles.

The HAIDA, who live on the Queen Charlotte Islands and on Prince of Wales Island, speak a language of their own, called Haidan or Skittegetan. The name "Haida" means "people". They were much like the Tsimshian in many ways, and differed from the Kwakiutl in having fewer and less-powerful societies. They were skilled canoe-builders, making some huge dug-outs sixty feet long or even more, able to carry forty people and all their trading goods with enough food and water for days. In these canoes they made long and sometimes dangerous voyages up and down the coast from

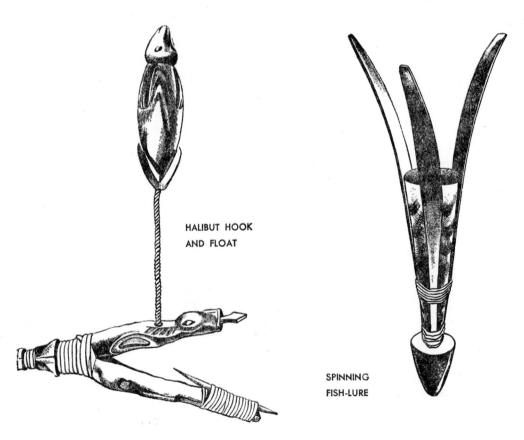

HALIBUT HOOK
AND FLOAT

SPINNING
FISH-LURE

Alaska to Puget Sound, raiding peaceful villages for slaves, and trading with other tribes.

They lived almost entirely on the coast of their island home, seldom going inland except occasionally to hunt bears and the rare Queen Charlotte Island caribou, which may now be extinct. They took almost all their food from the sea. They were expert carvers of masks and totem poles, and in recent years carved small totem poles in black slate. They also made beautiful silver bracelets in later years. They tattooed their bodies more than did most of the coast tribes.

The TLINKIT, the most northerly of the British Columbia coast tribes, also spoke a language of their own, Tlinkit. Their name, as is so often the case, means just "people". They live along the coast and on the islands that form the panhandle of Alaska; some of them moved inland to the southern Yukon where they have mingled with the interior people, the Kutchin. Not many Tlinkits actually live in Canada (for Alaska, of course, belongs to the United States), but they are an essential part of the group of northwest coast tribes. Their legends say that they moved to their present home from some-where in the interior, a bit farther south, and they still trade with the inland people. It was the Tlinkit who burned the Hudson's Bay post at Fort Selkirk in 1852 because they were afraid it would take away their trade with the Kutchin. The goods they dealt in were furs, copper, Chilkat blankets, sea-shells, and slaves. Slave trading was so important that they, like the Haida, made long trips to the south to capture slaves and they owned so many that only about two-thirds of the population were freemen, the other third being slaves. A man, no matter how high his rank, lost it when he was cap-tured, so that even the greatest Tsimshian chief was no more than a common slave if he fell into the hands of the Tlinkit.

They depended almost entirely on the sea for their food, of which seals, porpoises, sea-otters, and fish were the chief items, though the Tlinkit, like all the other coast tribes, ate a good deal of vegetable food too.

POPULATION

The west coast of British Columbia was one of the most densely populated parts of Canada, for here were abundant food supplies and a climate that was mild and pleasant. It is difficult to guess how many Indians lived here before white men came to the coast but fifty thousand may be a low estimate. Today there are perhaps fifteen thousand left.

PHYSICAL APPEARANCE

The people of the west coast tribes were not unlike each other in appearance, except perhaps that the Coast Salish were not quite as tall as the others and were lighter in skin color. The Nootka and Kwakiutl were a bit taller, and the Haida, Tsimshian, and Tlinkit a little shorter. Though many of them were not tall men, they had long and strong arms and thick heavy chests. Some people have suggested that generations of canoe paddling may have had something to do with this, but it is not at all certain that it did.

Some of the west coast people look amazingly like Chinese and it has often been said that a west coast Indian dressed in a Chinese costume might easily be mistaken for a Chinese. There is one difference that some people may not have noticed and that is the heavy dark eyebrow of the Indian, quite unlike the thin Chinese eyebrow.

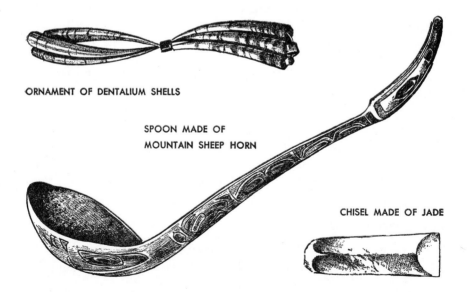

ORNAMENT OF DENTALIUM SHELLS

SPOON MADE OF
MOUNTAIN SHEEP HORN

CHISEL MADE OF JADE

As a whole these people have broad round faces and large heads, especially noticeable in the men. It was the custom, among the noble classes, to deform their heads. This was done by binding the skulls of little babies tightly while the children were still in the cradle. Among the Coast Salish, the forehead was flattened so that the head sloped back in a straight line from the eyebrows to the top of the head. None of the slaves were allowed to flatten the heads of their children, so a sloping forehead indicated noble birth.

The Kwakiutl practised another kind of head deformation. Bandages were wound tightly round the head, forcing it to grow up to a high point in the middle like an old-fashioned sugar-loaf. The Indians say that the children did not feel any pain from the bandages and never complained except when they were taken off to be re-adjusted and then the babies would cry till the bandages were replaced. The Haida, Tsimshian, and Tlinkit did not deform the heads of their children. This custom is no longer practised, nor is that of boring a large hole in the lower lip in which to wear an ornament called a labret. This was an oval plug of wood, as much as two inches long and an inch wide, which made the lip stick out

FISH RAKE FOR HERRING

TWO-PRONGED PORPOISE HARPOON

FLOAT MADE FROM
A SEAL'S STOMACH

in a strange way. When the labret was taken out, the lip flopped down on the woman's chin. Few men, if any, used labrets.

Men, and women too, often bored a hole in the gristle between their nostrils and wore a large bone pin in it. Holes were cut in the edge of the ear too, to wear ornaments such as shells or beads in.

NATURE OF TERRITORY

The west coast, with its thousands of islands, its narrow fiords, and steep mountains has often been compared to the coast of Norway, where the scenery is much the same. On the whole, the climate is wet; heavy rains fall all along the west flank of the Coast Range and there is deep snow in the mountains. As a result, innumerable streams and rivers pour down the hillsides, most of them short and swift, but other larger ones take their rise far inland and break through the coast ranges. Notable among these are the Stikine, the Nass, the Skeena, and the Fraser.

The largest of the many islands is Vancouver Island, about three hundred miles long and forty to eighty wide. The Queen Charlotte Islands consist of two large islands, Graham and Moresby,

CHILKAT BLANKET DESIGN

and many smaller ones, the whole group being about a hundred and eighty miles long and sixty across. The coast, because of the many islands and the deep fiords which run for many miles inland, has a very long shore line, about seven thousand miles in British Columbia (but only about five hundred miles in a straight line), and the Alaska panhandle coast line is longer still.

The heavy rains have encouraged the growth of a dense forest which is difficult to travel in, for not only is the growth thick but the hillsides are often steep. There are a few trails that run from the interior to the coast and these were used in early days as native trade routes. One benefit from the thick forest was the growth of giant cedar trees which the Indians used in building their houses, canoes, and totem poles.

Some of the islands in the southern part of the area have a much drier climate than has the main coast line, and the eastern side of them is often so dry that cactus grows there, a plant we usually think of as belonging in the deserts of the south.

FOOD

Food was of three principal kinds for all the tribes of the coast. A large and important part of it was derived from the sea; smaller quantities of animal food came from the land; and vegetable food, mostly from the land but some from the sea, was used by all of them.

The principal food from the sea consisted of salmon, cod, and halibut, whales, sea-lions, seals, porpoises, sea-otters, sculpins, and oolakan, as well as other kinds of fish, sea-urchins, cuttle-fish, and clams.

The land animals most hunted were deer, on both the coast and the islands, moose and elk which were not found on the islands as a rule, caribou and bears, mountain sheep and goats on the mainland.

Vegetable food from the sea consisted of edible seaweed, and eel grass; from the land, they got fern roots, camas, clover roots, berries, and the inner bark of hemlock and other trees. There were other foods too, of course, that were less important and not eaten so often.

Many of these foods were preserved for use in the winter. Salmon were smoked and dried, and so were clams. Seaweed and berries were pressed into cakes and dried, and herring spawn also was dried for later use. These preserved foods were important because they ensured a varied winter diet at a time when fishing and hunting were more difficult and less rewarding than in summer. They were useful too as a means of gathering goods for distribution at the big winter feasts when the chiefs tried to outdo each other in lavish displays of wealth.

AGRICULTURE

These people knew nothing of farming and had no idea of planting and harvesting crops. Some of them did grow a little tobacco in small gardens near their villages. They did not smoke the tobacco, but dried and powdered it and then chewed it with lime which they made by burning clam shells. They were among the very few people in North America who grew tobacco but did not smoke it.

There is a wild clover which grows in large patches in suitable places and these clover gardens were owned by certain families. The roots were dug up for food in the autumn but there was no attempt at cultivation, except that stones and weeds might be thrown out of the patch, and roots, that had been pulled up but were too small to use, might be replanted.

HUNTING

Much of the hunting of sea animals on the west coast was done from dug-out canoes of cedar, and the hunters, from centuries of experience, had developed great skill in many different ways of hunting.

One of the most spectacular hunts was that of the Nootka, who went whale hunting. Other tribes would gladly use whale meat if they found a dead one on the beach, but the Nootka went far out of sight of land and killed the whales in the open water. It was usually the California Gray Whale that was hunted and the right way of doing things was far from simple, for not only was skill in the actual hunting necessary, but the highly complicated rituals that the captain and crew of the whaling canoe had to go through must be most strictly performed too.

The captain, that is the man who actually struck the whale with the harpoon, was a man of great importance in his village. His father would probably have been a harpoon-man before him and the distinction might go back for several generations. Because of his importance he was less free than other men and had to submit to many restrictions on his behavior, almost as though he were a priest. When the right time came, he had to withdraw from other people and go alone to a special building where there were skulls of former harpooners and wooden figures of men. Here he had to pray for success, not eating or doing anything that might displease the spirits of the whales. He had to bathe in little lakes far from the village, plunging under the water and blowing as he came up, just like a real whale, and he had to scrub himself with bundles of hemlock twigs till the blood came, so that he might be quite clean both

RAIN CAPE OF
CEDAR BARK

RAIN HAT OF
WOVEN SPRUCE ROOTS

really and ceremonially before he started on the whale hunt. All
the other members of the crew had to be clean too and must bathe
and purify themselves. While they were away, the rituals and taboos
still held; their wives, who stayed behind, had to remain quiet and
do very little, avoiding anything that might frighten or displease
the spirits of the whales.

The whaling canoe was not very large, just big enough to carry
eight men, each one of whom had his special task. The harpoon-man
sat alone in the front seat; there were then three seats with two men
on each and the last man sat on a little seat at the stern. The harpooner carried a large harpoon made of yew wood, about three
inches thick and twelve feet long, tapered at each end. It was always
made in two pieces spliced together, probably so that it would not
be too springy. On the end of the shaft was the harpoon head, with
a sharp blade of mussel shell and two barbs of antler, to which was
attached a strong line of braided and twisted whale sinews. As a
rule a couple of small feathers were put in the cleft between the
barbs where the harpoon shaft entered, for good luck. Attached to
the harpoon line were long coils of rope made from twisted spruce
roots; these lay in the bottom of the canoe with large floats made of
seal skins taken off whole and blown up like footballs.

The canoe went many miles away from land, for the whales
seem to have the habit of swimming along parallel with the shore
but some distance out. Usually a whale was sighted by his blowing
for, being an air-breathing animal and not a fish, he has to come up
for fresh air every now and then. First he blows out all the stale

COPPER BRACELET INLAID
WITH ABALONE SHELL

WOODEN LABRET INLAID
WITH ABALONE SHELL

air from his lungs, and then takes a long deep breath. The expelled air is warm and damp and is often easily seen as it spouts up in the air, for the whale's blow-hole, through which he breathes, is on top of his head. The air he breathes out condenses like ours on a frosty morning.

As soon as a whale was sighted, the men paddled strongly to overtake him and they tried to come up alongside with the whale lying on their right. The harpooner stood in the bow of the canoe with the harpoon poised in his hands, waiting for the right instant to strike. If possible they liked to have the whale just coming up but still three or four feet under water. At the best moment the harpooner thrust the harpoon into the whale, just behind the head. The shaft came free and the harpoon head, to which the line was attached, stayed in the whale's body.

At once, the whale "sounded", that is made for the bottom of the sea, and the men got their long line over the side as fast as they could and tied the big sealskin floats on as the line ran out. The purpose of the floats was to tire the whale, make it difficult for him to dive, and force him up to the surface again as soon as possible. Fourteen was the traditional number of floats used.

At the very end of the line was another much lighter cord with a seal's stomach, dried and blown up, tied at the end. When the whale went so deep that he dragged all the floats down out of sight with him, this light little bladder would be the first to come to the top again and the men all watched for it eagerly and at once paddled towards it as soon as it showed so that they might be at the right place when the whale came up for another breath — as he must — or die.

As soon as he appeared the hunters thrust more harpoons into him, tied on more floats, and tried to kill him with long, sharp lances. Naturally, the whale struggled most furiously and sometimes succeeded in working the harpoon heads loose and getting away. If he was not successful in this, the men thrust and stabbed till at last he died. Then a man with a strong line, made of elk hide, slipped overboard, cut a slit in the whale's upper lip and another in the lower one, and lashed the huge mouth shut; otherwise it would gape open and the dead animal would swallow tons of water, making it much more difficult to tow him back to the village. The floats helped to keep him floating too but it was often a long and weary way home, towing a very heavy dead whale. These huge animals weigh about a ton for every foot of their length, so a seventy foot whale would weigh about seventy tons.

When at last the men reached the village the whale was drawn up on the beach, after being welcomed by men singing songs thanking him for coming to their home and praising him for his size and generosity in feeding them. The whale's body was cut up according to ceremonial rules, the most honorable piece being the one between the head and the fin on the whale's back. This piece was put on a framework and decorated with feathers, and the other pieces were distributed among all the people of the village. The blubber was cut off in large slabs, with hand holds cut in them so that one could get a good grip on the slippery mass. The meat was all eaten and so was the thin black skin. The sinews were used for cordage, the intestines to make containers for oil and water, and nearly all parts of the whale were of value in one way or another.

It is easy to see that a group of eight men, many miles from land, might get into trouble when they undertook to kill a huge animal several times as big as their canoe. One of the greatest

PAINTED WOODEN BENCH OR SEAT

dangers was that the fighting whale would strike the canoe with his huge flukes or tail and split it from end to end, for cedar splits very easily. Cases have been known when just this happened and the men, instead of losing their heads, slipped overboard, pulled the two sides of the split canoe together, lashed ropes round them, bailed out the water after stuffing the cracks, and paddled home, and sometimes with their whale at that! Men with such courage, such presence of mind, and such skill are surely worthy of our very genuine admiration.

Porpoises, which are much smaller animals, were also harpooned. A hunter and a steersman went out together and used a special canoe which was kept very smooth and well greased, so that it should be as silent as possible. The two men did not speak at all but the harpooner, in front, showed the steersman what to do by signs. The harpoon was double, each prong having a detachable head, and there was a float attached to the harpoon line just as in whaling. Seals were hunted in almost the same way.

Few land animals were killed, as we have already seen. Deer meat was used when it was to be had, but deer were valued more for their skins than for food. Some were shot with a bow and arrow, but more were caught in snares set in the trails or in pitfalls. Bears were generally killed in deadfalls, a kind of trap in which a heavy log falls on the bear when he releases a trigger by pulling at the bait. Mountain goats used to be numerous in the peaks of the Coast Range but not on the islands. Their wool was used for weaving and their sharp black horns for making spoons and other articles. The pale yellow horns of the mountain sheep were also used for spoons.

One kind of hunting that is not often seen was a special way of catching ducks. Flocks of ducks often fly from one pond to another and usually follow the same route every time. At suitable places, the Coast Salish people used to put up two tall poles, as much as eighty feet high. A net was stretched from one to the other at the top and a flock of ducks, on their way from one pond to another, would fly right into the net if it was at the right place and height. When the ducks struck it, the net was let down at once, entangling them in its meshes. Captain Cook saw these high poles here and there on the beach and was greatly puzzled as to what they could be used for.

FISHING

The west coast Indians were very clever fishermen and knew many different ways of catching halibut, cod, salmon, and other fish. The halibut, one of the largest fish they caught, has been known to weigh as much as four hundred pounds. They feed at the bottom of the sea where it is deep, and special hooks had to be let down at the end of a long line. This used to be made of kelp, a kind of sea-weed with a long thin stem. Some kelp plants have stems nearly a thousand feet in length. The hooks were sometimes let down in pairs with a wooden spreader to keep them apart. The way of setting them was quite complicated, with a float to hold the hook six inches off the bottom and a stone to keep the hooks and spreader down there. The halibut is a flat fish and swims along just above the bottom of the sea. When one was hooked his struggles were gener-ally enough to undo the special knot that was used on the sinker, so the fisherman did not have to haul the stone up to the top as well as the heavy fish.

Halibut hooks are of two kinds, one made of two wooden pieces and a bone point, the other of a single piece of hemlock twig, taken from a rotting log. When it had been scraped smooth, it was placed in a hollow kelp stem and buried in the ashes of the fire over-night. The heat made the kelp steam and in the morning the twig would

MORTAR AND PESTLE MADE OF STONE

BASKET WOVEN OF SPLIT ROOTS

be soft and flexible. It was then bent to the right curve and laid in a special groove cut in a plank; here it stayed till it was cold and dry. Then it was rubbed with grease, which was said to prevent it from straightening out again. Hooks of the same kind were used for cod, which were caught in much the same way as halibut.

Trolling was used for salmon fishing in salt water, the fisherman holding the line in his hand as he paddled. The movement of his arms made the troll speed up and slack off so that it behaved like a living fish and caught plenty of salmon. They also used a two-pronged spear for salmon, as well as nets and traps in the rivers when the fish went up into the fresh water to spawn.

One ingenious lure was something like a badminton bird. The fisherman made a very long thin pole by splicing lengths of cedar together. The pole might be as much as eighty feet long. Balanced carefully at one end of his canoe, he held the pole upright with the lure at the bottom end. Then he pushed the pole straight down into the water, hand over hand, till it was all in. A quick jerk freed the lure, which spun round and round as it rose slowly to the surface. A fish, seeing the flashing lure, would swim up after it. When the fish came near enough to the canoe, the fisherman speared it. At some seasons of the year herrings and oolakan swam in such dense shoals that there was no difficulty in catching them. One of the simplest ways was to scoop them out with a loosely woven basket,

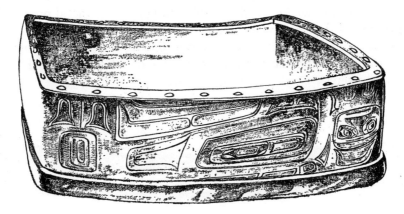

CARVED WOODEN BOWL

but some preferred to use a sort of rake, a long thin flat rod set with dozens of sharp teeth along one edge. The rake was swept through the shoals of fish and nearly always caught one or more. Many thousands of them were taken with nets.

Clams were dug in the sands at low tide and mussels were picked off the rocks; both of them were taken out of their shells and dried on racks for use in winter, except those which were eaten fresh. They were always to be had and were an almost certain guarantee against famine. Cuttle-fish were hunted at low tide in the rock pools and were used for food and also made good bait for halibut fishing.

Nets, made from nettle fibres, were used for salmon as well as for other fish, especially the oolakan or candle-fish. They come up the rivers to spawn about the middle of March and the run may go on till the end of April.

They are called candle-fish because their bodies are so full of oil that a dried one, lit at one end, will burn like a candle, with a smoky and smelly flame, of course, but still giving off light and heat. These fish come in millions, and there is great excitement when the oolakan fishing is on. They are not very large, only ten or twelve inches, but there are so many of them that their small size doesn't matter. They are stored in large wooden boxes or even in canoes and left to "ripen" for a few days. Soon fish oil begins to float to the top of the mass and then the Indians mash them up and add hot rocks to the decaying fish to hurry the extraction of the oil. After the fish are well cooked, the oil is forced out in metal presses, but in the old days the women used to press it out by squeezing the hot mess against their naked chests, letting the oil run down to be caught in the bags, made from sea-animal intestines, in which it was kept.

LONG WOODEN FOOD DISH

Ooolakan oil was used much as we use butter or ketchup. Dried fish was dipped into it, so were clover roots, and they even poured it over the cakes of wild strawberries which they dried for winter use. When it was well made and quite fresh it was said to taste sweet and have no unpleasant smell, but it was not long before it began to turn rancid; the Indians would go on using it just the same. Oil was traded into the interior of the province in great quantities and the trails along which it was carried soon got spattered with oil that dripped from the containers; because of this, these trails are known even now as the "grease trails".

DRESS AND ORNAMENTS

Because the climate was so mild, the native tribes of the west coast wore less clothing than did the people of any other part of Canada. While we might find it chilly, people who had been born to going without clothes were comfortable enough except in heavy rain and on the few really cold days of winter, and they had learned how to deal with those.

Most of the Indians of Canada, as we have seen, wore clothes made from skins, but on the west coast this was not the rule but the exception. Various other materials were used, such as mountain goat wool, dog wool, and shredded cedar bark.

Two kinds of blankets, perhaps three, were woven from mountain goat wool. The most remarkable sort was known as a Chilkat blanket because most of them were made by the Chilkat Indians, a band of Tlinkits, living near Skagway at the north end of the Alaska panhandle. It took the wool from three goats to make one blanket and, after it had been pulled from the hide, the coarse guard hairs had to be pulled out leaving the finer and softer wool. This was twisted into yarn and rolled up in balls ready for weaving. Wool that was to be used for the background was strengthened and thickened by having shredded cedar bark twisted in with the wool. The wool was dyed in three colors, black, yellow, and turquoise blue.

The heavier yarn with the cedar bark in it was stretched between two parallel rollers mounted on a frame, and the finer wool was worked into it in complicated patterns, generally intended to represent animals. They are much too difficult to explain, and only a picture can show what they were like. The men drew the patterns first on flat cedar boards and the women did the actual weaving. These Chilkat blankets are very seldom made now and those that are still to be had cost two or three hundred dollars each. Although it was the Chilkats who made them, it is believed that the Haidas really invented them; they were traded all up and down the west coast as far as the southern part of British Columbia.

The Coast Salish people made another kind of blanket, sometimes of goat wool and sometimes from the wool of a special breed of little white dogs, something like spitz dogs, which they bred for their wool alone. They were kept in flocks of two or three hundred on small islands from which they could not escape. Their wool was sometimes mixed with goat wool and sometimes with soft feathers, and the yarn that was spun from it was a good deal coarser than that used by the Chilkat blanket makers. These dogs are extinct now.

The third kind of blanket, also of wool, is quite rare. It was made only on the lower part of the Fraser River from Hope to Vancouver, and was woven with geometrical patterns.

Cedar bark does not sound like good material to make clothes from, but if it is properly treated it can be twisted into fairly satisfactory thread and woven into a sort of cloth. It is soft and warm and was used a good deal by the women on the west coast who wore aprons made of it when the weather was warm and cloaks when it was cold. They also had long dresses reaching from the neck almost down to the ankles and held in by a belt, all made of shredded cedar bark, with the neck trimmed with a band of sea-otter fur.

In summer, the men wore no clothing at all, but they would put on a robe of fur or cedar bark if they felt cold, or for ceremonial occasions. Many of the fur robes they wore were made of sea-otter fur and it was the discovery of this fact by Captain Cook that led to the important fur trade and the exploration of the west coast of Canada. Sea-otter fur was in great demand in China, where it was used for trimming the coats of important officials, and the fur traders were able to sell at a good profit all they could buy from the Indians.

Children, of course, wore nothing at all as long as they could get away with it, and it had to be a cold day indeed before one of them would admit that he wanted a fur robe. Wet weather was more likely to make people wrap up, for it sometimes rains for days on end in that part of the world. If they had to go out in wet weather, the west coast Indians sometimes wore a sort of poncho woven from narrow strips of cedar bark, not shredded as when cloth was made from it. These rain capes were quite efficient but not very comfortable or convenient.

The Nootka had special hats that they wore when out in their canoes, and the Tsimshian made beautiful hats of finely woven spruce roots, showing patterns in the weaving and then painted with other patterns on top of that. These were chiefly for use in rainy weather.

West coast Indians usually went barefoot, though they knew about moccasins and sometimes used them. Most of their time was spent either in the house or in canoes, where moccasins were not needed, or on the wet beach where moccasins would soon have become so soaked and slippery as to be more trouble than they were worth. These were the only people in Canada who usually went barefoot.

Many of the men wore their hair long, and either let it fall about their shoulders or bunched it up on top of their heads. Slaves often cut their hair short. Beards and moustaches were not common, but if a few hairs did sprout, the men usually pulled them out with tweezers.

What the men fell short of in the way of clothes, they more than made up in ornaments. They wore pins through their noses, and pierced the edges of their ears with a row of holes so that they could put sea-shells, beads, and anything else they fancied

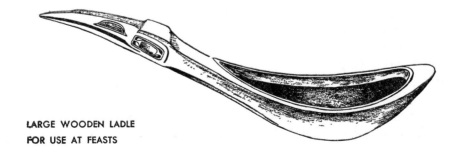

LARGE WOODEN LADLE
FOR USE AT FEASTS

in them. The women wore anklets, necklaces, and bracelets, and also, in the case of the Tsimshian, Haida, and Tlinkit, labrets in their lower lips. They also perforated the nose and wore rings in the hole.

The bone pins the men wore in their noses were often six or eight inches long and stuck out on both sides of their faces. Two white sailors were taken prisoner by the Nootka and kept as slaves for three years or more. One of them, a man named Thompson, loved to annoy the Indians by "accidentally" giving their nose-pins a jerk or twist as he passed.

Among the Haida, tattooing was common with both men and women. It was a most painful process, so much so that it often was done in three separate stages, to give the patient a chance to recover in between operations. Here both red and black pigments were used. The black looked dark blue when seen through a thin layer of skin. The designs were usually the family crests of the person tattooed.

When a man was dressed in his Chilkat blanket and wore a high carved head-dress with a trembling fringe of sea-lion bristles and a long train of ermine skins hanging down behind, he was a most impressive figure, showing quite clearly that these people got along with little clothing because that was the most comfortable thing for them, and not because they were unable to make clothes.

DWELLINGS

The most remarkable thing about the houses of the west coast Indians was their great size. One of the biggest ever measured stood near Seattle until about 1900; it was 520 feet long and 60 feet wide, so big that young men used to run races inside it. Not all the houses were as big as that, and some of the northern tribes built much smaller ones. The Coast Salish houses, of which the Seattle example was one, were the longest and had a flat roof. The front edge of the house might stand fifteen feet high and the back ten or twelve. This gave just enough slope to shed the rain, and there was seldom enough snow to worry about.

The Nootka people built smaller houses than did the people to the north or south of them, and theirs, instead of having a flat roof, were gabled. The Kwakiutl had houses which were larger than those of the Nootka, varying in size from twenty by thirty feet to some as big as fifty by sixty. These were more nearly square than those of the Coast Salish. Tsimshian houses were much like those of the Kwakiutl and so were the Haida dwellings. Farther north, the Tlinkit had comparatively small houses, but all along the coast the houses were huge when compared with the wigwams, tipis, igloos, and tents of other Canadian tribes.

Nearly always the houses were built in a row along the sea beach with their entrances facing the water. Sometimes there was an entrance in the back of the house too. In large villages there might be two or three rows.

The general structure was much the same in all cases. Huge logs were stood upright where the house was to be, sunk deeply enough in the earth for them to stand firmly. The tops of these posts had a notch cut in them to hold the long logs that stretched from one end of the building to the other to carry the roof. Some tribes, the Coast Salish for example, squared the sides of the upright posts and others left them round. The Kwakiutl put their house posts up in pairs with a short cross log on top. The exact shape of the main framework depended on the type of house, whether it was to be of the shed roof kind or gabled, and on how big it was to be. In any case, the framework was next covered with large planks split from cedar. These might be placed horizontally, as the Coast Salish did, or vertically as among the Kwakiutl, though these people

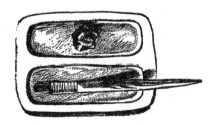

STONE PAINT-DISH
AND BRUSH

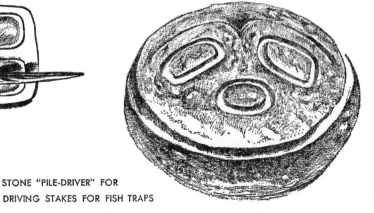

STONE "PILE-DRIVER" FOR
DRIVING STAKES FOR FISH TRAPS

too had once laid them horizontally. The planks were sometimes set in slots cut in the posts of the framework and sometimes lashed into place with flexible twigs or cords, but they could always be taken down easily when the people wanted to move.

Many groups had two villages, one in which they lived during the summer and the other for the winter. When it was time to move, the planks were taken off the house framework and laid across two canoes, making a sort of raft. When this was ready, the household possessions were piled on and the people started off to the other village, leaving the framework of the house standing. At their destination, the planks were again put on the framework waiting for them and the people moved in, a simple and convenient way of moving to the summer cottage.

The interior of the houses differed with the tribes. Because they were so big, a great many people could live in each house, all of them under the authority of the chief who had built the house and who was responsible for it. Each separate family had its own section, which was closed off more or less from the others by mats of cedar bark hung on rods. These mats not only gave the people a little privacy but also cut down the drafts which whistled through the long cracks between the planks. There was generally a wide platform running all round the inside wall and on this the people slept and stored their possessions. Some of them built shelves above the sleeping platforms to make room for other things, baskets, boxes, and so on. There was often another platform along the front of the house outside; here the people sat to work or rest in fine weather.

A separate fire was built for each family, or two families might share a fire. The smoke found its way out through the roof and in some cases there was an adjustable flap that covered a square hole in the middle of the roof. This flap could be so turned as to help the wind draw the smoke out.

Inside a Haida house there was a series of two or even three terraces with a fire in the middle of the lowest level. These terraces had sleeping platforms built round them, so that a comparatively small house could accommodate quite a large number of people. The roofs were made of cedar boards laid overlapping each other to keep the rain out, and they were held down with long heavy poles and big stones so that the wind could not blow the boards away, for the Indians used no nails and did not even peg the roof down with wooden dowels. Men often had to go up on top of the house to see that everything was undisturbed. They made ladders from thick broad planks with steps cut in them.

Many of the houses were decorated with designs painted on the front, with carved house posts, and with big totem poles standing in the middle of the end or side. Often there was a hole cut in the totem pole large enough to serve as a ceremonial entrance to the house, but this was not always used, for the people found it easier to move one or more of the wall planks aside and go in and out in that way.

There are not many of the old houses left, though they once were very numerous. The house posts have rotted in the wet climate of the west coast and now there are only a few crumbling ruins left. Fortunately we have photographs and descriptions of them so the memory of these remarkable buildings will not be lost.

FURNITURE

Most Indians lived such a roaming life that they were not able to carry much in the way of furniture, except bedding and the few

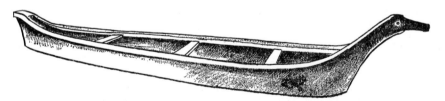

WEST COAST DUG-OUT CANOE, SOUTHERN TYPE

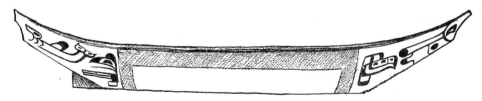

WEST COAST DUG-OUT CANOE, NORTHERN TYPE

bags and baskets they found essential. On the west coast, the situation was quite different. Here were permanent villages with large and solid houses and the people seldom went far from home or, if they did, expected to return before long. As a result they could accumulate great stores of possessions which they would have found quite impossible to carry about with them.

Not only were the men good canoe builders, but they were among the cleverest carpenters ever known. They had the big red cedar to work in, a wood which is soft and straight-grained, and with which they were able to do work that even our best cabinet-makers say is very skilful indeed. They had no chairs as we know them, but they did make settees, and the sleeping platforms took the place of our beds. Boxes, chests, and bowls, all made in wood, were their chief form of furniture. Some of these were carved out of solid blocks, often maple or alder, and others, especially chests and boxes, were made from long thin planks of cedar, carefully cut and grooved so that a plank could be steamed and then bent at right angles to make the four sides, and sewn together at one corner. The bottom was a separate piece pegged or sewn into position. The lid was also separate, cut so that it fitted down over the sides.

These boxes were made so well and the joins fitted so tightly that they would hold water and many of them were used for cooking with hot stones, for these people made no pottery at all.

The boxes and chests were used for keeping dried food in, as well as blankets, masks, and other possessions. Yet another use was as coffins for the dead.

Cedar was used extensively because of the ease of working it and of splitting off planks and boards. This was done with wedges, often used in sets of seven, each one a little larger than the other. They were usually made of yew wood, one end thinned down and the other squared off and bound with a twisted ring of cedar roots to prevent its splitting. Planks produced in this way were adzed smooth and finished with shark skin, which was used as we use sandpaper.

Bowls, made from a single piece of wood, were often used to eat from and some of those used at feasts were very big, large enough for several people to share at once. Some were carved in the forms of animals or they might be long, narrow, shallow dishes something like a flattened canoe.

Mats and baskets, made from cedar bark or spruce roots, were of many different sizes, weaves, and shapes, and some of the women were most skilful at making them. They served for all sorts of purposes, such as gathering clams or carrying fish, picking berries, storing wool for blankets, and so on. In some of the mats, the weave was twilled which means that the cross pieces went over one and under two, instead of over one and under one, which gives a plain checker weave. The better mats had dyed strips worked in to make a pattern, and baskets had patterns woven into them too. Black dye from the mud of springs, orange from alder bark, and a purplish stain from berries were the most usual dyes. Other mats were made from rushes, not woven together but sewn with a special wooden needle three or four feet long made of spirea wood.

Spoons were made of goat or sheep horn, and both spoons and ladles were also made of wood. Some of the ladles used at feasts

"PORTRAIT" MASK, REPRESENTING
AN ACTUAL PERSON

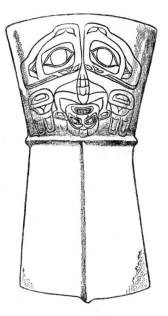

CEREMONIAL "COPPER", A SYMBOL OF WEALTH

were so enormous that a man could not handle one without help. They were used for ladling out meat and soup that had been cooked with hot stones in a canoe, for a chief liked to be able to boast that he had so many guests that the ordinary cooking boxes were not nearly large enough.

Some smaller bowls were pecked out of solid stone; they were generally used as mortars, for grinding up the tobacco they chewed, for instance. Some of these are carved in animal forms and others have decorative rings on them.

TOOLS

Naturally men who did so much woodwork had good sets of tools. There were all the usual kinds, such as hammers, chisels, drills, and so on, but they were much more varied in shape and more numerous than among other tribes. Here again the fact that they had safe places in which to leave them while not in use made a big difference.

Stone, shell, antler, and bone were the materials most often used for making tools. Hammers, adzes, and chisels were made of stone, tough fine-grained stone being preferred for the hammers, and jade for the chisels and adzes. The jade was traded down the Fraser from the Thompson River people who found it in boulders and pebbles in the river gravels round about Lytton.

Most of their stone tools were ground into shape, and not chipped as was usual in other parts of Canada. There had been other Indians living on the coast previously who did chip their

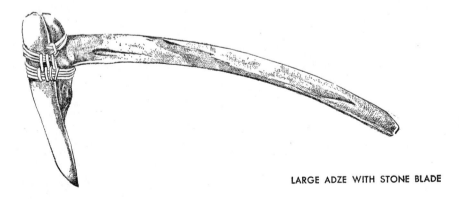

LARGE ADZE WITH STONE BLADE

stone tools and weapons, and these are still to be found in the old shell heaps.

Adzes were of two types, a large one with a long handle, for rough work, and a smaller one, for finishing, made with a D-shaped handle; both used blades of jade. Sometimes thick mussel shell, ground to a sharp edge, was used as a blade. These two types of adzes served instead of axes, which do not seem to have been used much on the coast.

There were many other tools, far too many to list and discuss in detail. The stone pile-drivers used in making fish weirs are interesting. They are flat rocks with a grip carved in each side so that they can be handled easily. Drills were used for making holes for wooden pegs and in woodwork. There was a whole battery of palettes and brushes for painters and special implements for shredding cedar bark and for many other crafts.

TRANSPORTATION

Travel, for west coast people, always meant a canoe trip, except for treks inland with goods to trade, on foot carrying a pack. Sleds and toboggans were not used on the west coast. Canoes were of many sizes and styles, each with its own special job. There were small hunting dug-outs, only about fifteen feet long, intended for one or two men, and great big ones, sixty-five feet long, which could carry forty or more people on voyages of hundreds of miles. They were all of cedar, except some on the rivers which were made from big black poplars, known as Balm of Gilead trees.

On salt water, canoes were of two principal styles: the northern type, in which both the bow and stern project and overhang the water; and the southern type, in which the bow projects, but the stern is straight up and down; these were used by the Coast Salish and the Nootka. The purpose of the raised and projecting bow is to enable the canoe to cut better through rough water. All canoes were paddled but the river canoe was usually poled along where the water was shallow enough. Sails do not seem to have been known until the Indians saw white men using them.

Paddles varied in shape, but most of them had leaf-shaped blades, and a little cross-piece for a handle. Many of the paddles came to a sharp point, especially those used for steering. It is

said that these made less noise than other kinds and so were preferred for getting near sleeping seals and sea-otters. Also, they
made effective weapons and many a man has been wounded by
them in fighting.

Building a canoe is a long process, but the workmen were so
skilful and had built so many thousands of them, that they knew
just how to go at it. The first step was to select a suitable tree,
large enough for the canoe they planned to build. Then the tree
had to be tested to make sure it was sound at the heart, for many
cedars which look quite strong are hollow and rotten at the core.

The tree chosen was cut down with adzes and sometimes with
the help of a carefully controlled fire. Then a log of the right length
was cut off and floated to the village where the canoe was to be
built. It was laid on trestles and the upper half of the log was
split off, leaving a flat surface. Then the outside was adzed roughly
into shape and the wood was chopped out of the inside. Sometimes fire was used here too, to char the wood and make it easier
to cut away. As the sides got thinner, they were tested again and
again by running the hands over them inside and out, noting any
variation in thickness. In places that were hard to reach, a hole was
drilled right through the wood, its thickness carefully checked, and
then a dowel was driven in to fill the hole again.

At last the hull would have taken the shape the canoe builder
wanted. There was no keel, though the bottom line of the body
was carried out in front to make a cutwater. Nor were there any
ribs, such as we use in making a boat or a canoe. A missionary
did persuade some Indians once to add ribs to a canoe, but they
never took to the idea.

The next step was to make the hull wider by stretching it.
It sounds impossible to stretch a piece of wood, but they did it
by pouring water in, bringing it to a boil with hot stones, and
covering the canoe with blankets while it steamed. When it was
thoroughly hot, they spread the sides apart and put stretchers in
to hold them open while the canoe cooled. The stretchers were
sometimes hundreds of bent saplings side by side, or at other
times the flat boards which eventually formed the thwarts or
seats. In this way a canoe could be made a good deal wider, safer,
and more comfortable than it would have been otherwise.

The last step was to add the extra bow and stern pieces. The bow piece is a decorative figure which, many people think, looks like the head of a deer or of a dog, but the Indians insist that it is not meant to be either of these. The two surfaces where the bow and the bow piece are to fit together are smoothed as well as possible, and then the face of one of them is smeared with black grease. It is put carefully in place and lifted off again. Any spots where the black grease had offset on the other surface must be too high and had to be adzed down till the whole thing fitted evenly and could be pegged securely in place.

The canoes were generally painted black on the outside after being made as smooth as possible and the inside might be painted red, or decorated with designs, or just left plain. Often the adze marks, which formed an amazingly even pattern, were left as a decoration and as a proof of the skill of the adzeman. Canoes had to be well cared for, never dragged over rough stones, and always kept in the shade or covered with wet mats when not in use. A well-cared-for canoe would last for years but it took only a few weeks of abuse to ruin the best one ever made.

DOMESTIC ANIMALS

The only domesticated animals on the west coast were dogs. These were of at least two breeds, one the little spitz-like animal which was kept by the Coast Salish for its wool, which was woven into blankets; the other breed was a larger kind which haunted the native villages in numbers. They seemed to have had but little

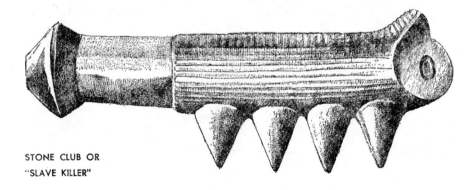

STONE CLUB OR
"SLAVE KILLER"

to do, for they were seldom used as pack animals and the people apparently did not use them for food.

SOCIAL ORGANIZATION

We have already seen that the native tribes of the west coast differ in many ways from those living in other parts of Canada, but it is in the organization of their society that they differ most of all. The natives of the west coast built up a system of secret societies and intricate rules governing the inheritance of crests and songs and rituals, the right to marry in this group and not in that, the right to perform certain dramatic plays showing real or imaginary incidents, the right to names and titles, in a most bewildering tangle.

There were three principal ways in which their society differed from that of other Canadian Indians: first, in the recognition of a definite aristocracy, something much more advanced than the system of chiefs among the Iroquois; secondly, the custom of accumulating large quantities of goods and distributing them at great feasts known as potlatches; and thirdly, a well-organized system of slavery.

It would take a great many pages to explain all these things in detail, nor is it really possible. We know a good deal about the secret societies of the Bella Coola and the Kwakiutl, but much less about

WAR CLUB MADE OF COPPER

WAR CLUB MADE OF BONE

those of other tribes. We know something about the totem poles, but much less about the crests that were used in the old days, and we know more of the Tsimshian people than we do of the Coast Salish, for example. This is because scientists had time to study only certain groups and certain subjects before the native system broke down under the pressure of new customs and new ways which came in with the white man.

The elaborate structure of society typical of the west coast is seen at its best in the tribes of the central part of the area, among the Haida, Tsimshian, and Kwakiutl. As one goes south, to the Coast Salish, the system grows weaker and disappears entirely in the state of Washington. Going north, too, there is again a weakening of the system and the Tlinkit, though they had more of it than the Coast Salish, also show a less complicated society than those in the middle, the Haida, Tsimshian, and Kwakiutl.

There are few statements that can be made to fit all the tribes, but the general practice among them was to regard the aristocracy as superior in birth and in prestige to the nobles, and definitely superior to the commoners or freemen. The slaves, of course, had no social standing at all. The important chiefs were the heads of large groups of families, all related or of the same clan, much as the chief of a Scottish clan was responsible for all the members of it, though related to some of them only remotely. These chiefs erected and owned the large houses in which most of the people lived and had many public duties and responsibilities.

There was great rivalry between them, each seeking to outdo the others and to acquire greater prestige, which was based in the long run on wealth. The right to use certain crests, to sing certain songs, and so on were all inherited; in some tribes (Tlinkit, Haida, and Tsimshian) through the mother's side of the family and in others through the father or through either. Such rights could also be sold, or given away, as was frequently done. Other rights could be acquired through marriage, and it was a matter of great concern to the older men and women to keep exact record of just who was allowed to do what. Naturally there were often differences of opinion, sometimes honest mistakes, sometimes attempts to cheat a little, and a great deal was made of all these points of right and prestige. The situation was not very different in the aristocracy of the Old World a hundred years or so ago and, indeed, until fairly recently.

Men of the class of nobles, who were not quite of the aristocracy, often accumulated wealth by their own efforts and, by giving great feasts, could improve their position and eventually be accepted by the true aristocrats, though they always ran the risk of having their comparatively recent honors laughed at by those who considered themselves to be of better birth and older family. This situation too was not unknown in Europe, where men who have made a fortune in beer, or bacon, or boots, have recently been given titles. The rivalry for prestige was intense and continuous and a man who wanted to advance in social standing did so by shaming his rivals by the profusion of his gifts at the great winter feasts.

Just as the prairie tribes put war deeds first, so the west coast people made wealth and the generous distribution of gifts the really important thing in life. Wealth was in the form of goods, for there was no money in our sense of the word. It is true that certain seashells, called tusk shells or dentalium, were considered almost as we consider money, but they were used in certain ways only and not as a standard currency. The kinds of goods recognized as wealth were canoes, slaves, furs, oolakan grease and, in later years, blankets and other goods obtained from white men, even such things as sewing machines and enamel basins.

A chief intending to give a feast or "potlatch" would accumulate great quantities of goods, all he and his followers could get together. Invitations were sent out weeks in advance to neighboring villages of the same tribe and, if a really big event were being arranged, to villages of other tribes too. There was a certain proper way of doing things, which varied from tribe to tribe and from

DAGGER, MADE OF COPPER

generation to generation, but as a rule the visitors began to arrive a day or so ahead of time. They were welcomed and feasted and, when all those expected had arrived, the important proceedings would begin. There were officials appointed to act as masters of the ceremonies with long speeches and much etiquette. The prestige of a chief would suffer severely if he were not given his proper place in the seating, if he were not addressed by his right titles, or if he were neglected in any way.

Gifts were distributed, several slaves to this one, canoes to another, great quantities of grease to a third, and so on. Sometimes a chief, to show his greatness and his contempt for mere wealth, would destroy as much as he gave away and perhaps even more. He would pile canoes on top of each other, pour quantities of valuable grease over them, and set fire to the whole heap. He would kill three or four slaves and throw their bodies into the sea. He would take a "copper", a shield-shaped sheet of copper, and break it up, throwing the pieces away, or giving them as presents to his rivals. This has more meaning when we understand that these "coppers" were symbols of great wealth. While of little or no value in themselves, they meant a lot; each of them had a name and had been sold in previous potlatches for large sums, perhaps five thousand blankets, or for ten slaves. One "copper" was called the Salmon, because it was so "slippery" that few men could afford to hold it, and so on.

Wealth that was destroyed and wasted in this way was lost forever, but it did add to the chief's prestige. He also paid out great sums in return for services, such as payment to the men who distributed the goods, and to those who announced the names of the chiefs to whom presents were to be made. The "gifts", however,

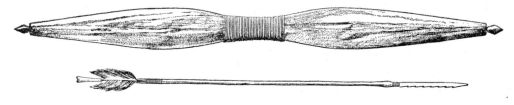

BOW, OF YEW WOOD, AND ARROW WITH BONE POINT

whether of canoes, slaves, or grease, were loans rather than gifts
and the chiefs who received them were expected to pay them back
with high interest when they in their turn gave a potlatch. It was in
this way that it was possible to shame and outdo one's rivals. Giving
a chief five thousand blankets made things very awkward for him;
he had to accept them, or be shamed, but he knew that he would
have to return ten thousand blankets when the time came, and
that was not always possible. Almost never was it easy.

A chief, therefore, who intended giving a potlatch generally
had a number of these "gifts", which were really loans, already outstanding, and he collected as many of them as he could beforehand.
Men who had given many potlatches in the prime of their lives
would have great wealth owing to them which they could get back
as they grew older. It was a form of insurance, though our bankers
would consider the rate of interest wickedly high.

So much wealth was wasted in the last fifty years of the nine-
teenth century in the efforts of chiefs, who had grown rich through
the fur trade, to outrival each other that the government prohibited
potlatches altogether, a step which may have been necessary but
which hastened the breakdown of the Indian social organization.
Canoes became less essential than they had been, slavery was prohibited, the use of oolakan grease lessened as new foods were intro-

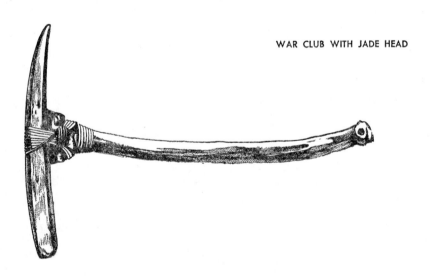

WAR CLUB WITH JADE HEAD

duced, and the old scale of values became meaningless. A chief's prestige was no longer based on the number and splendor of the potlatches he gave, and what had once been wealth no longer had any value.

The system of slavery, once so well established, was one of the first to break down under white government. Slavery had been abolished in the United States and the British government had been fighting slavery in the East for many years, so that when it was found to be a common practice among the natives on the west coast of Canada, it was looked upon with no favor at all by the white men.

Slaves had not been ill treated as a rule. They did much of the work, but their condition was little worse than that of their masters. Their situation was bad in that they must always remain slaves if they were born of slave parents and a man who was captured and made a slave lost any rank he had once had among his own people. Slaves had no opportunity of improving their condition by acquiring wealth or by marriage, for they could marry only other slaves.

Slaves were a form of property and a chief or noble had complete rights over them. He could sell them or give them away at feasts or potlatches. He could even kill them to show his contempt for mere wealth. Among some of the west coast people there were actually special stone clubs known as "slave killers" which were used for this purpose. Among the Tlinkit, slaves are said to have been killed and buried under the posts of a new house as a way of making it strong and free from evil influences. The Cannibal Society of the Kwakiutl used to kill slaves, too, and eat them at their ceremonies.

John Jewett, the armorer of the ship *Boston*, was kept a prisoner by the Nootkas from March 1803 to July 1805, and then he was rescued. He and one other man alone were spared when the Indians killed the rest of the crew. Jewett was saved because they wanted him to teach them how to work metals, and the other man, Thompson, owed his life to Jewett's quick thinking when he urged the Indians not to kill Thompson who, he said, was his father. Though they were both given a lot of hard work to do and were not very well fed, most of their difficulties came from the fact that they were unable to speak the Nootka language and were not used to the comparatively comfortless life the Indians found normal.

WARFARE

There was a good deal of fighting among the people of the west coast. The motive might be revenge for an actual or imaginary injury, or for some act that had lowered a chief's prestige, or simply a raid to capture slaves. There were feuds, too, which often led to wars and might go on for a long time. If a man were murdered, his fellow clansmen would demand the killing of a man of equal importance in the murderer's group, or they might kill the first one of the enemy they could get their hands on. In slave raids, they killed as few as possible, trying to take their prisoners alive.

Men who were going on a war party or on a slave raid had to go through rituals and ceremonies, just as the Nootkas did when they went whale hunting. They must purify themselves by bathing and scrubbing with hemlock twigs and their wives had to behave properly while they were away. In war, they believed, as in any other kind of hunting, success was to be had not only through skill and bravery but also by the proper observance of all the rituals and taboos and magic that were involved.

Surprise attacks were the most popular method of fighting. The evening before a raid or an attack the enemy would send a single

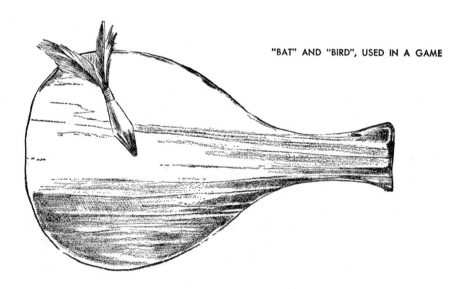

"BAT" AND "BIRD", USED IN A GAME

small canoe, apparently peaceful enough, to spy on the village. Its crew would note how many houses there were and anything else that might be important. Then the main body of the enemy, in several large canoes, would approach the village at the earliest light of dawn. Each canoe would select a certain house for attack; a man would be provided with pitchy wood, which would blaze furiously, to set each building on fire, another would have cords to tie captives with, and yet another would stay with the canoe to protect it.

When everything was ready, they all attacked at the same moment, rushing into the houses and killing or capturing the sleeping inhabitants before they realized what was happening. In a successful raid, there would be almost nobody left except the fortunate few who were away from the village at the time, or who managed to escape unobserved and hide in the dense forest, where they were usually safe.

Bows and arrows were used as weapons, but most of the fighting was hand to hand, and then they preferred clubs and knives. Some of the clubs were made of the bones of whales, others of stone, and some of copper. They were usually slung by a cord round the warrior's neck or wrist so that the club would not be lost if it slipped from his hand. There was one peculiar form of war club shaped something like a pickaxe, with a jade head and a wooden handle. Spears were used for throwing and stabbing at short range. The Tlinkit made daggers of copper which had a curious handle and a grip lashed with smooth roots.

Defence was not well organized and the practice of having a sentry posted to warn the people does not seem to have been adopted unless an attack was actually expected. Some villages were built on a spit of land so that they could be defended by ditches and palisades, and a few even had fortresses nearby to which the people could retire. Most of these places could have been forced to surrender by laying siege to them, but that was not the Indians' way of fighting.

For armor, there were wooden helmets, and protectors for the neck and throat also made of wood. There were suits or coats of armor, made of slats or rods of hardwood lashed together, and these did well enough against arrows and knives. Some men wore long coats of several folds of thick leather and these, too, were strong and thick enough to stop an arrow, but the Indians were much astonished when one of Captain Cook's men shot a musket ball right through six layers.

Usually a single attack was the whole war but, if it seemed likely that an attack would be followed by revenge, peace was brought about by paying what was claimed as the right value for the men killed and the damage done. There was a certain amount of prestige in having fought well and bravely and men used to cut off the heads of their victims and take them home as trophies. In later years, they found it simpler to take only the scalp including the ears. War honors were not inherited as other distinctions were.

SOCIAL LIFE

Daily life on the west coast was not the difficult kind of living that the people of the Northwest Territories knew, for example. As a rule, food was abundant and not difficult to obtain. Men spent most of their time, especially in summer, in hunting and fishing, mostly in the sea. The women did all the tasks that fall to their lot the world over, bringing up the children, looking after the food and clothing, and keeping the house, as well as all the related crafts and arts that go with it. In ordinary times, life was pleasant enough but not perhaps especially exciting.

MEDICINE MAN'S CEREMONIAL RATTLE, CARVED FROM WOOD

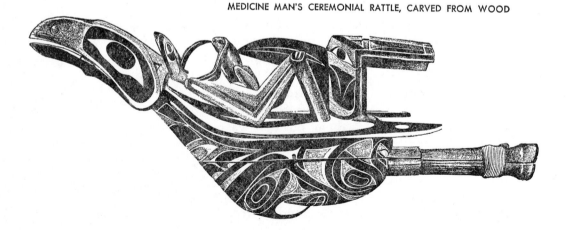

The winter was different. It was then that most of the secret societies performed their rituals and that the big potlatches were given. The word *potlatch* means "to give". It comes from the Chinook jargon, a curious combination of Indian languages with English and French, that was used by whites and natives on the west coast. The big feasts were called potlatches because things were given away at them. Almost any important event in the life of a child or adult was an excuse for a potlatch and men gave as many of these feasts as they could for this was a way of increasing their prestige. When a child was born, or took a new name, or became engaged to be married, or did get married, or built a house, or put up a totem pole, or wished to shame a rival, his parents or he gave a potlatch and a great feast.

When the secret societies, such as the Cannibal Society, or the Seal Society, were going to perform a ceremony, there was a strange feeling in the village. Spirits were supposed to be about, not as they are at Hallow-e'en, but in a much more real sense. Strange whistling sounds could be heard, but not explained, and the women and children would be careful to keep out of sight. Suddenly one of the young initiates of the Cannibal Society might be heard approaching, running pell mell down the hillside, bursting through the brush, and dashing into the village, running up to people and pretending to bite, or actually biting, pieces out of their arms. Many men bore

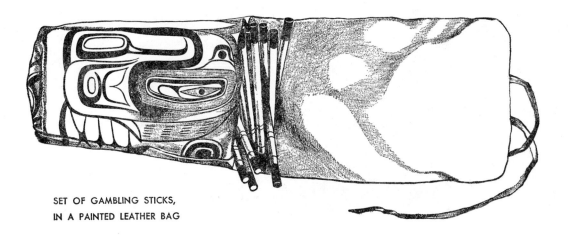

SET OF GAMBLING STICKS,
IN A PAINTED LEATHER BAG

scars showing where one of the *Hamatsa* (Cannibal) Society members had bitten him. Sometimes they held rituals in which they had to eat slaves or corpses, and other revolting practices are reported.

Some ceremonies were more like theatrical performances and the players rehearsed for a long time before they played a scene which showed how an important family first gained its name or the adventures of a mythical ancestor. These performances, half dramatic and half religious, were most impressive. The performers wore carved wooden masks and were seen only by the flickering light of the fires in the huge shadowy houses. Some of them hid small whistles in their mouths to imitate the cries of the spirits, and voices came from the middle of the fires. This was done by having a long hollow kelp stem running under the floor from the fire to the outside of the house, where an accomplice spoke through it to make the voice seem to come from the fire. At times men were seen to be killed; the blood poured out when they were stabbed and then they

MASK REPRESENTING A BIRD

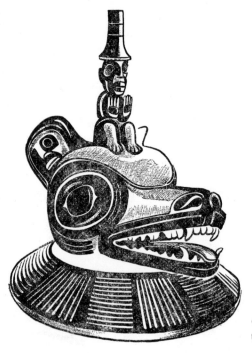

CARVED WOODEN HELMET,
USED IN WAR

were healed again, for the blood really had been hidden in a bladder that the medicine man cut with his knife.

Marriages were elaborate affairs among the wealthy and were considered most important because many crests and songs and names were transferred at a marriage. A man might marry several wives and acquire new honors with each marriage. Children were often betrothed when they were very young, and presents were exchanged between the two families to seal the bargain, so that the advantages of the marriage might be enjoyed by both families even before it actually took place.

Now and then it was much to the advantage of one family or the other to marry an old man with a young girl, or an old woman of wealth and social position might be married to a youth not yet old enough to go hunting or fishing for himself, but the difference in their ages was not thought to be an objection. The Nootka and the Kwakiutl of the west coast of Vancouver Island sometimes made the bridegroom undergo tests of his courage, such as passing close to a very hot fire, before the wedding took place, and a man not willing to take the dares himself would hire another man to do it for him, which was just as good.

GAMES

Many of the adult men were so much pre-occupied with holding and improving their social position that they looked down upon games as a waste of time, if not unmanly, but that did not prevent them from gambling and, like most of the native tribes of Canada, they often risked high stakes on such games as *la-hal* which is much like our "Who's got the button?" Many of them owned most beautifully carved and painted sets of sticks to play with, which they kept in special leather cases; they had mats to play on and shaggy gloves of shredded cedar bark to wear while playing to make it harder for their opponents to guess which hand held the "button".

They also had a kind of dice, shaped a little like arm-chairs. A primitive kind of badminton was played with a cedar-wood bat and a shuttlecock, and spinning tops were used, especially when the few cold days of winter made ice to spin them on.

Archery contests were popular and a special moving target, a doughnut-shaped disc of lava rock, was rolled along the ground.

The archers tried to shoot an arrow into the hole before the target stopped rolling.

They played cat's cradles, and at times the boys pretended they were whale or seal hunters, dragging a thick piece of kelp along the beach and stabbing it as they ran.

MUSIC

Music was not much more advanced than in other parts of Canada, but the west coast people had a larger variety of instruments than most, including drums, rattles, whistles, and clappers. The ordinary tambourine type of drum was used as well as a much larger one which was a shallow box of cedar wood, hung from the roof and pounded with the side of a man's fist. It could make quite a loud noise. Rattles were of several kinds, the most remarkable of them being carved in a very intricate shape, resembling a bird, with the tail making the handle. On the bird's back are a little hut, a medicine man, and a frog, with the man and the frog touching each other's tongue to pass magical power from one to the other. Other rattles were made of sea-shells, or the beaks of puffins, and also of circles of wood with compartments built in them containing small pebbles that would rattle.

Whistles were of many sizes and shapes, some with high notes and others with low. Sometimes several whistles were built side by

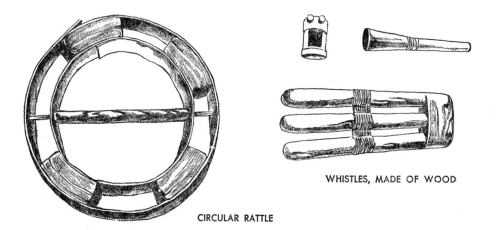

CIRCULAR RATTLE

WHISTLES, MADE OF WOOD

side so that different notes could be produced; others were double-ended, with two notes. One of the strangest types was fastened to a man's belt in such a way that when he breathed in, the belt would tighten, press a valve, and blow the whistle. Hidden under his robe, it would sound like the voice of a spirit performer in the winter ceremonies. The clappers consisted of two pieces of wood fastened together in such a way that one of them could be made to clap against the other when the clapper was shaken.

The west coast people had many songs that they used in their rituals and the music for some of them was quite beautiful. Musical instruments were not used to provide an accompaniment, as a rule, except the drum.

ART

The natives of the British Columbia coast were by far the most advanced artistically anywhere north of Mexico. In painting and carving, their work is equal to that of almost any native race in the world, and was far ahead of the comparatively crude and simple designs of other tribes.

In carving and painting, animals provided the designs most frequently used, including human beings and also, at times, other forms. These were seldom made to look just like the animal intended, but they were altered to fit the space that was to be carved

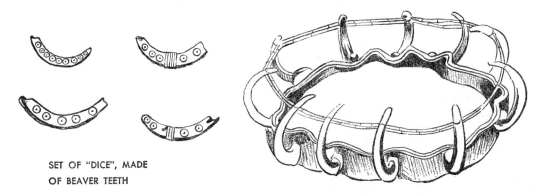

SET OF "DICE", MADE
OF BEAVER TEETH

MEDICINE MAN'S HEAD-DRESS OF GRIZZLY BEAR CLAWS

or painted. Quite often it was as if the animal had been skinned and the hide stretched and cut up to make the design fit the area to be filled or the surface to be covered.

The famous totem poles of the west coast are among the best examples of native skill in carving. Many people, when looking at a totem pole for the first time, think it ugly and grotesque, but those more familiar with west coast art find them strong and dignified. Most of them show a series of family crests, generally the crests of those who had the pole carved, and a few poles illustrate myths and legends connected with the owner's family.

Some people believe that totem poles can be "read", much as we read a book, but that is not true. It is true that tales and legends are known about most of the crests and that some people can recite these legends, but that is not "reading". In the same way, if we see a picture of a little girl with bright golden hair and three bears, one large, one smaller, and one tiny bear, we know that it is a picture of Goldilocks and the Three Bears, but we have not "read" the picture, although we do know the story about them.

The animal forms used on totem poles often looked so much alike that the carvers got into the habit of using certain features to distinguish one from the other. Thus the position of the ears will tell us whether a man or an animal is meant, for a man's ears are level with his eyes and an animal has his ears above them. A long straight beak on a bird means a raven, a curved beak is for an eagle, and a beak so much curved that it touches the lower lip indicates a hawk. A fish with gills and a high forehead is a shark; a beaver has

HORN SPOON SHOWING ELABORATE CARVING

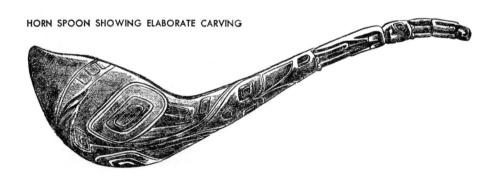

big front teeth, a scaly tail, and a stick in his mouth; a grizzly bear
is shown with big claws, sharp teeth, and his tongue out, and so on.

Totem poles were not the only things carved, for masks used
in the winter ceremonies were a most important form of art too. The
big ones were carved in cedar wood because it was light, and the
smaller ones were usually in alder wood. Some represented animals,
some human beings, and others spirits or imaginery beings. Not
only were they skilfully carved but most of them were painted
too. Some were double, and were worked with strings, so that the
outer masks could be opened by pulling the cords to show another
one inside, quite different from the first. One large mask had ten
different mouths which could be changed by the man wearing it,
each mouth giving the face a different expression.

For the last hundred years or more the Haidas of the Queen
Charlotte Islands have carved objects for sale to tourists in a smooth
black slate which is found at just one place on the islands. They
made dishes, and mugs, and pipes, and flutes, as well as groups of
figures, and miniature totem poles. Few of these are being made
now and collectors are very keen to buy those they can find. Silver
bracelets, engraved with west coast designs, were made too, generally of silver from Mexican dollars. They say the Mexican silver was
softer than ours and easier to work.

Many other objects were decorated, fish hooks, food bowls,
fish clubs, almost anything that possibly could be carved, but never
was the decoration allowed to make the thing itself less useful, or
awkward to handle. A fish club was designed first of all for killing

BONE "SOUL CASE",
INLAID WITH ABALONE
SHELL

fish when they were pulled alive into the canoe so that they would not flop about and upset things, and the decoration had to come second. This is not always true in our art, for we have many such things as gaudy decorated jugs that won't pour without dripping, and that is poor designing.

Painting was a highly developed art and many objects were painted. Totem poles were painted, but the extent of this varied from time to time and from tribe to tribe. Masks, too, were painted and so were the sides of chests and boxes. This was done freehand on cedar wood and required great skill for there was no chance of correcting a mistake because the paint soaked into the wood quickly and could not be erased.

Black from charcoal, red and yellow from ochre, green from copper ore, and white from a fine clay, were the colors most commonly used. The painting of delicate work was done with small brushes, the handles of which were sometimes carved too. Stone palettes were used to grind up the paint on, and the artist chewed

MECHANICAL MASK, WORKED
BY STRINGS, SHOWING A
BIRD WHEN CLOSED AND
A MAN WHEN OPEN

up a mixture of salmon eggs and cedar bark and then spat it into the palette to mix with his paint so that it would not rub off easily.

Weaving was well advanced; they made blankets of goat's or dog's wool, and mats and baskets. In all of these, patterns were worked in, both in the weave and by dyeing. Some of the baskets, such as those of the Nootka, are unusually fine and perfect.

LITERATURE

Not having any way of writing, the west coast people had to memorize all their songs and stories and there were thousands of them. Nobody knew them all, of course, but some of the old women had amazing collections.

They told tales of the early days of the world, and Raven often comes into them, for he seems to have been mixed up with just about everything from stealing the sun to stocking the rivers with salmon. There are legends of the origin of all the noble families and many other tales, as well as the songs sung in the winter rituals and in the secret society meetings. Some of these are in an old language that the people have now forgotten, or that perhaps they themselves never knew, just as some of our songs are in Latin.

SCIENCE

In most cases, when people settle down in villages and lead a reasonably safe and secure life, art and science begin to develop. We have seen that this was true on the west coast as far as art was concerned, but science seems to have been slower. Some of the medicine men were beginning to take an interest in the movements of the sun and stars and marked the change of the seasons by noting which peak or valley the sun set or rose near, but they had made little progress beyond this. They still believed that illness was caused by magic and tried to cure it by stronger magic, though they did have some crude ideas about surgery, the setting of broken bones, and the lancing of boils. Several skulls have been found on the west coast with holes intentionally cut in them; the edges of these holes have healed, showing that the patients lived for some time after the operation. It was done, we believe, in an effort to relieve bad headaches, or perhaps to cure the insane.

RELIGION

Like most of the other natives of Canada, the west coast
Indians had no idea of a Supreme Being in our sense of the word.
They did believe in the existence of spiritual beings of various
degrees of importance, who had different roles to play, if not exactly
duties to perform. There was no general agreement about these
things and not only did the various tribes have different sets of
spiritual beings, but men of the same tribe were quite likely not
to agree on these matters; in fact, most of them gave very little
thought to anything more than being careful to avoid taboos and
to make sure they were ceremonially clean before going hunting
or fishing.

The Haidas told of a spiritual being whose name meant something like the "Power of the Shining Heavens" and it was from this
source that minor spiritual beings drew their strength. This great
power had nothing to do with human beings, for these could deal
only with the lesser spirits.

Another Haida spiritual being was Wigit, who lived in a magical house hung from the sky. It was he who decided the length of
each man's life and, when a child was born, Wigit reached blindly
behind him and chose a stick from a great mass of them. If the stick
was short, the child would not live long; if it happened to be a very
long stick, then the child would live to an old age.

Then there was the Thunderbird, whose wings flapped together
to make thunder and whose flashing eyes caused the lightning. The
Thunderbird was enormous and caught whales in its talons and
carried them to the mountain tops to devour them. Tsonoquoa, the
wild woman of the woods, was a Kwakiutl being, who wandered
through the woods with a basket in which to put the children she
caught; then she would carry them off to kill them and eat them.

The Creek-women controlled the streams and brooks, and
among the most powerful of the spiritual beings were the Killer
Whales. These small whales were always looked upon with fear
and respect. They are vicious animals which attack and eat other
whales many times their own size. The Haida insist that they are
really powerful spirits and have their own villages under the sea
in which they live just like people. The natives can tell you just

where these villages are and even know the names of them. All living beings, they believe, have some supernatural powers and can take on human form at will, but the Killer Whales do this more than other animals.

Naturally, with so many spiritual beings about and some of them very powerful, one has to be careful not to offend them in any way. There are many taboos which must be observed, many rituals that must be followed. The really important thing is to keep quite clean, so that the animals which are hunted or the fish that are to be caught will not be offended. Men bathed four times in four different lakes on four successive days, and performed other ritual acts in fours, for this was the sacred number. They would make pads of folded twigs of cedar or hemlock and scrub their bodies till the blood ran and, when the occasion was important enough, would go without food or drink for a long time, all to make sure of being completely clean.

There were some ceremonies which many of the people participated in, such as the First Salmon ceremony, in which the first

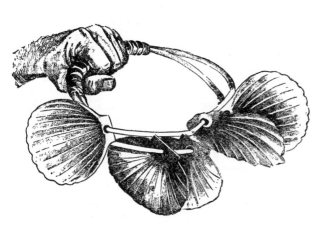

RATTLE OF PECTEN SHELLS

CARVED AND PAINTED
WOODEN CLAPPER

salmon of the year's run was laid on a clean mat of woven bark, and eagle's down, the symbol of peace and friendship, was scattered over it. When Alexander Mackenzie came down the Bella Coola River, he found it difficult to buy salmon from the Indians. Though he did not know it, the reason was that they feared he would not treat the fish with proper respect and might even cut them with metal knives instead of stone ones as the ritual ordered.

The Nootkas treated a bear, if they killed one, with great respect; they brought it into the house and made it sit up and wear a ceremonial hat like an honored guest. They offered food to the dead bear and begged it to eat, and tossed handfuls of eagle-down in the air to show their good will.

The medicine men, as in other parts of Canada, were priests, doctors, and fortune tellers all at the same time. They professed to foretell the future, and to be able to see what had happened to war parties or whaling canoes that had not returned when they should. They went along on slave-raiding expeditions to steer them clear of such dangers as the magic of the enemy medicine men or the accidental breaking of little-known taboos. Many of them dressed in a strange way, and never cut their hair or even combed it. They wore great nose-pins and looked just as dangerous as the people believed them to be. They cured the sick by magical means,

MASK REPRESENTING
A MYTHICAL BIRD

with drums and rattles, the blowing of whistles, and the pretended
sucking of pebbles and twigs from the bodies of their patients.

Some medicine men taught that every man had two souls or
perhaps even three, and that if he fell sick it was because one of his
souls was out of his body, either stolen or strayed away. Among the
Salish, four or eight medicine men would climb into an imaginary
canoe and undertake the long voyage to the land of the spirits to
see if they could find the sick man's soul and bring it back. The
ceremony might go on for a long time, the medicine men acting out
all the stages of their journey, first paddling and then poling their
canoe up a stream. When they got to the land of the spirits, they
left the canoe and went on still farther on foot. They knew when
they had reached the land of the spirits because the people, who
looked normal enough otherwise, walked with their legs crossed
and whistled instead of talking. Here they would hunt about for the
sick man's soul, and sometimes had to cross a stream by walking
over on a slippery pole. This was a moment of great danger, but
always they seemed to succeed and at last found the soul they were
seeking.

All this was played almost as if it were on the stage of a theatre
and generally the sick man was placed where he could watch and
see what was being done for him. When the missing soul was found
the medicine man caught it in his hands and placed it carefully in
a bone tube, about six inches long, beautifully carved and inlaid
with brightly colored abalone shell. Then they started the journey
back to the land of the living, going through all the same dangers

LARGE MASK
REPRESENTING A RAVEN

and difficulties they had first met on their way. At last the soul was brought right to the patient and, some of the old medicine men used to say, they could prove it was the right one by singing the patient's own song which nobody but he could possibly know. Whether they were really able to do this, we cannot tell.

Burials were of many different kinds on the west coast. The simplest form was that used for the unfortunate slaves who, when they died, were simply thrown into the sea and forgotten.

More important people were buried in a variety of ways. The Nootka and their Kwakiutl neighbors used to place the coffin high up in a tree, generally on a small island which was used for nothing else except burials. Sometimes the body was placed in a sea cave and, as some families owned the caves and used them again and again, there might be a number of bodies in one cave. The salt in the air seems to have had some preservative action for, in spite of the damp climate, many of these bodies were found so dried and shrunken as to remind one of the mummies of Egypt, though no chemicals or bandages were used.

The Salish sometimes placed the dead man in a small canoe and then hoisted the canoe high up in the tree, almost out of sight among the branches. The Tsimshian used to take the heart out of the dead body and bury it, the rest of the body being cremated. The Tlinkit cremated the whole body and the bones and ashes were kept in little boxes, some of them in fairly recent years being bought from traders who got them from China by way of Siberia and Alaska. Tlinkit medicine men were not cremated, but buried in grave houses in isolated spots where people seldom had occasion to go.

When mourning a death it was not uncommon for the nearest relatives to blacken their faces and cut their hair short. The clothes

CARVED WOODEN CLUB FOR KILLING FISH

and other personal belongings of the dead were often burned or
left on the grave; monuments, sometimes carved in wood, in the
form of a human being, or a special totem pole would be put up to
mark the place of the grave, if the body had been buried, or as a
memorial if it had been cremated. Sometimes the monument would
bear the family crest of the dead person.

PRESENT CONDITIONS

The white men who first met the natives of the west coast,
from about 1780 on, were in a more advanced stage of civilization
than had been the early French fishermen of the Atlantic coast and
the effect on the native people was much more intense. For a while
the natives profited from the rich fur trade but soon they began to
adopt the customs of the white man, some of which were not to
their advantage, to eat his foods, and to wear his clothes. Then
they grew discontented with their own ways of doing things and
later discontent turned to shame, and they no longer wanted to be
thought of as Indians. The white men called them Siwashes, a mis-
pronunciation of the French word "sauvage", meaning savage, and
the Indians resented the slur, as they still do and with good reason.

Many of the most aristocratic of the Indians, who had been
wealthy men among their own people and who could trace their
ancestors back for many generations, found that all their riches and
pride of race meant nothing to the white men, who neither understood nor bothered to try to.

For one or two generations, the Indians went downhill fast and
there seemed little hope that they would be able to get themselves
settled in the new ways of life that had come with the white man,
but today things are much better. Now, an Indian in British
Columbia has a vote just as a white man has and they have even sent
one of their own people to the Provincial Legislature in Victoria.
They are finding work in the canneries, the hop fields, and the apple
orchards, and many of them are now healthy and happy people. A
few still wish for the old days, but for the most part, even the
memory of the old times has faded. The children go to school, dress
as we do, and talk our language. In another generation or two, the
change from the native ways to ours may be almost complete.

The flying chain

A Legend of the British Columbia Coast

Along the coast of British Columbia, the land and the sea do not meet in a straight and clean-drawn line; they run together in a tangle of bays and inlets, points and islands. There are hundreds of islands, thousands of them, more islands than one could believe possible, and this is how it happened.

Many years ago, when the world was still tender and green, an Indian village stood near the mouth of the Nass River. To the west lay the great ocean, sparkling in the lazy sunlight. From the east came the river, flowing out of the great snow-capped mountains, down through a rocky canyon where the eagles nested.

The people were happy there. The sea and the river, the tide-flats and the hillsides, gave them plenty of food: seals, clams, and fish, and mountain goats. Theirs was a life of ease, with time for repose and pleasure, and the play of children.

One morning a little boy was out in front of his house, busy with a bow his uncle had made for him. When a great shadow moved slowly along the ground before him, he looked up and saw a huge eagle flying low over the village, as though looking for game.

"Oh, look, Daddy! There's a great big eagle, and he's down ever so low. Look, Daddy. I'm going to shoot him with my bow. Look, Daddy! Watch me!"

"It'll take a stronger arm and a longer bow than yours, my boy," his father laughed.

"No, it won't. Truly. Look, Daddy!"

The little boy loosed his arrow. The eagle was low indeed, but the arrow fell to the ground without coming anywhere near the bird at all.

Dropping lower and lower, the eagle circled slowly over the village.

"Just look at that! I never saw one down so low!"

"No," agreed another. "And see how big he is. It must be the Thunderbird."

"Of course not! It's not nearly big enough for a Thunderbird. It's just a big eagle, flying a little lower than usual. Why doesn't somebody shoot it?"

Old Lokoma, the medicine man, spoke up at once. His voice trembled with anxiety.

"No, no. Don't shoot it. Don't dare to try!"

"Why not?" asked one of the younger men. "I need some eagle feathers for my arrows. We always shoot eagles if we can. And why not this one?"

"This is no ordinary eagle," Lokoma explained. "It's either a powerful medicine man, or it's the Chief of All the Eagles, and only a fool would shoot at either one of those. You know that!"

"Oh, stick to your medicine-making and your silly spirits," the youth replied. "What harm can it possibly do, to shoot an eagle?"

"Harm enough! I've been a medicine man for many years, before most of you here were born. I tell you plainly, if you shoot that bird, all the village will suffer for it."

Everybody within earshot jeered and mocked at him, for the whole village was now in an uproar of excitement. Never had they seen an eagle behave in such a strange way. The birds were common enough. One or more could nearly always be seen, circling high above the river, but nobody could remember having seen one so obviously anxious to be noticed.

Every man in the place, every boy and girl, every woman who could possibly leave her cooking, and there were few who couldn't when there was so much excitement, was on the spot.

Most of the men and boys had run for their bows and by now there was a steady stream of arrows flying upwards, but not one of them came close enough to the great bird to make it pause in its slow and steady gliding.

"Where is Stokos?" somebody asked. "He has the strongest bow. Let him shoot."

Other people took up the cry.

"Stokos!" they shouted. "Stokos! Stokos!"

"He has gone up along the river bank," his wife told them, "and he's taken his bow with him."

"Look, here he comes now, running. Hurry up, Stokos, and bring that strong bow of yours."

"What's it all about?" panted Stokos. "What are you all looking at?"

At once a hundred people began to tell him all about the great eagle and its strange behavior, and they all urged him to see if he could shoot it, for nobody else had been able to.

"Shoot it? Of course I can shoot it. How could I possibly miss? Why, it's so low down you can hear the wind whistling through its feathers!"

Following the bird with his eye, Stokos strung his bow, and nocked an arrow on the string.

"Don't shoot, Stokos," urged old Lokoma. "That's no common eagle. You can see that, for you know more about such things than most people do. This is either some great medicine man who has come to visit us, or it is the Chief of All the Eagles himself."

Stokos paused, stared at the old medicine man for a moment, and then he laughed.

"Well, he's certainly big enough to be the chief, if size has anything to do with it, but once I've shot him it won't matter whether he was chief, commoner, or slave.

Stand clear, all of you. If that huge bird drops on you, you'll never know what he was."

Some people made a half-hearted move to get out of the way, but nobody really did anything about it, just as people usually behave in a crowd. So Stokos put an arrow on his string and shot.

There was a dead silence as everybody fixed his eyes on Stokos and then on his arrow. Nobody who lived through the rest of that awful day could ever forget the sound of the twanging bowstring and the whistling arrow when Stokos shot at the eagle.

Up and up went the arrow. Now the bird and the arrow appeared to be but one.

"He's got him!" shouted a young man. "See? It can't miss. He's got him!"

"No, no. The arrow can never reach him. See, it's a miss. Why, look! Look at that! The eagle is watching the arrow as it rises towards him!"

Sure enough, they saw the great bird's head turn to watch the arrow as it reached the top of its flight and turned lazily over, hung still for a moment in mid-air, and then plunged swiftly to the earth.

"Ah! He missed. Try again, Stokos, he's lower than ever now. Try again!"

"Stop, you fools, stop!" old Lokoma shouted once more. "I've warned you, warned you again and again. This is no common bird. Stop now, before some great evil comes to us."

By now, everybody who had a bow was shooting and the arrows were certainly going as high as the eagle, and even higher. But not one of them touched him. It was very strange that so many arrows should all miss.

Was the old medicine man right after all? Was this really some great magician who had come to visit them, only to meet such unfriendly people? Or was it indeed the Chief of all the Eagles?

The people were standing as closely together as they could get and still find room to draw their bows. Why none of them was killed by the shower of arrows falling back to the ground it is difficult to guess. Lower and lower the huge bird circled until they could see his glittering eyes, the cruel talons, and count each burnished feather as it glistened in the sunlight.

"I believe he is coming right down among us. Take care, he may strike at somebody!"

"Shoot him now!" cried another. "Shoot him now, before he does us any harm."

Old Lokoma slipped into the house to fetch his magical rattle, carved like a bird with a little magician lying on its back. He put on his goat's-wool blanket with the secret woven designs, and the high, carved head-dress, bright with ermine skins and trembling sea-lion bristles, inlaid with iridescent abalone shell.

Now he came back, shaking his rattle, and singing a magical song, which he had just made up of course, for there was no chance of having one ready for such an event as this, but he hoped the big bird would understand and fly away.

> "Hai, hai, hai. Hy-ah, hy-ah, hy-ah!
> Chief of All the Eagles, we welcome thee!
> Chief of All the Eagles, we are thy children!
> Chief of All the Eagles, we sing to thee!
> Leave us in peace, O Chief, as we leave thee!
> Hy-ee, hy-ee. Hy-ah, hy-ah. Hai, hai, hai-i-i!"

All the people stood silent as he sang. At last his rattle grew still and his voice faded away on a high, long note. Then, not a sound was to be heard, only the thin, sweet tune of the wind whistling through the great bird's wing feathers, as he swung and balanced at ease on the air currents.

Slowly the men's arms relaxed and their bows dropped to their sides. Listless fingers slid back into their quivers the arrows they had only just drawn out and, for a long moment, it seemed as if the life of the whole village had come to a stop.

Suddenly, in the flash of an eye, the eagle dropped. Dropped down into the crowd of Indians, huddled so close and tight that not one of them could have run to save his life. And who was his victim?

Stokos, of course. Stokos, who had tried so hard to shoot him. Stokos, who had jeered at him, who fancied himself so much as an archer.

"Look, look! The eagle has caught Stokos by the hair!"

"He's carrying him off!" shouted his wife. "Look out! He's away with him. Quick, quick! Grab him by the ankles. Hold him, hold him!"

Well, they tried to hold him, of course. Just as Stokos was about to be lifted out of reach, one of the tallest men seized him by the ankles and held on like a clam. He clasped his hands round the slowly rising legs and then, to his horror, he found that his fingers were locked tight, and he couldn't let go, try as he would.

The old medicine man, Lokoma, had been right.

"Let go! Let go!" they all shouted.

"I can't! I can't let go!" and there was a deadly fear in his voice.

Naturally, they all turned to Lokoma. He was the medicine man, the magician. This was his affair now and he would tell them what to do.

"Of course he can't let go. It's magic. Didn't I warn you all a dozen times? Here, let me try. Perhaps I can hold him."

The brave old man hung on to the tall Indian's ankles in the vain hope that he could hold down the great eagle, risking his life for his people as so many good doctors have done before and since. And he couldn't let go either!

Up the eagle struggled, slowly, not too fast.

There was a deep and awful cunning in his slowness. Anybody could see that the load he now had to lift was so great that, magician or not, he could barely manage it and that if they added the weight of just one more man they could pull the whole long and growing chain back to earth.

One by one they linked on, and one by one the eagle lifted them off the ground till at last every man, youth, stripling, boy, and male child in the village, right down to the little boy who had first shot at the eagle, was hanging in a desperate long chain, hands locked to ankles, hanging from the bird's great talons.

"Oh, look! My little boy. My own little, little boy. Let go! Let go at once, before you go too high. Let go quickly!"

There wasn't one of them who could let go.

Up and up flew the great bird, right into the eye of the sun. Higher and higher till he could hardly be seen at all, till he looked like a mosquito with a long, thin tail, or a skein of geese high in the clouds.

The women and the girls of the village were the only ones left behind.

"What shall we do?" they asked each other. "What shall we do? There is not a man left in the whole village. There will be nobody to go out hunting or fishing. There will be nobody to protect us when the Haidas come raiding for slaves. Nobody to comfort us in the long cold nights of winter."

Their tear-filled eyes followed the eagle's flight far above the earth.

"Look! Look! He's coming down again. He grows bigger every moment. Perhaps he just wanted to punish the men for having shot at him. That's it, of course. He just wanted to teach them a lesson. Soon he'll put them all down again, safe and sound. Oh, how noble, how kind. They'll all be safe on earth again."

Weeping with relief, hardly breathing, the women watched as the big bird loomed larger and larger. But he didn't come down.

When the lowest link of the flying chain of men was so close to the ground that he could almost touch it, the eagle flew off towards the open sea, flying so fast that the chain of bodies strung straight out behind him like the smoke from a torch in a strong wind.

Then he stopped suddenly and the chain swung the other way. Again and again, he flew and stopped, now this way, now that, until he had all the people swinging backwards and forwards at a furious rate.

Then, all at once, he let go!

And, as soon as he let go, everybody else let go too, for he had broken the magical spell which had held them all locked so tightly together.

Still driven by their dizzy swinging through the air, they spread out in a long line of falling bodies. Some went a long way, others fell near by, but they all fell sooner or later, up and down the coast and far out to sea. And, as they hit the water, they all turned into islands.

The big men of the village made big islands, and the middle-sized people, of no great importance one way or the other, made middle-sized islands, and the dozens and dozens of children made the little islands.

The small boy who started all this made the smallest island of them all and, if you listen carefully on a fine day when tiny waves beat gently on his shores, you can hear him calling with a little chuckle in his voice, "Look, Daddy! Look, Daddy!" just as he did on that sad day when the Chief of All the Eagles made the islands.

CHAPTER 9

CONCLUSION

CONCLUSION

No SINGLE BOOK HAS YET been written that tells everything we know about the Indians of Canada, nor is it likely that one ever can; it would have to be very large indeed. In the one you are reading now, an immense amount of detail has been left out, for almost every sentence could have been expanded. Though the life of an Indian was not nearly as full as ours is, yet every day of it was taken up with occupations of one sort or another.

In trying to find out how the Indians did things in the old days before the white man came, scientists make use of three different methods: questioning living Indians; studying the writings of early travellers; examining things found in old camps and villages.

THOSE WHO TELL US ABOUT THE OLD TIMES

In the few Indian communities in which life is still much as it was years ago, there may be found an occasional Indian who is interested in the old ways and is glad to talk about them. There are few things so heart-breaking as the pathetic joy and eagerness of an old Indian, who feared the things he knows and remembers would die with him, when he finds someone who wants to know everything that can be told of the old wisdom, so that it may be preserved in a book and never forgotten. Generally, the Indians of today know little about the old times, often a good deal less than the person who is asking about them. In eastern Canada many of the Indians have been living under white influence for three hundred years and most of them know little or nothing of how their ancestors lived. On the coast of British Columbia, white men have been present for only about a hundred and fifty years, but even that is time enough for great changes to have taken place.

In the Northwest Territories and the Yukon the Indians and Eskimos have lived under less pressure from white neighbors and many of them are still able to speak from personal knowledge of the ways in which things used to be done. Some of them know how to make stone tools and still even use them at times, preferring them to those of steel. A few people still observe the old taboos and know something of the system of thought that gave them meaning. It is from such people as this that we get the most reliable information, but these old timers are disappearing year by year, and our chances of learning what they remember are vanishing with them.

A great deal was written in early descriptions of the Indians by explorers, traders, missionaries, and soldiers. These accounts are nearly always incomplete, largely because the study of the Indians and their customs was not the principal interest of the writer. Not only are these accounts likely to be incomplete, they are almost certain to be inaccurate; the writers were often mistaken in their conclusions about what they saw and, also, they frequently showed a good deal of prejudice in what they wrote. The explorers were likely to magnify the strangeness of native customs and the dangers of their travels, the traders had their own interests to serve, the missionaries were concerned with the salvation of pagan souls, and the soldiers with the destruction of their bodies, so each group formed a different mental picture of the natives.

In the same way, the authors of books of fiction about the Indians seldom showed them as they really were. We might suppose, from reading books of this kind, that there were two different types of natives. Some authors pictured the Indian as a "noble savage", a tall and handsome warrior, brave and skilful, generous to his enemies, filled with love of the woods and affection for his family, free from all the sorrows and faults of mankind.

Other writers took an opposite view and spoke of the Indians as "fiends" who:

". . . on midnight errands walk
And bathe in brains the murderous tomahawk."

Needless to say, both of them were wrong. The Indian was no noble savage, nor was he a treacherous fiend. There could be, in fact, no one description that would fit all the Indians of Canada, for they differ greatly as we have seen.

The specimens collected in abandoned villages, in graves, and at casual camp sites give us a great deal of information which, while it is incomplete because many things have rotted away, is at least unprejudiced. If we find deer bones and arrowheads in the same place, it is reasonable to suppose that the people who lived there made the arrowheads to kill the deer with. If we find skin-scrapers, we assume that the people tanned the hides of the animals they killed, and other similar conclusions can be arrived at. Reconstructing native life and history in this way is the work of the archaeologist.

THE REAL INDIAN

The many facts obtained from these various sources of information are like pieces of an enormous jig-saw puzzle. Bit by bit we fit them into place to form a picture of the life and history of the Indians from the time of their first arrival in North America. This picture is slowly becoming more detailed and more accurate, but it will always be unfinished and only partly right, for some pieces of the puzzle have been lost forever.

From what we can see of this huge picture now, we believe that, with the exception of the Iroquois, the people of the prairies and of the west coast, the average Canadian Indian lived in a state of savagery. He spent his days hunting and fishing and making the tools and weapons necessary for self-preservation; he knew nothing of agriculture, nothing of the domestication of animals (except the dog), he knew almost nothing of science, and little of art. He was often hungry, often cold, often tired, and seldom lived in comfort and security. In most cases, conditions were so difficult that he had time for nothing but the efforts necessary to enable him to stay alive and support his family.

It was not realized at first that this was the condition of most Indians for it so happened that, except for the Beothuks and Algonkians of the Maritime Provinces, the Indians whom white men first met on the east side of Canada were the comparatively civilized Iroquoian people. As a result, the descriptions of the Indians that reached Europe in those early days were misleading because they applied to tribes who were better off than most. In British Columbia, almost the same thing happened, for the coast Indians were the first to be met and, as we know, they were more advanced than the people of the interior, so again a false idea of native life was formed.

THE INDIAN POINT OF VIEW

It is not possible to be quite unprejudiced in describing the details of Indian life, for we are almost certain to color our statements; we white men always look at things through our own eyes, taking it quite for granted that our way of doing things or of thinking about things is the "right" way. Actually, our way of thinking or of doing things is not always the "right" way, it is merely one of several possible ways. The Indian's way of doing things was just as "right" for him as ours is for us, and he is as much entitled to think our way "wrong" as we are to think of it as "right". It is clear that ways of doing things, such as hunting or fishing, or building a canoe, or performing a ceremony, are "right" if they bring about the desired results and "wrong" if they fail. From this standpoint, the Indian is just as likely to be "right" as we are.

One of the important differences between white men's ideas and the Indians' is the way in which the world around us is looked at. We hardly realize how much what we think and do is influenced by what we have been taught, what we have seen, and what we have read. We take many things for granted and forget that people with a different background might not take these same things for granted at all. For one example, if a white hunter wounds an animal he feels in honor bound to follow it until he can put it out of its misery. An Indian of the old school had no such feeling. He would never think of killing a wounded animal simply to cut short its suffering, but was more likely to be amused by its screams and struggles. On the other hand, as we have already seen, an Indian who killed a bear treated it with great ceremony and respect, which no white hunter dreams of doing.

The Indian point of view differed from ours in more than this, however; he felt there was a spirit in every bird and beast, in the waterfall, and throughout the great forest. Most of these spirits, he believed, were quite indifferent to man and would neither help him nor harm him, but others were dangerous and must be treated with caution and deference, offerings must be made to them, and care taken not to offend them by breaking any of the countless taboos. Some spirits could be controlled by charms and magic, and the professional medicine man was supposed to know far more about charms and have stronger magic than the ordinary individual. These beliefs are held by primitive people in most parts of the world, and were common in the British Isles and western Europe only a few hundred years ago.

We are so ready to assume that an Indian's thoughts are the same as ours that we sometimes try to explain his actions in a way that makes sense to us, but perhaps not to the Indian. We ask an Indian guide to meet us at nine o'clock in the morning and he comes at ten, if at all. We say he is lazy, or he is unreliable, or he is dishonest, or he is trying to get more money out of us, or something else that might explain a similar action on the part of a white man. In all probability, all these explanations would be wrong. It is simply that, to the Indian, clocks and watches mean far less than they do to us. To him nine o'clock might mean "some time after breakfast" and that is about all. So, in the middle of the morning he strolls in and is honestly surprised to find the impatient white man angry because his guide turned up an hour later than he was expected.

HAND WORK IS HARD WORK

There were two aspects of Indian life in the old days that we seldom think of, important though they were. First was the brake put on everything by inefficient tools. With a power saw, we can, in five minutes, cut down a tree that would have kept an Indian with a stone axe busy all day. Everything he did was slowed down in the same way. Making a basket or a pair of moccasins took hours of labor, days on end had to be given to building a canoe or making a tipi. Everything needed throughout a man's life had to be made, usually by the man himself or by his wife, using tedious hand methods, time consuming and laborious. Imagine our own situation if we had to make all the things we need ourselves — our clothes, shoes, knives, matches, everything. Making many complicated things, such as automobiles and radios, even building the houses we have today, would be quite impossible and we should find ourselves spending most of our time making things for daily use, with very little leisure for anything else. The advance of civilization would be slow indeed.

THE LACK OF PRIVACY

Another thing we seldom think about is the "private life" of the Indian. Living, as most of them did, in a small group of no more than ten or twenty people from the day of his birth to the day of his death, he would know each one of them intimately, know just what they did, be aware of almost every thought that went through their heads, and they would know equally well everything he thought or did. There could be no such thing as privacy as we know it, no chance of getting away from people, no way to escape "public opinion", what his fellows thought of him and said about him. The only privacy was to be found in the dreams and visions of the spirit quest of boyhood, and that may be one of the reasons they were held so dear.

If a man was a coward, everybody in his little group knew it. If he killed a deer and tried to keep it for his own family instead of sharing it with others who needed food, that would be known too. If he was more interested in another man's wife than in his own, all the people would see it and either laugh at him or scold him for it. It was as though each one of us was doomed to spend the rest of his life with the small group of people in his class in school, and it was only in those more advanced tribes, the Iroquoians and the west coast people, that there was any relief from this pressure. Here was some chance of living in a larger world, though never the great world that we know today, and here it was, too, that the most progress had been made towards a higher culture.

AND WHAT OF THE FUTURE?

If Columbus had not discovered America, what would have become of the Indians? That is a question that we can never answer, for so many things that could change the course of events might have happened. We may suppose, however, that the Indians would have continued to develop slowly but surely. Already the people of Central America had made great progress in art, science, architecture, mathematics, and government and they had reached a stage of culture not unlike that of the early Egyptians. Their influence would have spread, in fact it was already spreading. The population would probably have increased, but not very fast for the country was already supporting as many as it could, considering the low level of culture and the primitive ways of hunting, fishing, and farming known to the Indians. Better methods would have been introduced gradually and then the land would have been able to support a larger population.

Such things could not have happened, however, for even if Columbus had never made his famous voyage, somebody else would have crossed the Atlantic not much later in the world's history, and the fate of the Indians would have been just about the same. In Central America and Mexico the Spaniards treated the Indians with ferocious cruelty, almost beyond belief. In the United States, the whites were less barbarous though even there the natives were handled none too kindly, as the official records show. Nor may we in Canada feel any too proud of ourselves, though it is true that our Indians were, on the whole, better off than many others. There have been great changes in recent years and the whole Indian problem has been reconsidered and new policies have been adopted in an effort to give the Indians every advantage that white citizens enjoy. The aim today is to help them to adjust themselves to the new way of life as rapidly and as painlessly as possible. The older people will probably go on much as they are till their end comes, but the younger people show every wish to adopt white ways of living and, even more important, white ways of thinking too.

GLOSSARY

ABALONE — A large and brilliant blue and green sea-shell imported from California by the west coast tribes and used for jewellery and decoration.

ACCOMPLICE — A partner in crime, usually in a subordinate position.

ADZE — A kind of axe, but with the blade at right angles to the handle.

AFT — In or near or towards the stern end of a boat or ship.

ALDER — A tree related to the birch, common in Canada, whose bark yields a strong orange dye.

ALLY — A person or state joined with another for some special reason.

AMBUSH — Troops lying hidden to surprise a passing enemy.

AMULET — Something worn as a charm against evil.

ARCTIC FOX — A fox of the far north whose fur turns white in winter.

AUTHENTIC — Real, genuine.

AWL — Small sharp tool for making holes.

BABICHE — Rawhide cut into thongs or strings and used for lacing or lashing and for the webbing of snowshoes.

BALM OF GILEAD — A large poplar tree also known as black poplar.

BARB — A small point projecting backward from the main point of a spear or fish-hook, hindering its removal from the skin.

BARRENS — Land north of the limit of trees; flat, open, and infertile plains.

BEVEL — A sloping edge or surface.

BLUBBER — A layer of fat under the skin of arctic animals such as the seal, walrus, and whale.

BOLAS — A hunting weapon consisting of half a dozen weights tied to the ends of strings fastened together by a knot.

BOUNTY — A sum of money paid for the destruction of a dangerous or harmful animal or person.

BOW — The front part of a boat or canoe.

BOW DRILL — A tool that is used for making holes in wood or other materials. The drill bit (see Drill Bit below) is spun rapidly by means of a short bow.

BREECH-CLOTH — A strip of cloth that passes between the legs and is folded in front and back over a belt, worn by many primitive tribes.

BUCKSKIN — Soft tanned deer hide.

BULL-BOAT — A circular craft made by stretching skins over a wooden framework; it is used by prairie Indians.

CACHE — A hiding place where food and other goods may be placed for safety.

CAMAS — A lily whose bulbs were used for food.

CARIBOU — The North American reindeer.

CATLINITE — A red stone that was used in making tobacco pipes.

CHALDEAN — The language of the Chaldees who lived in Babylonia.

CHICLE — Gum made from the sap of a tree, used as the base of chewing gum.

CHILKAT BLANKET — An elaborate blanket of mountain goat wool woven by a Tlinkit group of Indians.

CHINOOK — A language made up of Indian, English, and French words used from about 1800-1930 on the west coast.

CINCH — The girth that passes under the horse's belly to hold the saddle firmly.

CLAN — A number of people claiming descent from a common ancestor.

COCKPIT — The hole in the deck of a kayak in which the person using it sits.

CONFEDERATION — A group of allies leagued together for defence and government.

CONJURER — Someone who uses or professes ability in magic or juggling.

COPPER — A shield-shaped sheet of copper used by west coast tribes as a symbol of wealth.

CORRAL — An enclosure, often circular, for horses or other large animals.

COTTON WOOD — A kind of poplar tree.

COUP — The act of touching one of the enemy in warfare with a bow, a rifle, or a specially made coup stick.

CRUPPER — A leather strap fastened to the back of the saddle and passed under the horse's tail to keep the saddle from slipping forward.

CUBICLE — A small separate sleeping room.

CULTURE GROUP — A group of people who have the same way of life.

CUTTLE-FISH — A sea-animal with ten tentacles armed with sucking discs by which it holds fish and other food.

DEADFALL — A kind of trap in which a heavy log falls on, and kills, any animal that disturbs the bait.

DENTALIUM — A sea-shell shaped like a small elephant tusk, used by the west coast tribes as a kind of money and as ornaments.

DEW CLAW — The inner false hoof of deer and cattle (not reaching the ground).

DIALECT — A way of speaking any language not quite like the standard way.

DIP-NET — A fish-net dipped by hand in the water when fishing.

DOGBANE — A kind of plant once thought to be poisonous to dogs. The tough fibres are used for making twine.

DOG-PACK — One of a pair of small bags used when dogs are trained to carry loads.

DOWEL — A headless wooden pin for fastening pieces of wood together.

DRESSING — The processes of cleaning and preserving animal hides to make leather.

DRILL BIT — The part of a drill that actually makes the hole.

DUFFLE — A coarse thick cloth used for making warm clothing.

DUG-OUT — A canoe made from, or dug out of, a single log.

EEL GRASS — A sea-weed with long narrow green leaves.

EXTINCT — Having died out, no longer living or in existence.

FIBRE — One of the thread-like strings used to make twine or cloth.

FILLET — A narrow slab of fish with no bones in it, prepared for drying.

FIORD — A long narrow arm of the sea running between high hills.

FISH GAFF — A stick with a hook on it for catching or landing fish.

FLAKING TOOL — A tool used by primitive people for removing small flakes of stone in making stone knives, etc.

FLINT — A kind of stone, hard and fine-grained, suitable for chipping into shape for making stone knives, etc.

FLINT AND STEEL — A combination of a piece of flint and a piece of steel which, when struck together, produce a spark that can be used for making fire.

FLUKE — One of the two broad pieces that make up a whale's tail.

FLYWHEEL — A heavy wheel which, like a top, tends to keep on spinning once it has been started.

FOOL HEN — A kind of grouse, so "foolish" as to let itself be caught easily.

FOSSIL — Remains of plants and animals that lived in past ages, found in rocks.

FUNGUS — A simple plant without leaves, flowers, or green coloring, such as mushrooms and toadstools.

GABLE — The triangular top of the end wall of a building.

GENS — A clan claiming descent through the male side of the families composing it.

GLOSSARY — A list of unusual or unfamiliar words with explanations.

GREBE — A kind of water bird with a short tail and feet far to the back.

GUNWALE — The top edge of the side of a boat or canoe.

HARPOON — A barbed spear, often with a line attached, used for capturing whales and large fish.

HEARTH (of fire drill) — The part of the fire drill that the drill bit or shaft rests on. It is here that the heat is produced.

HITCH — A knot by which a rope is made fast to some object.

HOMINY — Coarse ground Indian corn boiled with water to make gruel.

HORMONE — A substance essential to life, formed in the bodies of animals and men.

HOUSE-POST — An upright post supporting the framework of a house.

IGLOO — An Eskimo house, especially one built of blocks of snow.

INDIAN HEMP — A plant whose fibres were used for making twine. Also called dogbane.

INITIATE — A person who has been, or is now being, admitted to a secret society or special position.

INTRICATE — Involved or complicated.

IRIS — The colored part of the eye surrounding the pupil.

JADE — A hard tough stone, often green in color, used by the natives for making chisels, etc. Also called nephrite.

JAVELIN — A light spear meant to be thrown by the hand.

JIG — A hook used to catch fish by jigging it up and down where fish are believed to be numerous.

JUNIPER — An evergreen shrub having berries with a pungent smell.

KAYAK — A canoe used by the Eskimo consisting of a wooden frame covered with sealskins and propelled by a double-bladed paddle.

KELP — A large seaweed, often with a very long stem.

LABRET — An ornament worn in a hole in the lip.

LACING NEEDLE — A special needle used in lacing up tents, pack sacks, etc.

LANCE — A kind of spear, usually long and light, used as a weapon and also in hunting or fishing.

LAVA — Molten rock from a volcano.

LEAGUE — An alliance of tribes formed for their common advantage and defence.

LEAN-TO — A building which leans against something, such as a cliff, a tree, or another building.

LEISTER — A two-pronged spear with flexible prongs for taking salmon and other fish.

LICHEN — Small simple plants, often gray, yellow, or green, that grow on rocks or trees.

LING — A fish, common in Canada, used by the Indians for food.

LINGUISTIC — Having to do with languages.

LOBE — A rounded projecting part of anything, such as the lobe of an ear.

LURE — Something bright and shining, generally not good to eat, used to attract fish to a hook or spear.

MATTOCK — An adze-like tool for digging in hard ground.

MIGRATION — The movement of a large number of people, or animals, from one place of abode to another.

MOLESKIN — A strong, soft, thick cloth.

MORTAR — A cup-shaped stone vessel in which substances are ground up with a pestle.

MUSKEG — A wide marshy stretch of land, covered with moss and small plants, and often impassable.

MUSK-OX — A stocky, short-legged animal with a long coat, somewhat like cattle in appearance, living in northern Canada.

MUSSEL — An edible shell-fish found on both Atlantic and Pacific coasts.

NARWHAL — A whale-like animal of the Arctic seas with a long straight tusk.

NEPHRITE — A tough hard green stone, often called jade, used by the Indians for making chisels, etc.

OOLAKAN — The candle-fish found on the British Columbia coast, used for food and as a source of oil.

ORGANIC — A living plant or animal, as opposed to a mineral which is inorganic.

OSSUARY — A place where the bones of dead people are kept or buried.

PACKBOARD — A board or frame carried on the back, to which packs or bundles can be fastened.

PALETTE — A thin flat board or slab of stone on which paints are mixed or ground.

PALISADE — A strong fence or wall made of big stakes set upright in the ground.

PARFLECHE — A folded sheet of rawhide in which pemmican and other things can be carried.

PARKA — A common name for a warm winter coat with a hood that can be pulled over the head and round the face.

PECKING — A process of shaping stone by battering or "pecking" it with a smaller pebble held between the thumb and finger.

PEMMICAN — A food consisting of dried and powdered meat mixed with fat and (sometimes) berries.

PETERHEAD BOATS — Small sea-worthy boats often used by whalers and sealers.

PIGMENT — A coloring matter, such as a paint or dye.

PITFALL — A hidden pit dug in the hope that wild animals will fall in and be captured.

PONCHO — A kind of cloak, oblong in shape, with a slit in the middle for the wearer's head.

PORPOISE — A small whale-like animal only a few feet in length.

POTLATCH — A feast and ceremony at which a wealthy west coast chief gives away presents to increase his social importance.

POUND — An enclosure, usually circular, of logs or fencing for holding buffalo or other animals.

PREFIX — A syllable placed in front of a word to change its meaning; thus the prefix "dis-" changes the meaning of "please" to "displease".

PRESTIGE — Influence and reputation derived from previous character and achievements.

PTARMIGAN — A grouse-like bird common in the far north.

PYRE — A pile of wood on which dead bodies are burned.

PYRITES — An iron ore containing sulphur. Two pieces of this, when struck together, will produce sparks from which a fire may be started.

QUIVER — A long narrow open-ended bag or case for holding arrows.

RADIO-ACTIVE — Emitting rays of energy, such as x-rays.

RAWHIDE — Animal skins which have been dried and dehaired, but not yet tanned or smoked.

RED OCHRE — An iron ore, red in color, which makes a good paint.

REGALIA — The decorations and special clothes worn by a king or some lower official or a chief.

RESIN — The hardened sticky sap of pine and fir trees.

RITUAL — Having to do with rites and ceremonies.

RUSE — A trick or dodge to confuse and mislead the enemy.

SACHEM — An Algonkian word meaning "chief".

SAGEBRUSH — A low shrub, common in the west, that has a sage-like smell.

SALMON BERRY — A wild berry much like a raspberry.

SAP SCRAPER — A bone or antler tool used to scrape the inner bark from a tree (for food) after the outer bark has been peeled off.

SAPLING — A young tree, often slender and flexible.

SCALPING — Removing the scalp of a dead or wounded enemy.

SHOEING — A coating of frozen mud put on a sled runner to prevent its wearing out.

SKIN-SCRAPER — A tool of stone or bone used for scraping hides in tanning.

SLOUGH — A piece of wet, marshy, or muddy ground, sometimes covered with water.

SNARE — A piece of cord or sinew stretched tightly from side to side of a drum head. The snare vibrates when the drum is struck.

SNOW BEATER — A short rod of wood or antler, used by the Eskimo to knock loose snow from their fur clothing.

SOAPSTONE — A soft stone with a soapy feeling, easily carved to make pipes, bowls, etc.

SOCIAL ORGANIZATION — The system of customs and laws that enables a tribe or nation to govern its affairs.

SOUND — Verb. To go deep under the water.

SPATULA — A thin flat flexible piece of wood or other material used for stirring and other purposes.

SPAWN — A mass of fish eggs, often used by the Indians as food.

SPLICE — Verb. To join two pieces of rope without a knot; to join two pieces of wood by overlapping and lashing.

STAMPEDE — A sudden flight of a herd of animals.

STERN (of canoe) — The rear end.

STOP — A block of ivory or other material fastened to a line or thong to prevent objects from slipping out of position.

SUCCOTASH — A dish of Indian corn and beans boiled together.

SUFFIX — Syllable placed after a word to change its meaning, thus the suffix "-age" changes the meaning of "short" to "shortage".

SUPERNATURAL — Above or beyond the ordinary course of nature.

SYLLABIC — A form of writing in which the different characters represent syllables rather than simple sounds.

TABOO — A prohibition of any particular action, generally for ceremonial reasons.

TACTICS — The art and science of military and naval manoeuvres; also schemes and devices for attaining one's own ends.

TATTOO — To make permanent marks on the skin by rubbing pigment into a series of small punctures.

THWART — A cross-brace running from side to side of a boat, and sometimes made to serve as a seat.

TINDER — Any dry inflammable stuff that easily catches fire from a spark.

TOMAHAWK — A wooden war club (not a small steel hatchet).

TOM-COD — A small kind of codfish much used as food in the north.

TRACE (for sled dog) — The leather line connecting the dog's harness to the sled.

TRAVOIS — A pair of poles, drawn by a dog or horse, used to carry things on.

TRESTLE — A braced framework used to support a bridge or heavy weight.

TRIBE — A group of primitive people under a leader or chief.

TROLLING — A way of fishing, using a spinning lure or bait.

TUMP LINE — A strap across the forehead to assist in carrying a heavy pack.

TUNDRA — Wide, wet, treeless region in the far north.

TURF — A sod of grass, with roots and earth.

TWILL — Cloth so woven that the threads pass over one and under two, instead of over one and under one, as in plain weaving.

TYPICAL — Representative of its class or type.

ULU — A half-moon-shaped knife much used by Eskimo women.

UMIAK — An Eskimo open boat, consisting of a wooden frame covered with sealskins, capable of carrying a number of people; it is propelled by oars and not paddles.

WEDGE — A tool of hard material, thick at one end and tapering to a thin edge, used for splitting wood, etc.

WEIR — A fence or barricade built in a river to catch fish.

WHETSTONE — A specially shaped stone used to give cutting tools a sharp edge.

WOOD BUFFALO — A variety of buffalo living in the woods north of the prairies.

YEW — An evergreen tree with a strong elastic wood often used for making bows.

INDEX